THE SIXTH GUN

Book 8: Hell and High Water

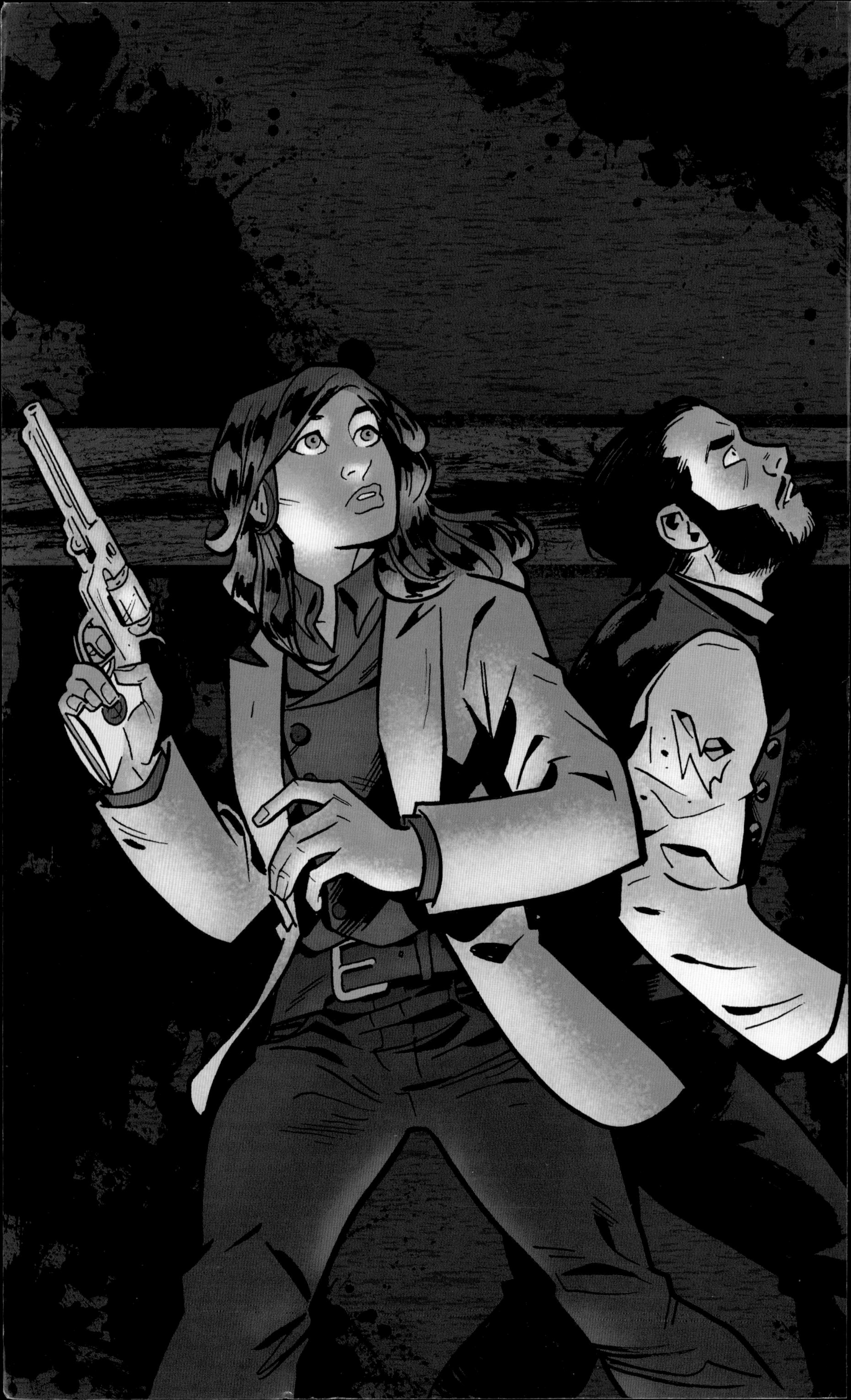

THE SIXTH GUN

Book 8: Hell and High Water

Written By

CULLEN BUNN

Illustrated By

BRIAN HURTT

Colored By

BILL CRABTREE

Lettered By

CRANK!

Edited By

CHARLIE CHU

Designed By

KEITH WOOD

AN ONI PRESS PUBLICATION

THE SIXTH GUN™
By Cullen Bunn & Brian Hurtt

PUBLISHED BY ONI PRESS, INC.

JOE NOZEMACK *publisher*

JAMES LUCAS JONES *editor in chief*

TIM WIESCH *v.p. of business development*

CHEYENNE ALLOTT *director of sales*

FRED RECKLING *director of publicity*

TROY LOOK *production manager*

HILARY THOMPSON *graphic desinger*

JARED JONES *production assistant*

CHARLIE CHU *senior editor*

ROBIN HERRERA *editor*

ARI YARWOOD *associate editor*

BRAD ROOKS *inventory coordinator*

JUNG LEE *office assistant*

This volume collects issues #42-47 of the Oni Press series,
The Sixth Gun.

ONI PRESS, INC.
1305 SE MARTIN LUTHER KING JR. BLVD.
SUITE A
PORTLAND, OR 97214
USA

onipress.com
facebook.com/onipress
twitter.com/onipress
onipress.tumblr.com
instagram.com/onipress

cullenbunn.com • @cullenbunn
brihurtt.com • @brihurtt
@crabtree_bill
@ccrank

First edition: July 2015

ISBN: 978-1-62010-246-6
eISBN: 978-1-62010-247-3

Library of Congress Control Number: 2014957506

10 9 8 7 6 5 4 3 2 1

Printed in China

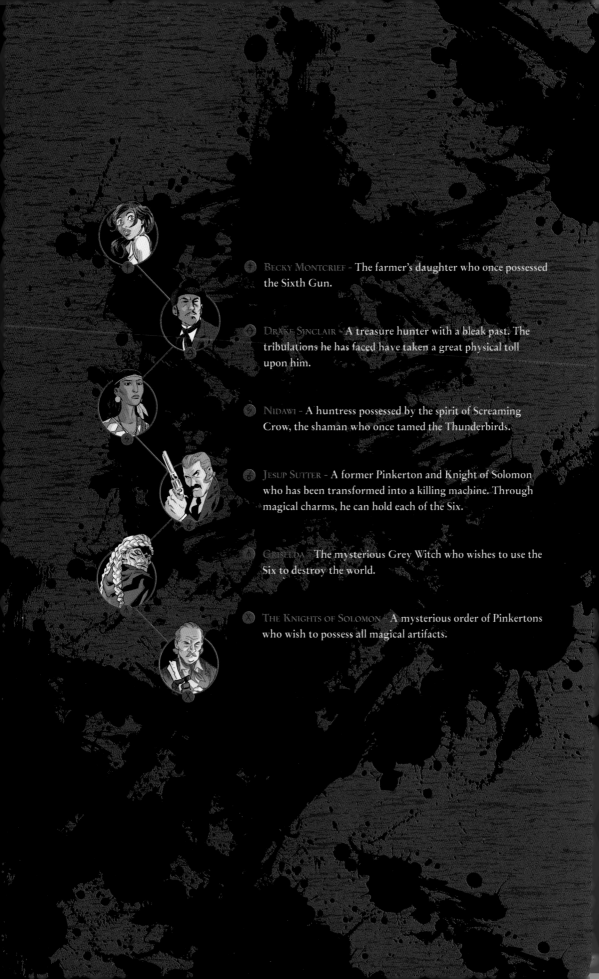

BECKY MONTCRIEF - The farmer's daughter who once possessed the Sixth Gun.

DRAKE SINCLAIR - A treasure hunter with a bleak past. The tribulations he has faced have taken a great physical toll upon him.

NIDAWI - A huntress possessed by the spirit of Screaming Crow, the shaman who once tamed the Thunderbirds.

JESUP SUTTER - A former Pinkerton and Knight of Solomon who has been transformed into a killing machine. Through magical charms, he can hold each of the Six.

GRISELDA - The mysterious Grey Witch who wishes to use the Six to destroy the world.

THE KNIGHTS OF SOLOMON - A mysterious order of Pinkertons who wish to possess all magical artifacts.

CHAPTER ONE

I've not been here before.

I've never *seen* this.

Few have, Mr. Mercer.

This place... it is typically *forbidden* to all but the highest circle initiates.

But you have served us well, and there's little time for the *proper ceremonies* to be performed.

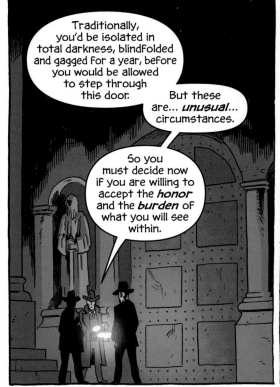

Traditionally, you'd be isolated in total darkness, blindfolded and gagged for a year, before you would be allowed to step through this door.

But these are... *unusual*... circumstances.

So you must decide now if you are willing to accept the *honor* and the *burden* of what you will see within.

After you.

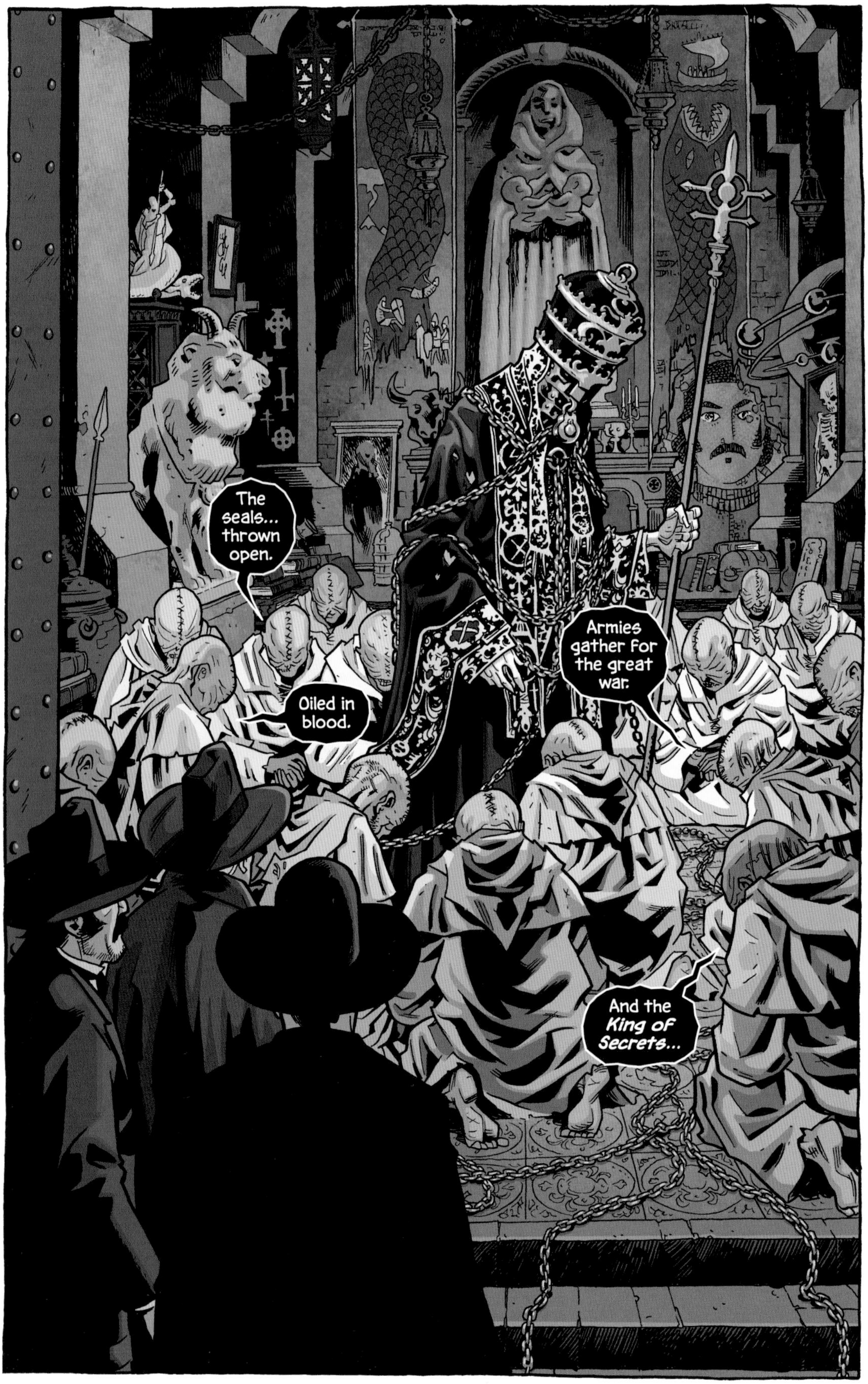
The seals... thrown open.
Oiled in blood.
Armies gather for the great war.
And the King of Secrets...

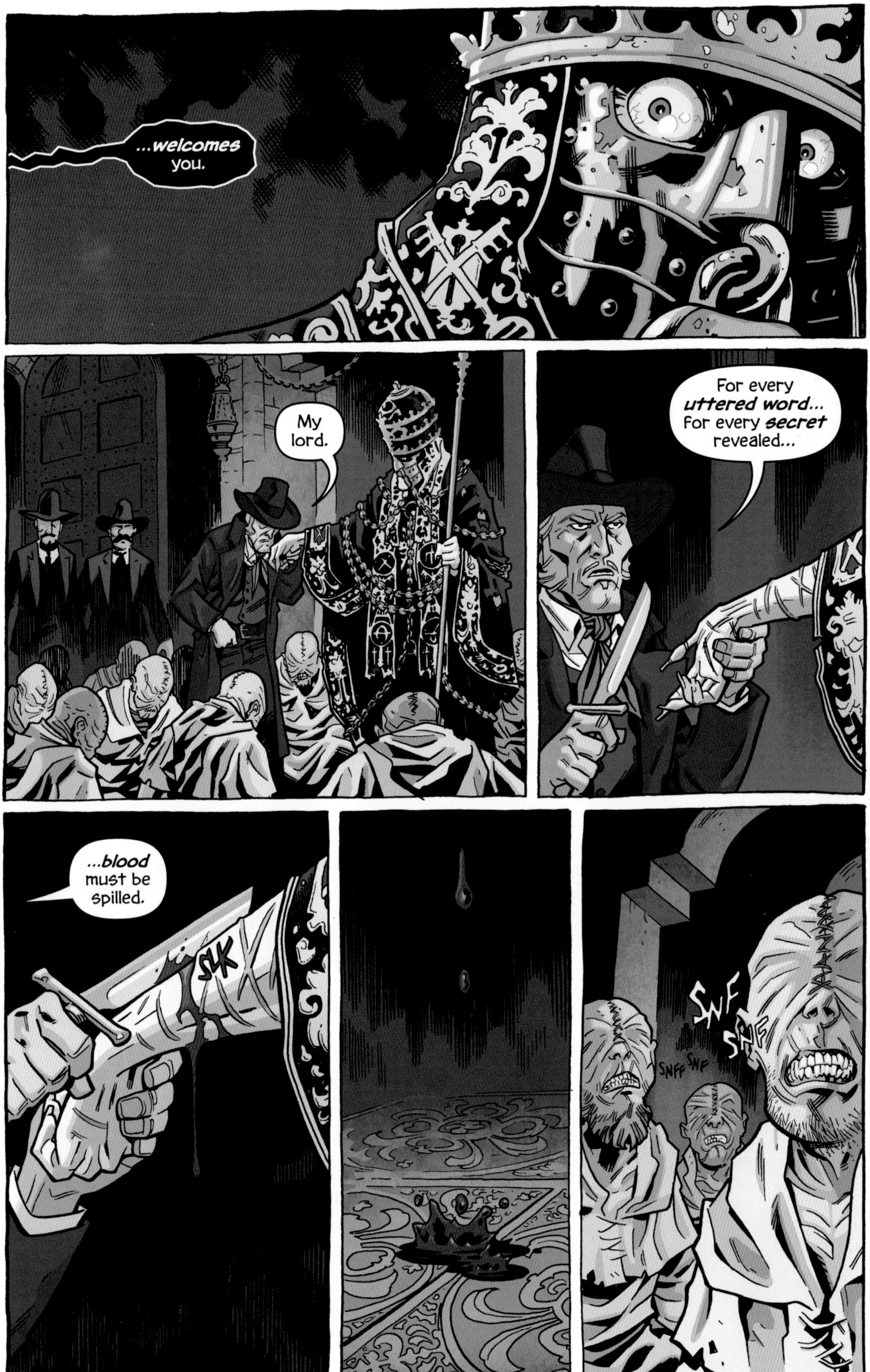
...*welcomes* you.
My lord.
For every *uttered word*... For every *secret* revealed...
...*blood* must be spilled.
SLK
SNF SNF
SNFF SNF

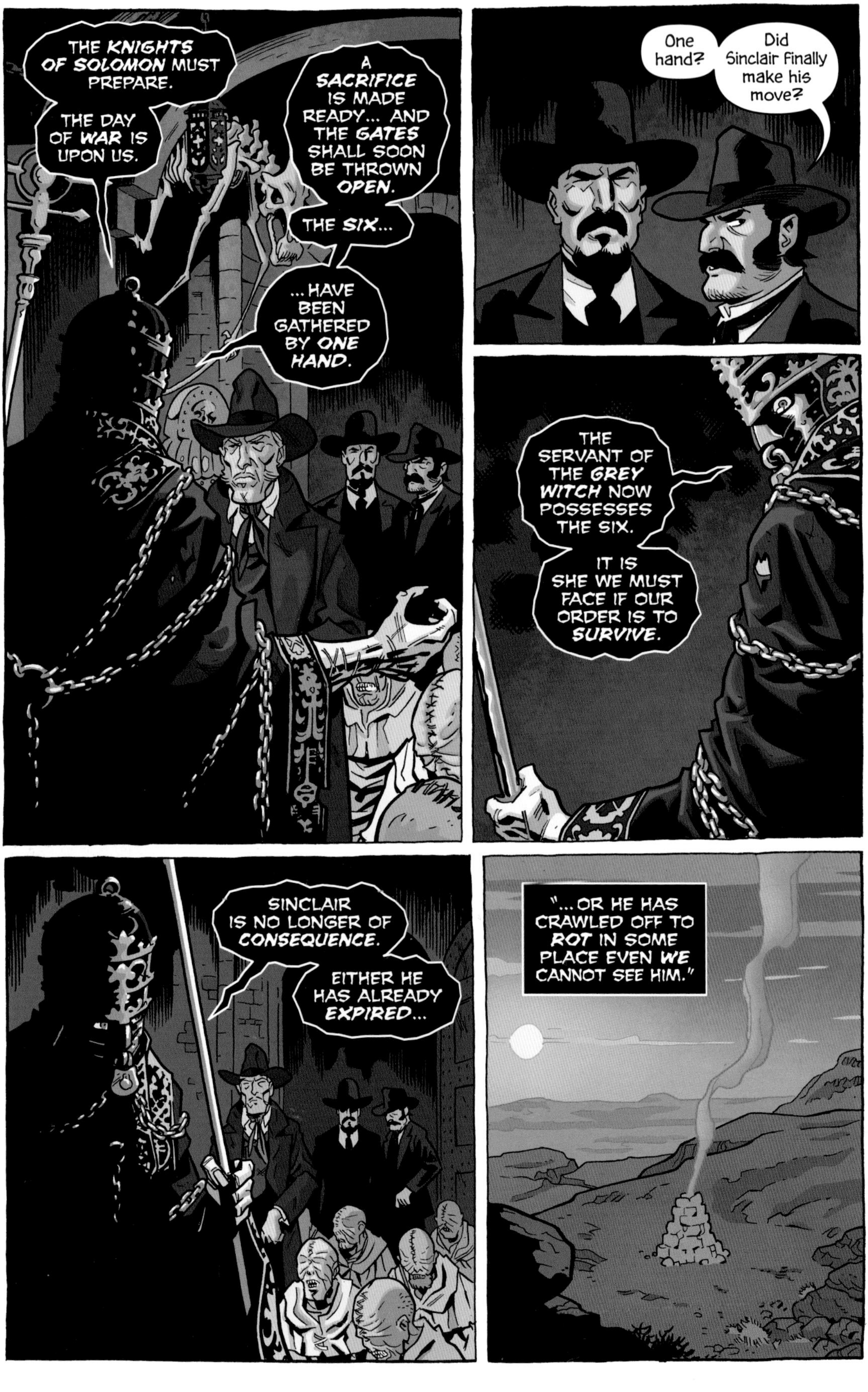
THE KNIGHTS OF SOLOMON MUST PREPARE.
THE DAY OF WAR IS UPON US.
A SACRIFICE IS MADE READY... AND THE GATES SHALL SOON BE THROWN OPEN.
THE SIX...
...HAVE BEEN GATHERED BY ONE HAND.
One hand?
Did Sinclair finally make his move?
THE SERVANT OF THE GREY WITCH NOW POSSESSES THE SIX.
IT IS SHE WE MUST FACE IF OUR ORDER IS TO SURVIVE.
SINCLAIR IS NO LONGER OF CONSEQUENCE.
EITHER HE HAS ALREADY EXPIRED...
"...OR HE HAS CRAWLED OFF TO ROT IN SOME PLACE EVEN WE CANNOT SEE HIM."

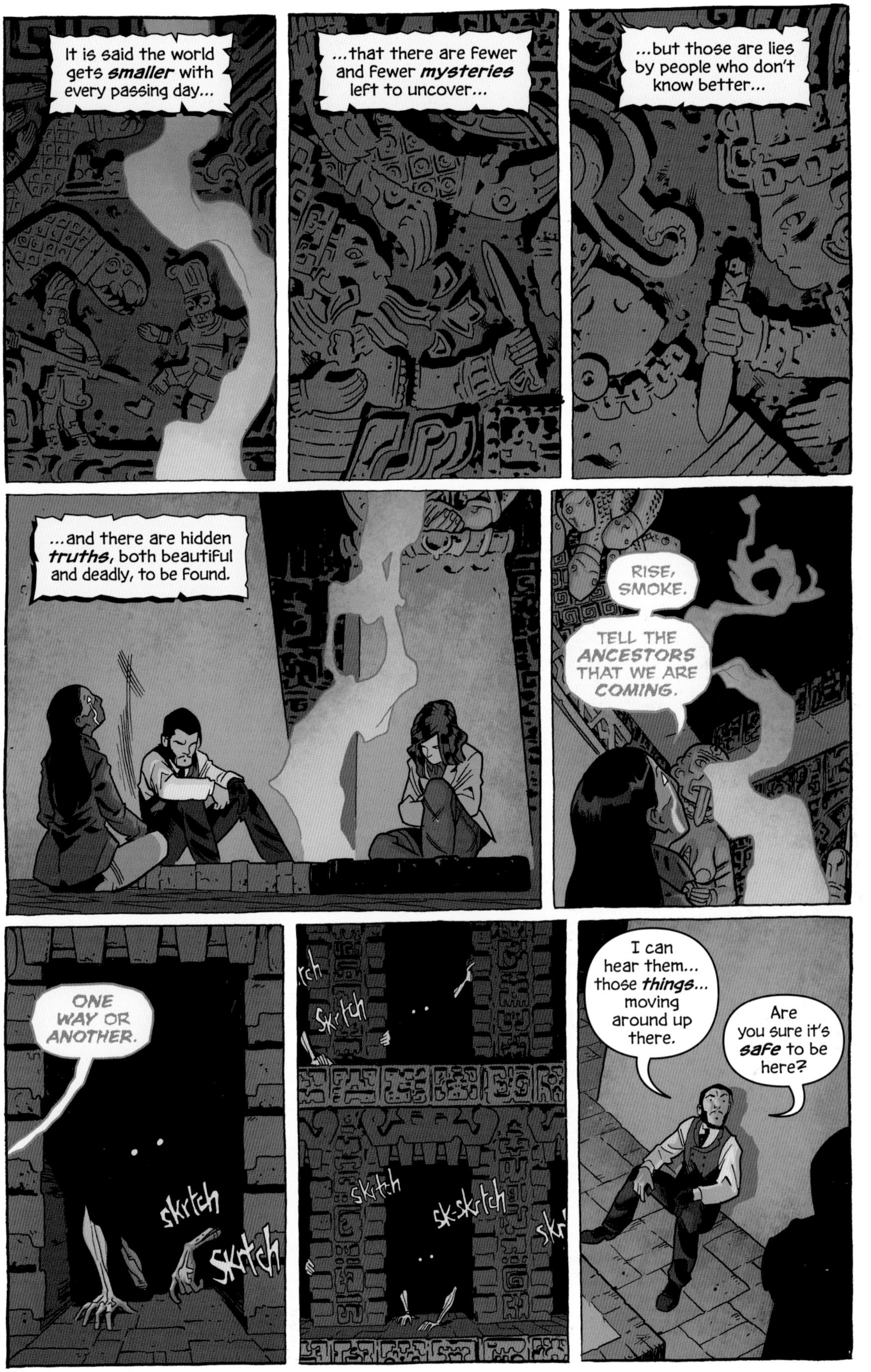

It is said the world gets smaller with every passing day...
...that there are fewer and fewer mysteries left to uncover...
...but those are lies by people who don't know better...
...and there are hidden truths, both beautiful and deadly, to be found.
RISE, SMOKE.
TELL THE ANCESTORS THAT WE ARE COMING.
ONE WAY OR ANOTHER.
skrtch
skrtch
skrtch
skrtch
skrtch
sk-skrtch
I can hear them... those things... moving around up there.
Are you sure it's safe to be here?

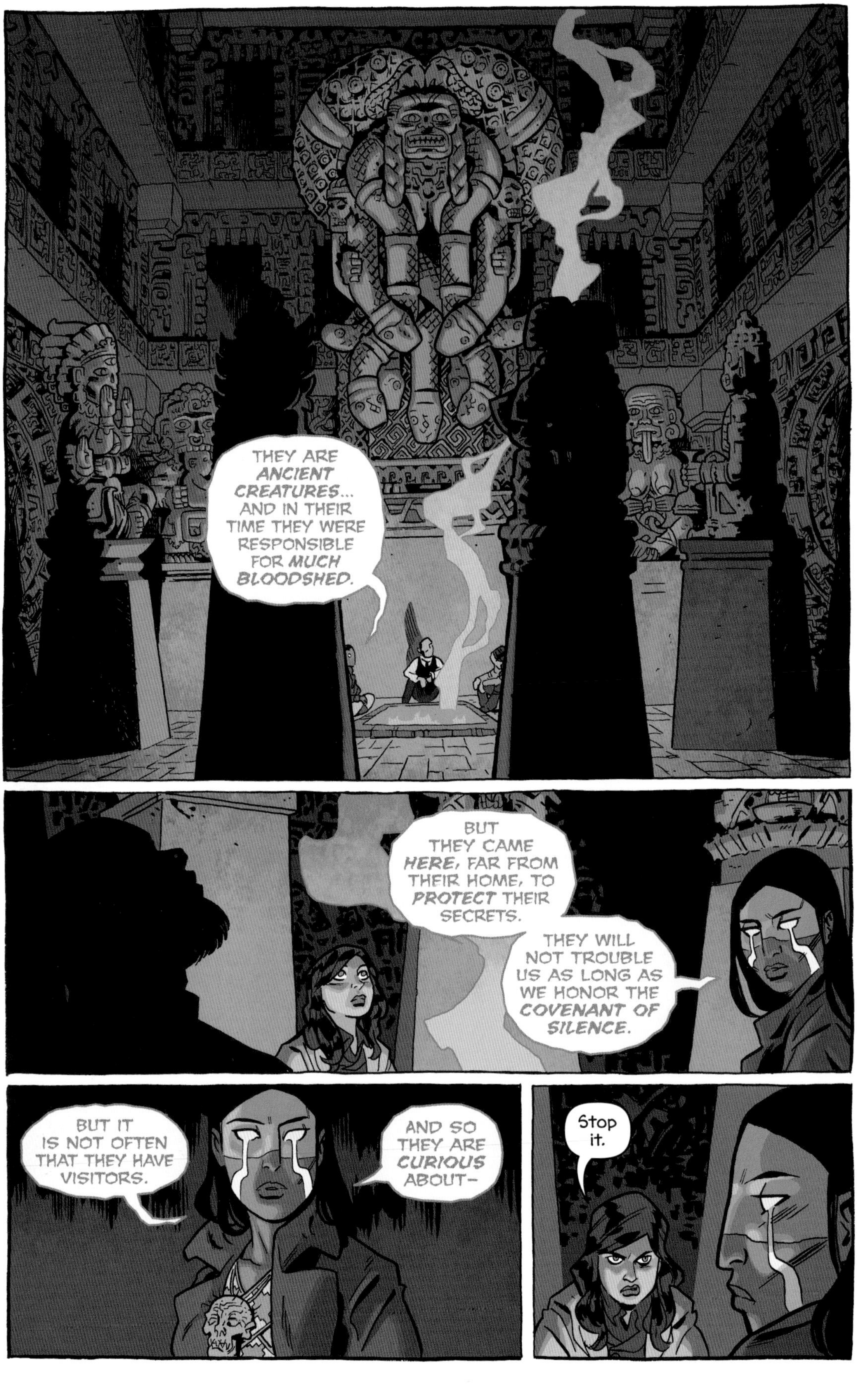
THEY ARE ANCIENT CREATURES... AND IN THEIR TIME THEY WERE RESPONSIBLE FOR MUCH BLOODSHED.
BUT THEY CAME HERE, FAR FROM THEIR HOME, TO PROTECT THEIR SECRETS.
THEY WILL NOT TROUBLE US AS LONG AS WE HONOR THE COVENANT OF SILENCE.
BUT IT IS NOT OFTEN THAT THEY HAVE VISITORS.
AND SO THEY ARE CURIOUS ABOUT-
Stop it.

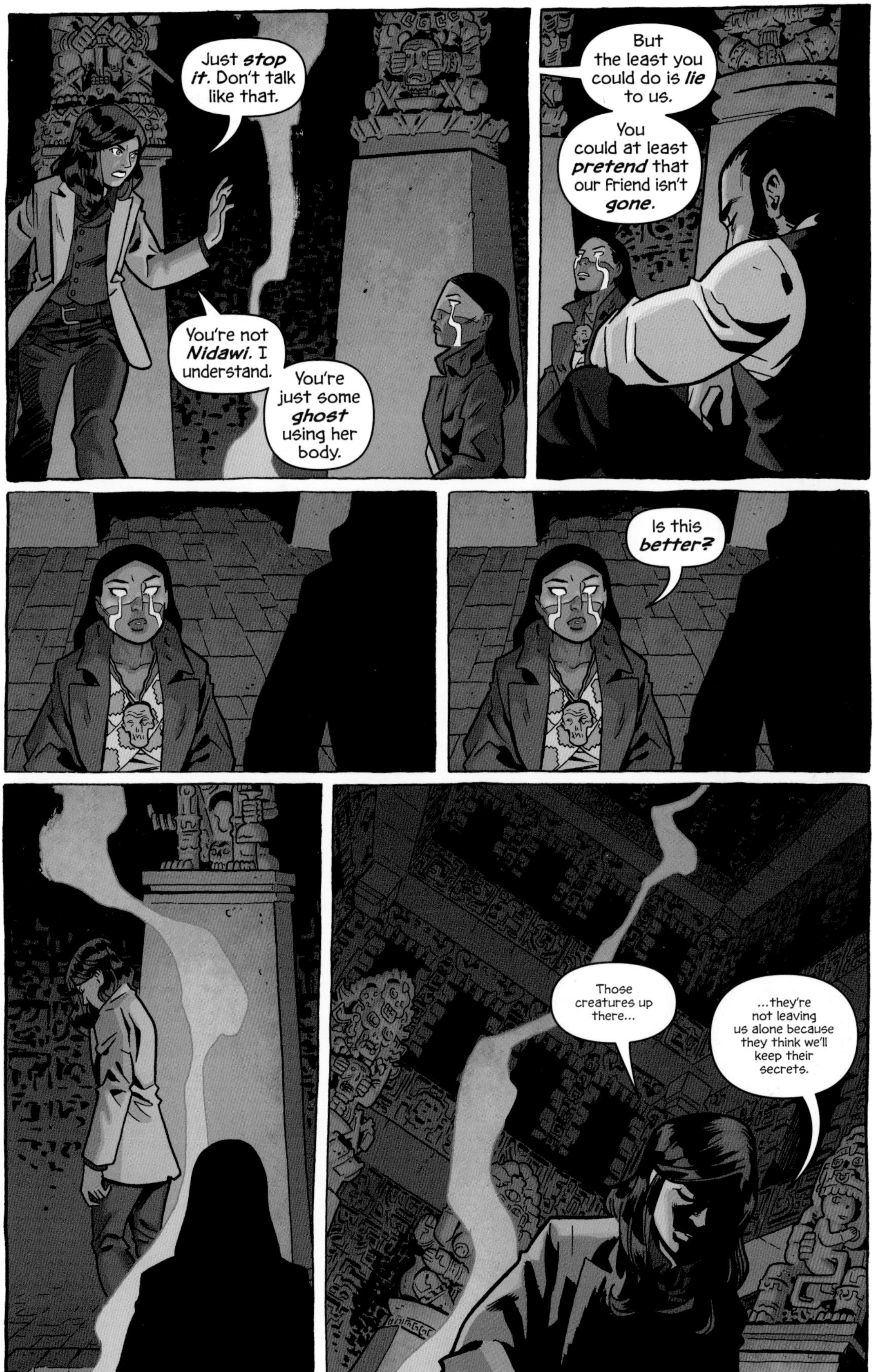
Just *stop it*. Don't talk like that.
You're not *Nidawi*. I understand.
You're just some *ghost* using her body.
But the least you could do is *lie* to us.
You could at least *pretend* that our friend isn't *gone*.
Is this *better?*
Those creatures up there...
...they're not leaving us alone because they think we'll keep their secrets.

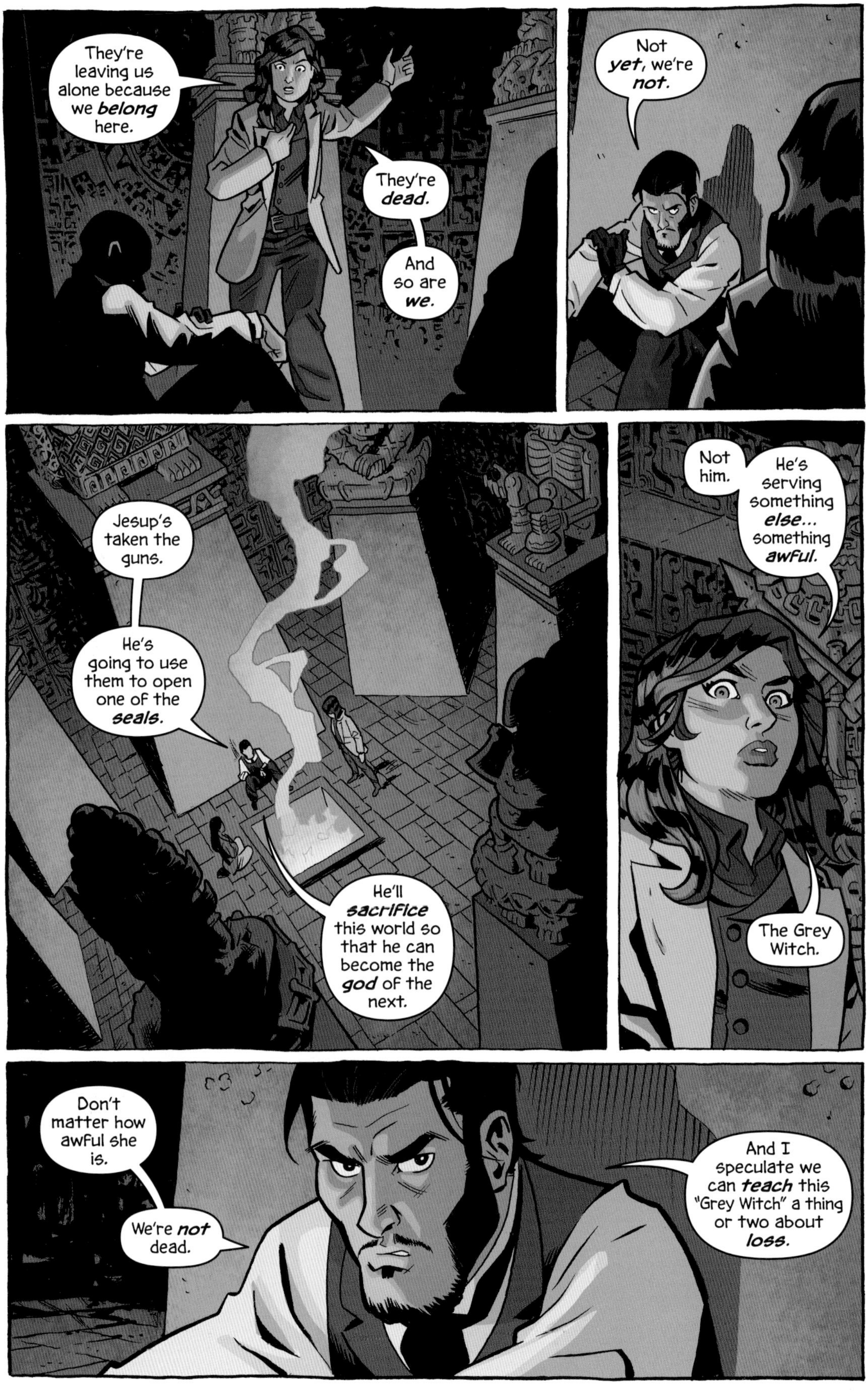

They're leaving us alone because we belong here.
They're dead.
And so are we.
Not yet, we're not.
Jesup's taken the guns.
He's going to use them to open one of the seals.
He'll sacrifice this world so that he can become the god of the next.
Not him.
He's serving something else... something awful.
The Grey Witch.
Don't matter how awful she is.
We're not dead.
And I speculate we can teach this "Grey Witch" a thing or two about loss.

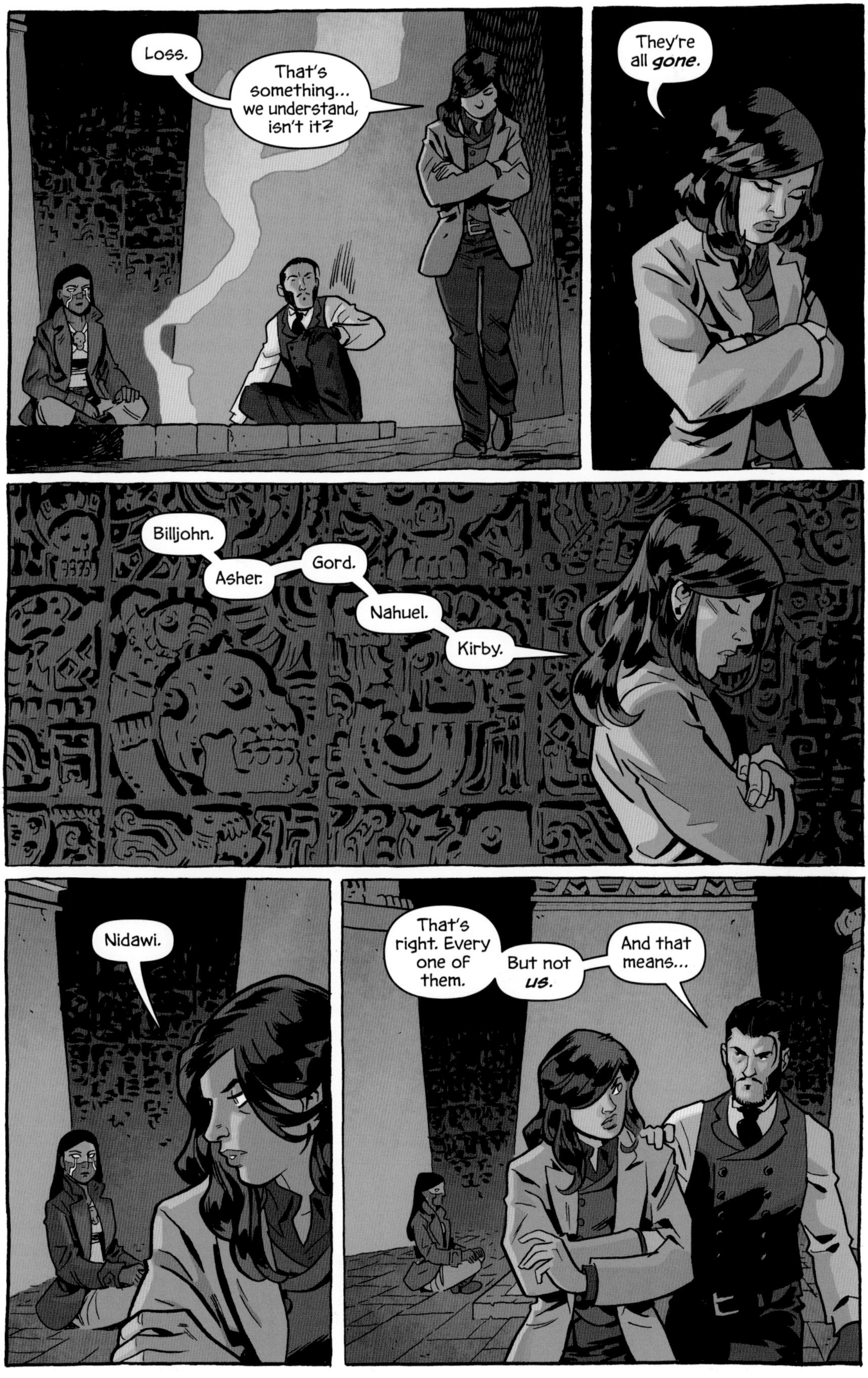
Loss.
That's something... we understand, isn't it?
They're all *gone*.
Billjohn.
Asher.
Gord.
Nahuel.
Kirby.
Nidawi.
That's right. Every one of them.
But not *us*.
And that means...

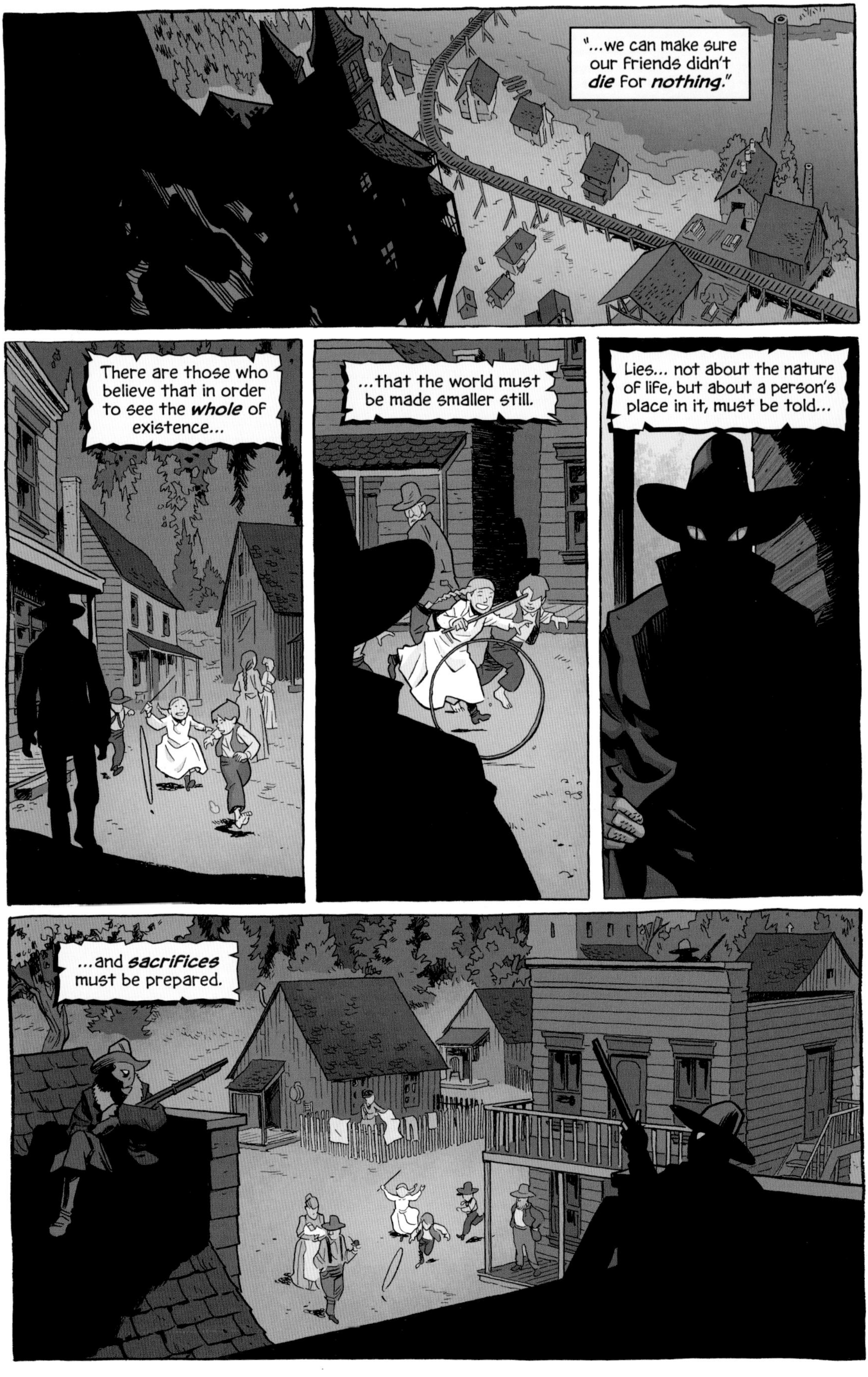
"...we can make sure our friends didn't *die* for *nothing*."
There are those who believe that in order to see the *whole* of existence...
...that the world must be made smaller still.
Lies... not about the nature of life, but about a person's place in it, must be told...
...and *sacrifices* must be prepared.

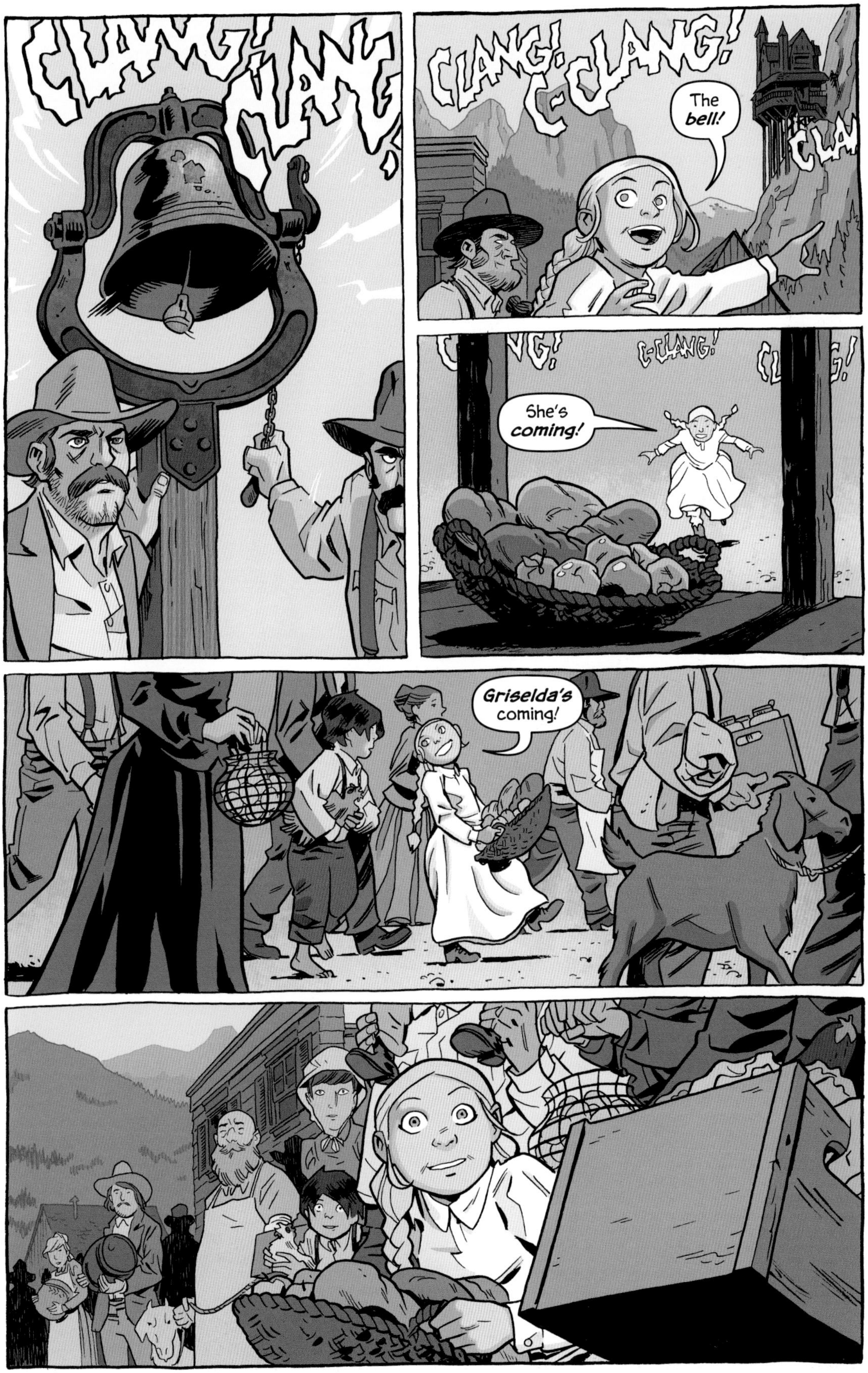
CLANG! CLANG!
CLANG! C-CLANG!
The *bell!*
CLA
C-CLANG!
She's *coming!*
Griselda's coming!

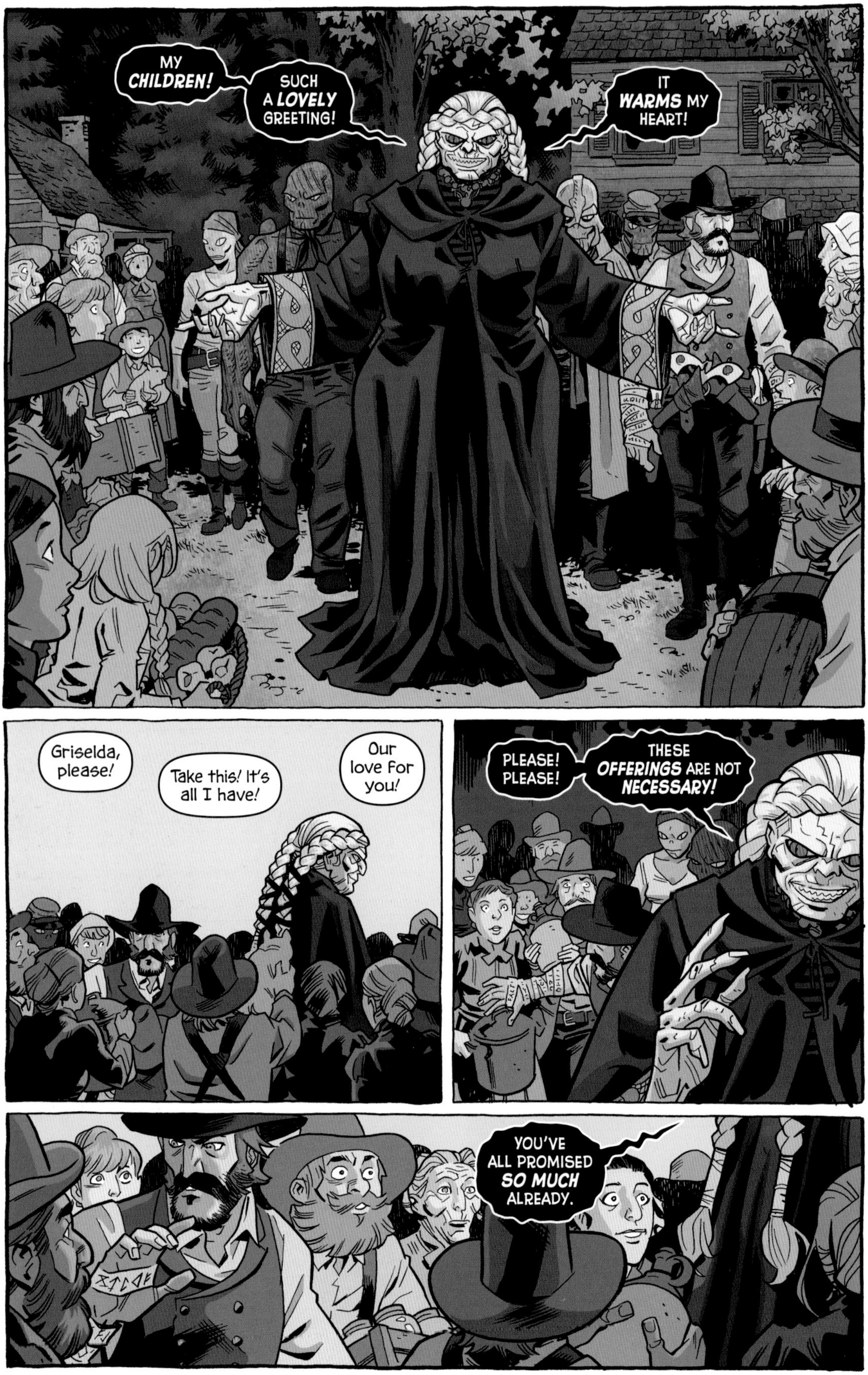
MY CHILDREN!
SUCH A LOVELY GREETING!
IT WARMS MY HEART!
Griselda, please!
Take this! It's all I have!
Our love for you!
PLEASE! PLEASE!
THESE OFFERINGS ARE NOT NECESSARY!
YOU'VE ALL PROMISED SO MUCH ALREADY.

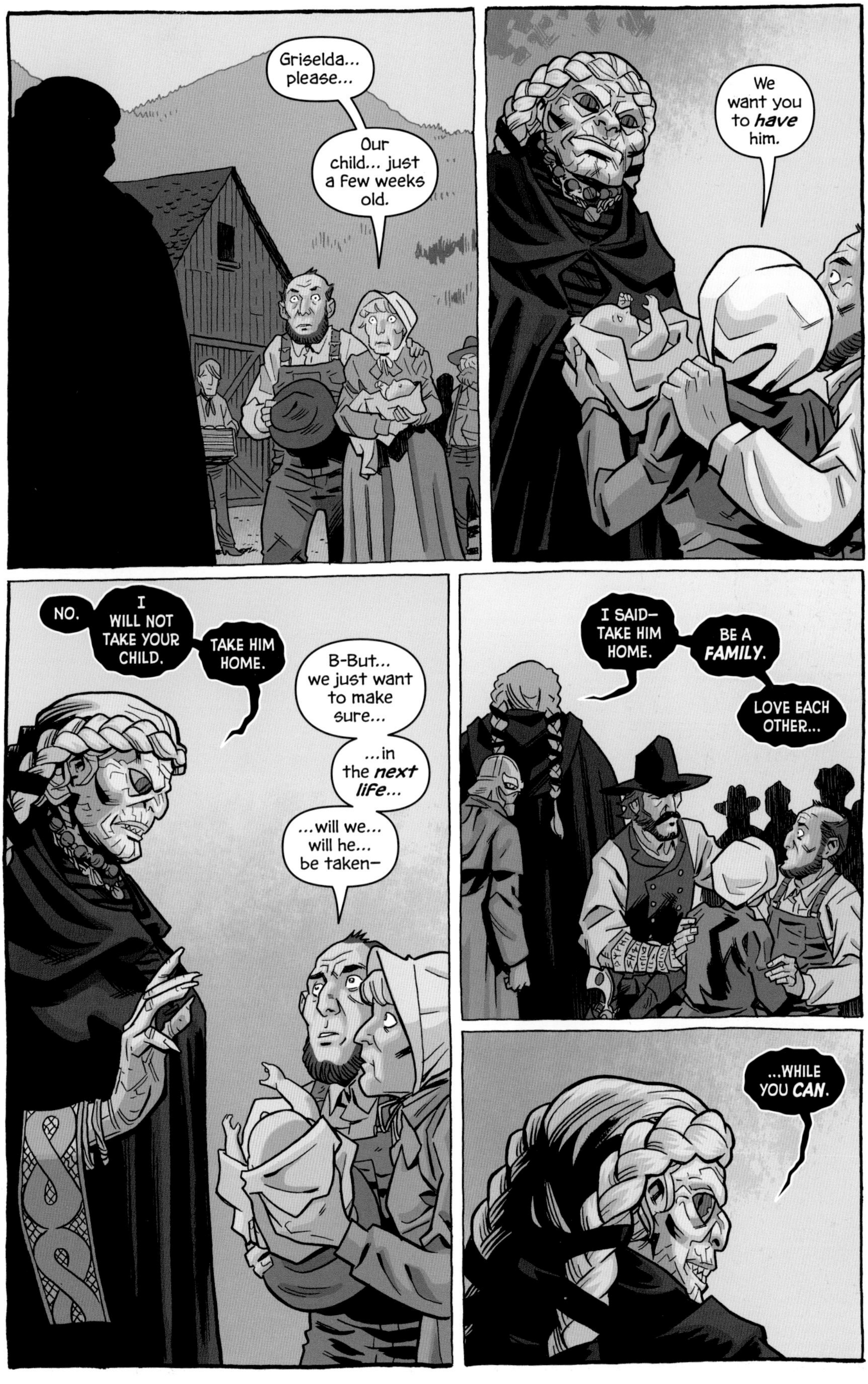
Griselda... please...
Our child... just a few weeks old.
We want you to *have* him.
NO.
I WILL NOT TAKE YOUR CHILD.
TAKE HIM HOME.
B-But... we just want to make sure...
...in the *next life*...
...will we... will he... be taken—
I SAID— TAKE HIM HOME.
BE A *FAMILY*.
LOVE EACH OTHER...
...WHILE YOU *CAN*.

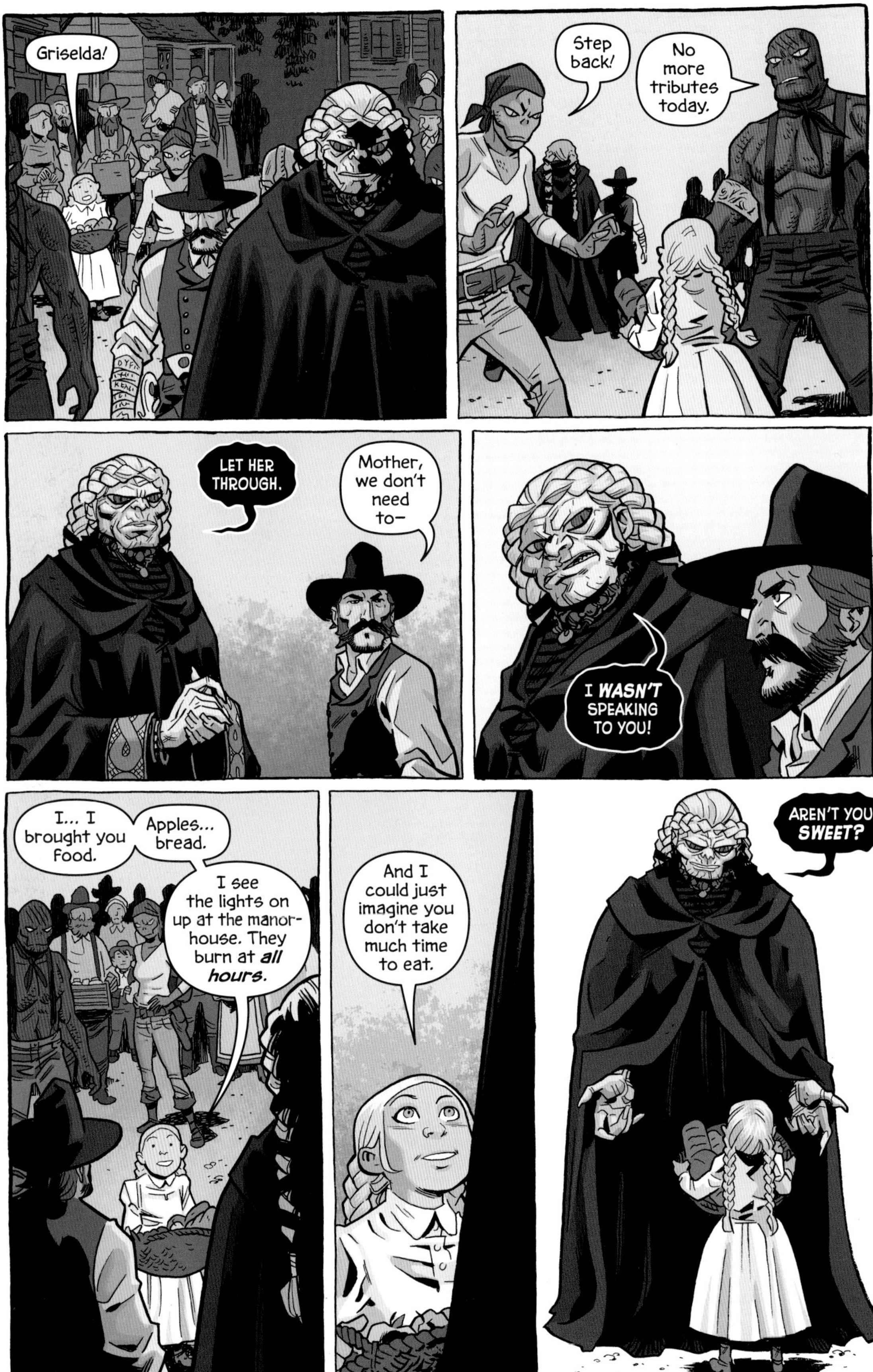
Griselda!
Step back!
No more tributes today.
LET HER THROUGH.
Mother, we don't need to–
I *WASN'T* SPEAKING TO YOU!
I... I brought you food.
Apples... bread.
I see the lights on up at the manor-house. They burn at *all hours*.
And I could just imagine you don't take much time to eat.
AREN'T YOU *SWEET?*

GO, NOW.

PLAY.

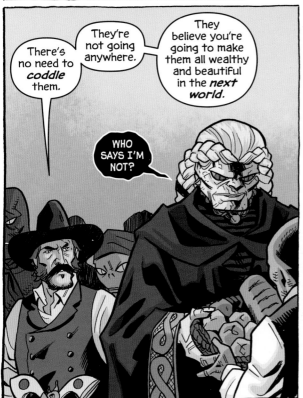

There's no need to **coddle** them.

They're not going anywhere.

They believe you're going to make them all wealthy and beautiful in the *next world*.

WHO SAYS I'M NOT?

If I thought you might do something like that, I'd **beg** you to bring my Abigail back.

But I'm no *fool*.

Not like these people.

WHY HELP ME AT ALL THEN?

YOU'VE ALREADY GOTTEN YOUR **REVENGE** ON SINCLAIR.

YOU'VE **BROKEN** HIM.

Way I see it...

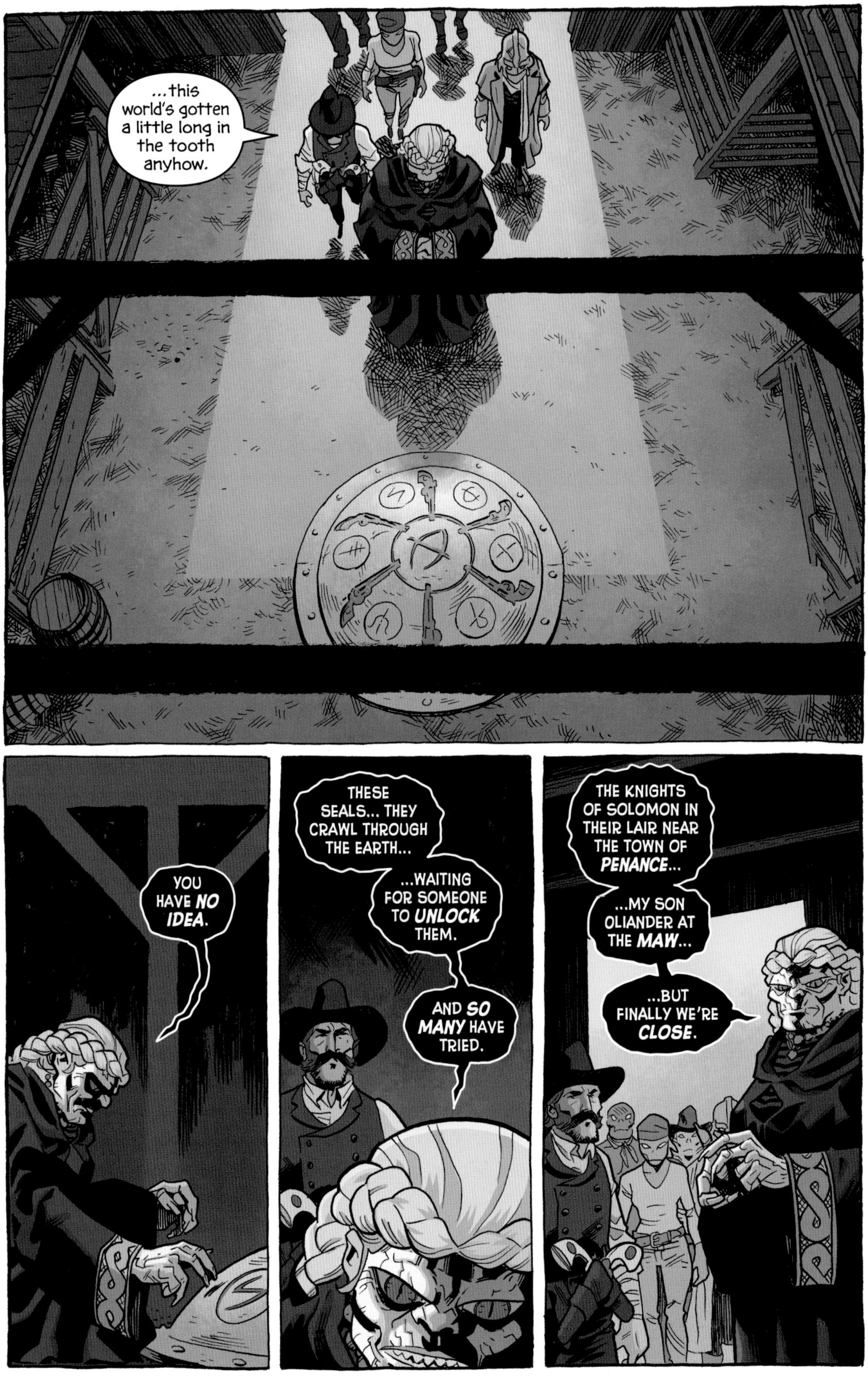
...this world's gotten a little long in the tooth anyhow.
YOU HAVE NO IDEA.
THESE SEALS... THEY CRAWL THROUGH THE EARTH...
...WAITING FOR SOMEONE TO UNLOCK THEM.
AND SO MANY HAVE TRIED.
THE KNIGHTS OF SOLOMON IN THEIR LAIR NEAR THE TOWN OF PENANCE...
...MY SON OLIANDER AT THE MAW...
...BUT FINALLY WE'RE CLOSE.

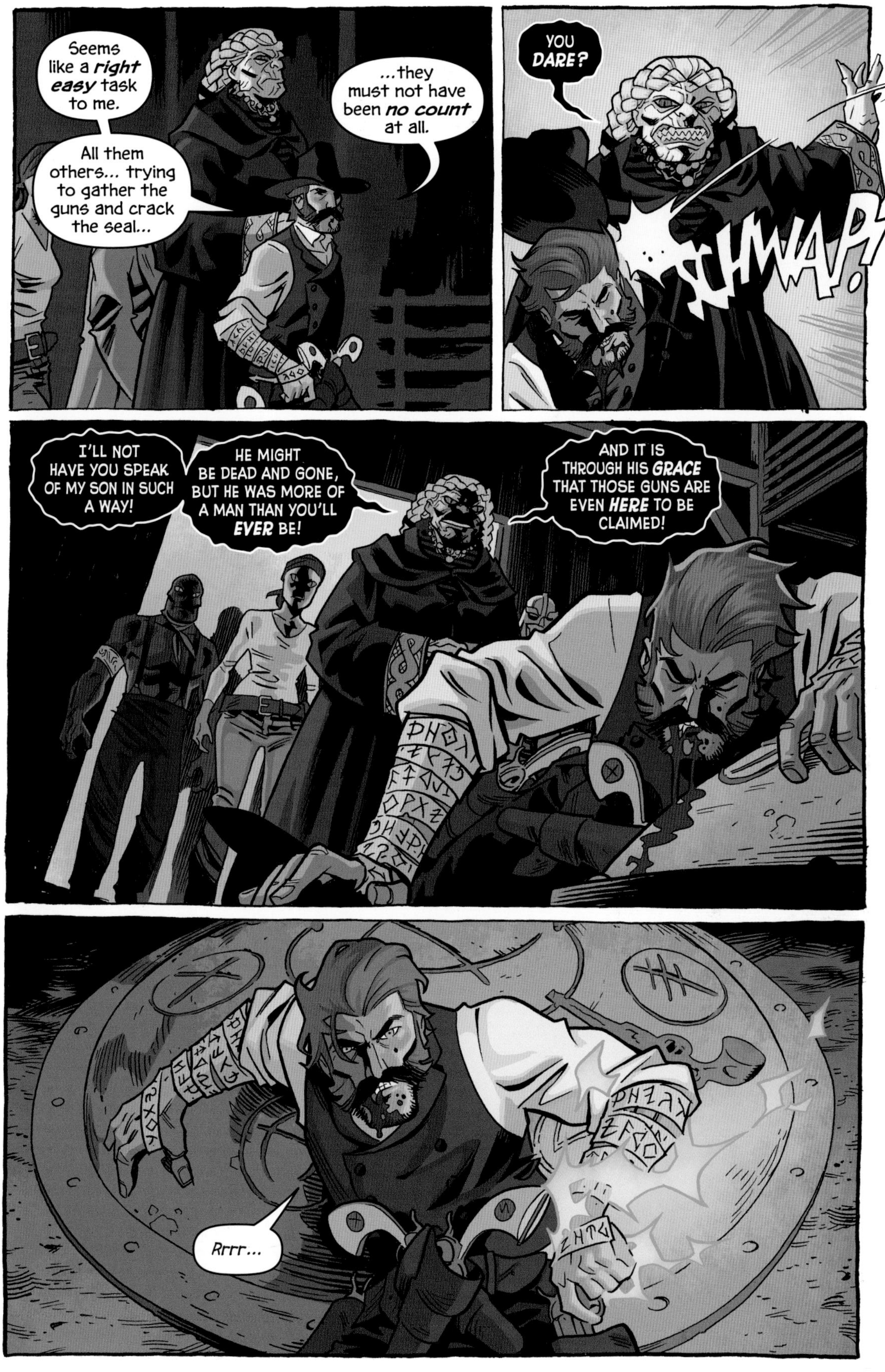

Seems like a *right easy* task to me.
All them others... trying to gather the guns and crack the seal...
...they must not have been *no count* at all.
YOU *DARE?*
THWAP!
I'LL NOT HAVE YOU SPEAK OF MY SON IN SUCH A WAY!
HE MIGHT BE DEAD AND GONE, BUT HE WAS MORE OF A MAN THAN YOU'LL *EVER* BE!
AND IT IS THROUGH HIS *GRACE* THAT THOSE GUNS ARE EVEN *HERE* TO BE CLAIMED!
Rrrr...

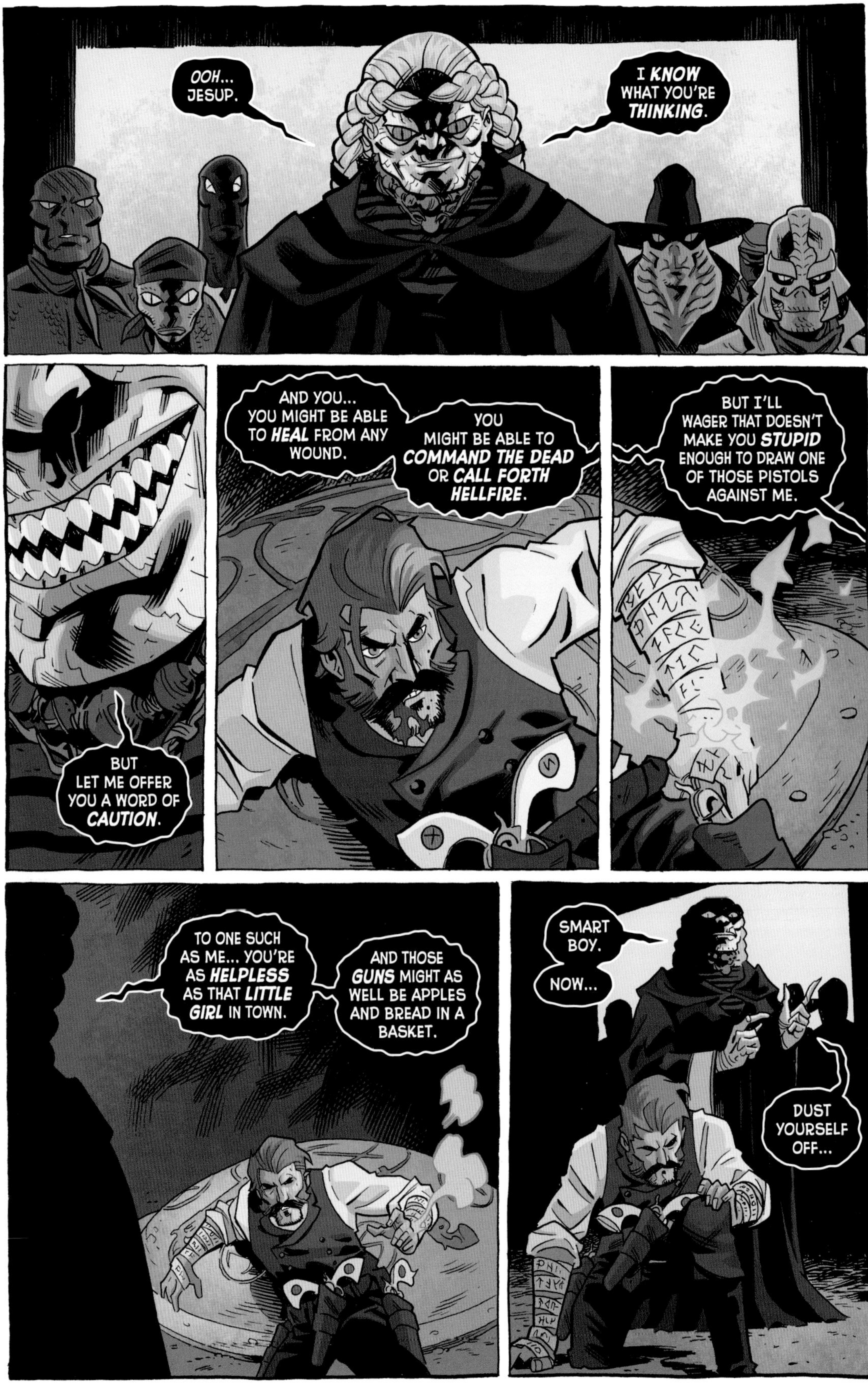
OOH... JESUP.
I KNOW WHAT YOU'RE THINKING.
BUT LET ME OFFER YOU A WORD OF CAUTION.
AND YOU... YOU MIGHT BE ABLE TO HEAL FROM ANY WOUND.
YOU MIGHT BE ABLE TO COMMAND THE DEAD OR CALL FORTH HELLFIRE.
BUT I'LL WAGER THAT DOESN'T MAKE YOU STUPID ENOUGH TO DRAW ONE OF THOSE PISTOLS AGAINST ME.
TO ONE SUCH AS ME... YOU'RE AS HELPLESS AS THAT LITTLE GIRL IN TOWN.
AND THOSE GUNS MIGHT AS WELL BE APPLES AND BREAD IN A BASKET.
SMART BOY.
NOW...
DUST YOURSELF OFF...

"...BECAUSE WE HAVE A **SACRIFICE** TO PREPARE!"

There were...

...a lot of things written in those books.

If you ask me, most of it was **nonsense**.

But there were bits and pieces... about the Six... about what must be done to **destroy** them...

...that ring **true**.

To **destroy** them.

That's what Gord wanted.

But how do we do that—**especially** now?

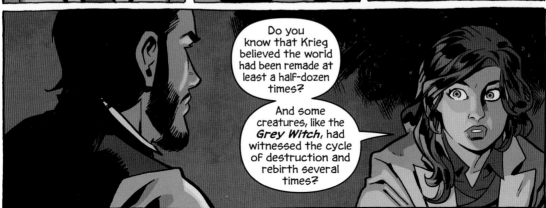

Do you know that Krieg believed the world had been remade at least a half-dozen times?

And some creatures, like the **Grey Witch**, had witnessed the cycle of destruction and rebirth several times?

27

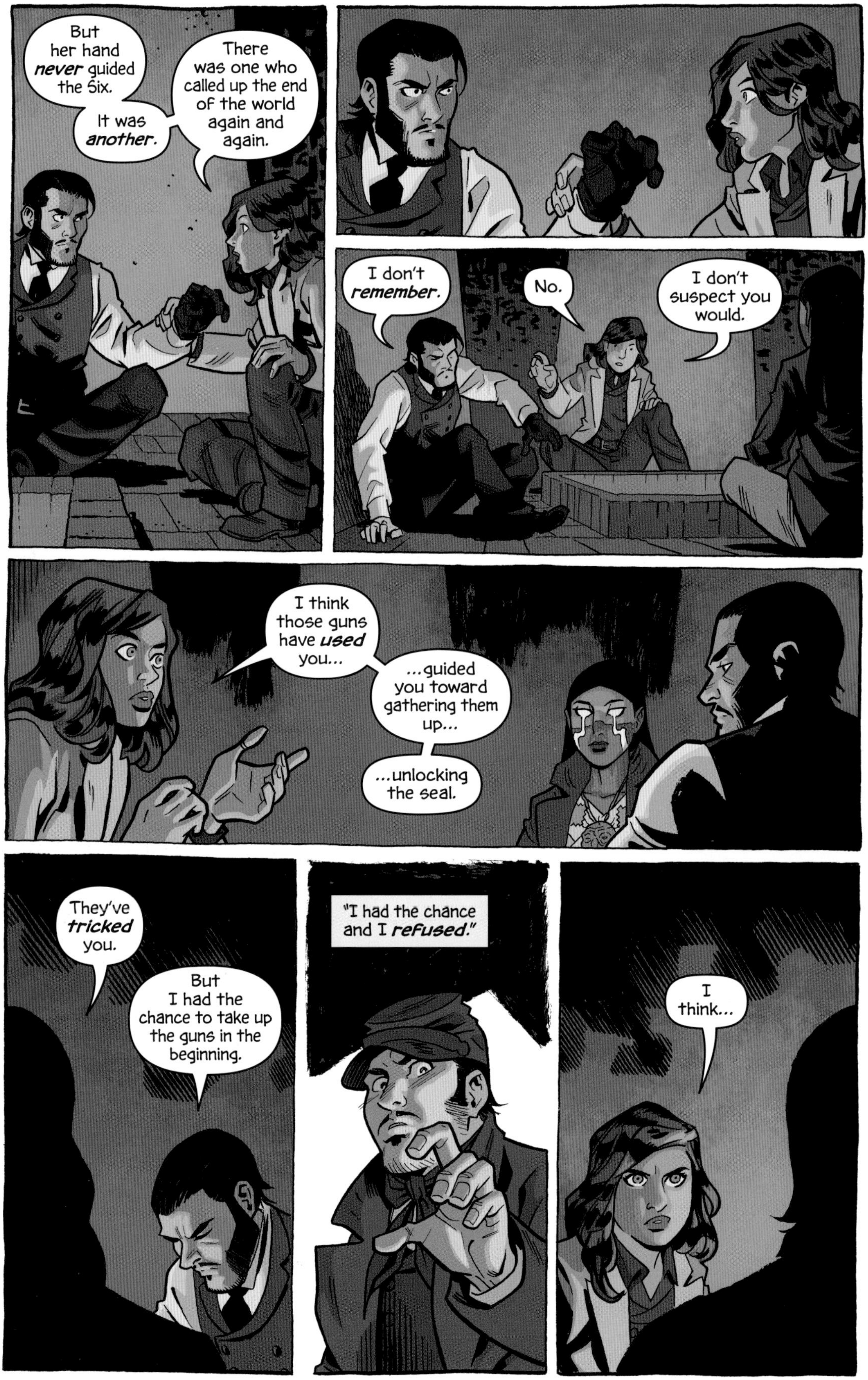
But her hand *never* guided the Six.
It was *another*.
There was one who called up the end of the world again and again.
I don't *remember*.
No.
I don't suspect you would.
I think those guns have *used* you...
...guided you toward gathering them up...
...unlocking the seal.
They've *tricked* you.
But I had the chance to take up the guns in the beginning.
"I had the chance and I *refused*."
I think...

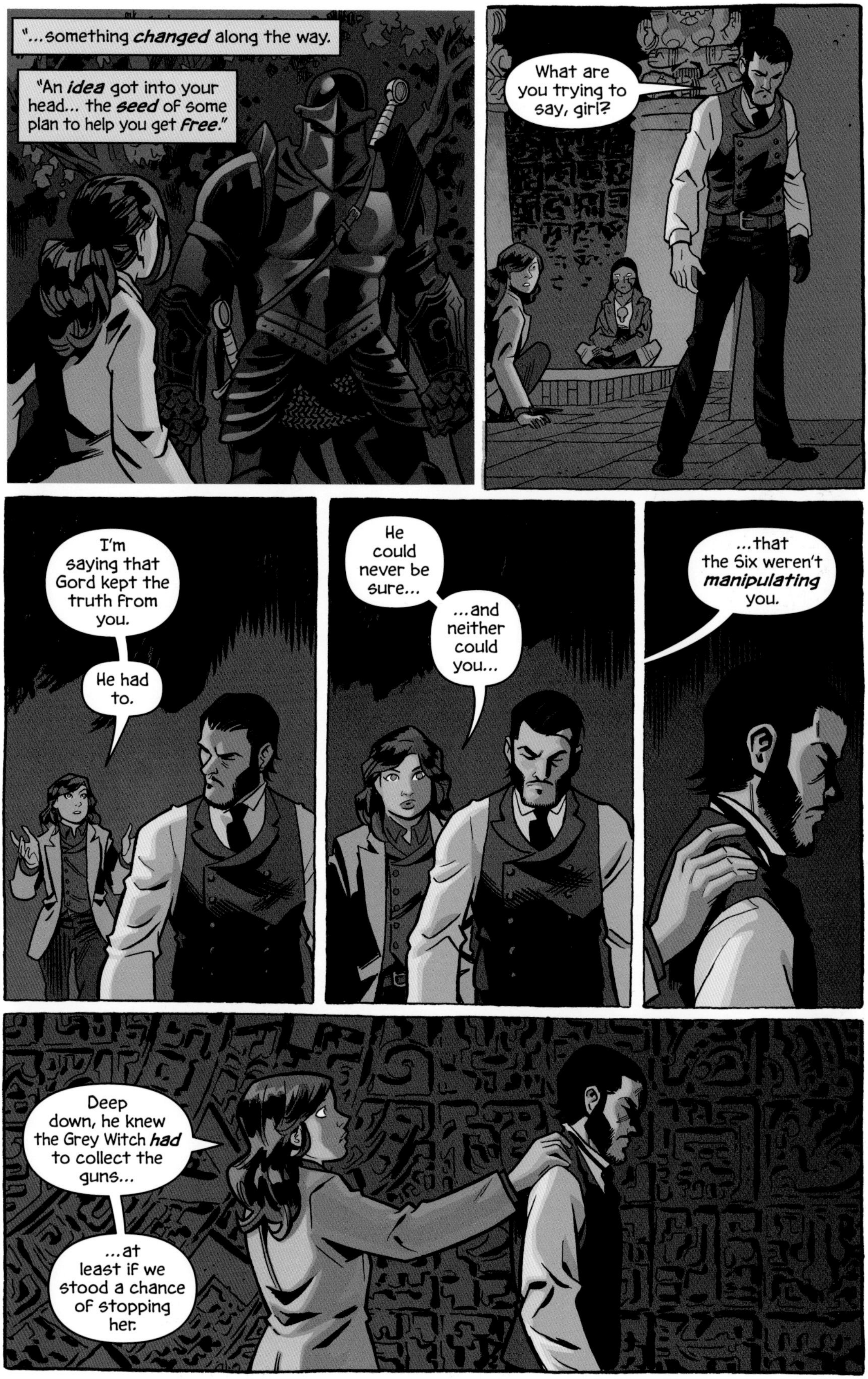
"...something *changed* along the way.
"An *idea* got into your head... the *seed* of some plan to help you get *free*."
What are you trying to say, girl?
I'm saying that Gord kept the truth from you.
He had to.
He could never be sure...
...and neither could you...
...that the Six weren't *manipulating* you.
Deep down, he knew the Grey Witch *had* to collect the guns...
...at least if we stood a chance of stopping her.

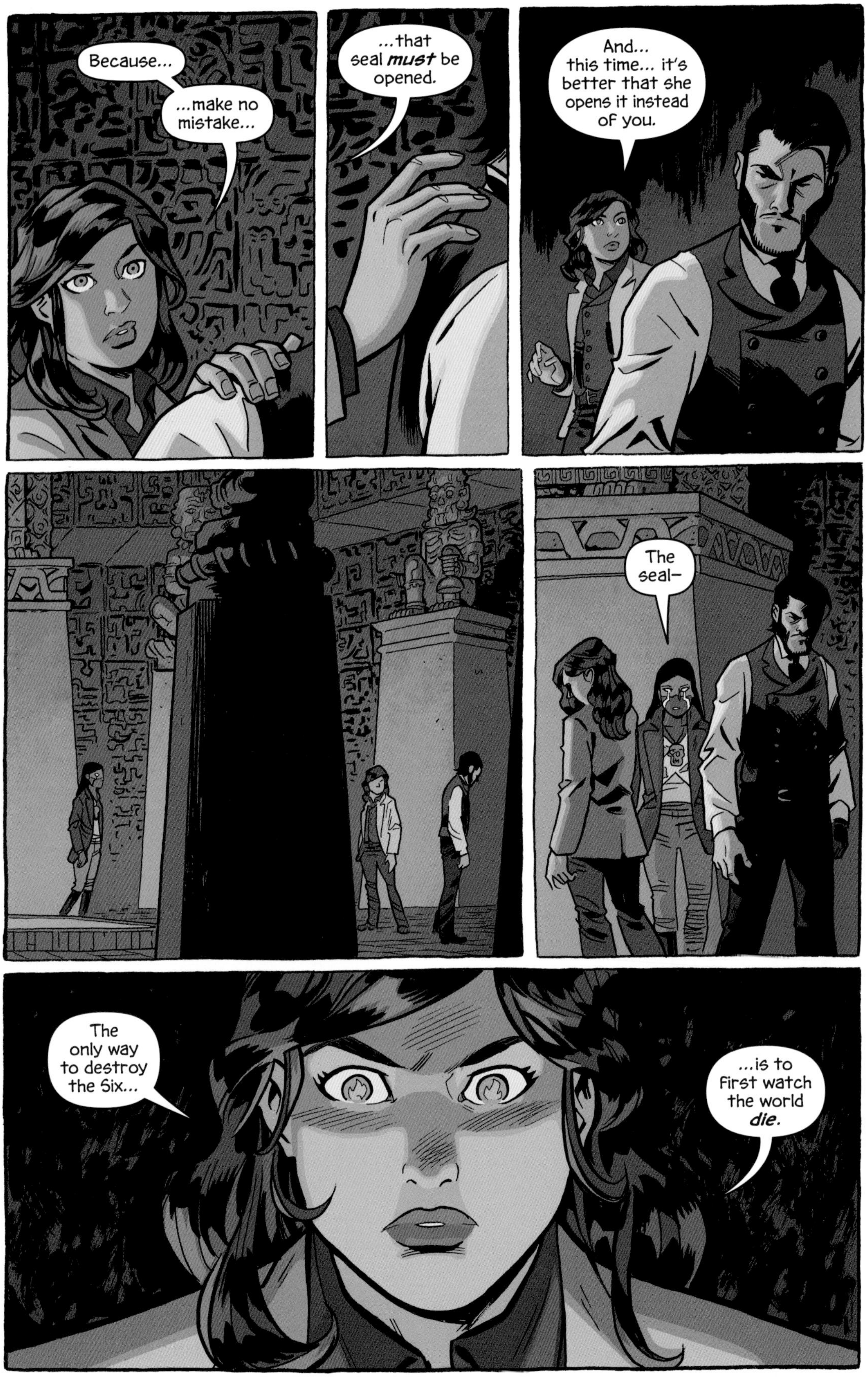
Because...
...make no mistake...
...that seal *must* be opened.
And... this time... it's better that she opens it instead of you.
The seal–
The only way to destroy the Six...
...is to first watch the world *die*.

CHAPTER TWO

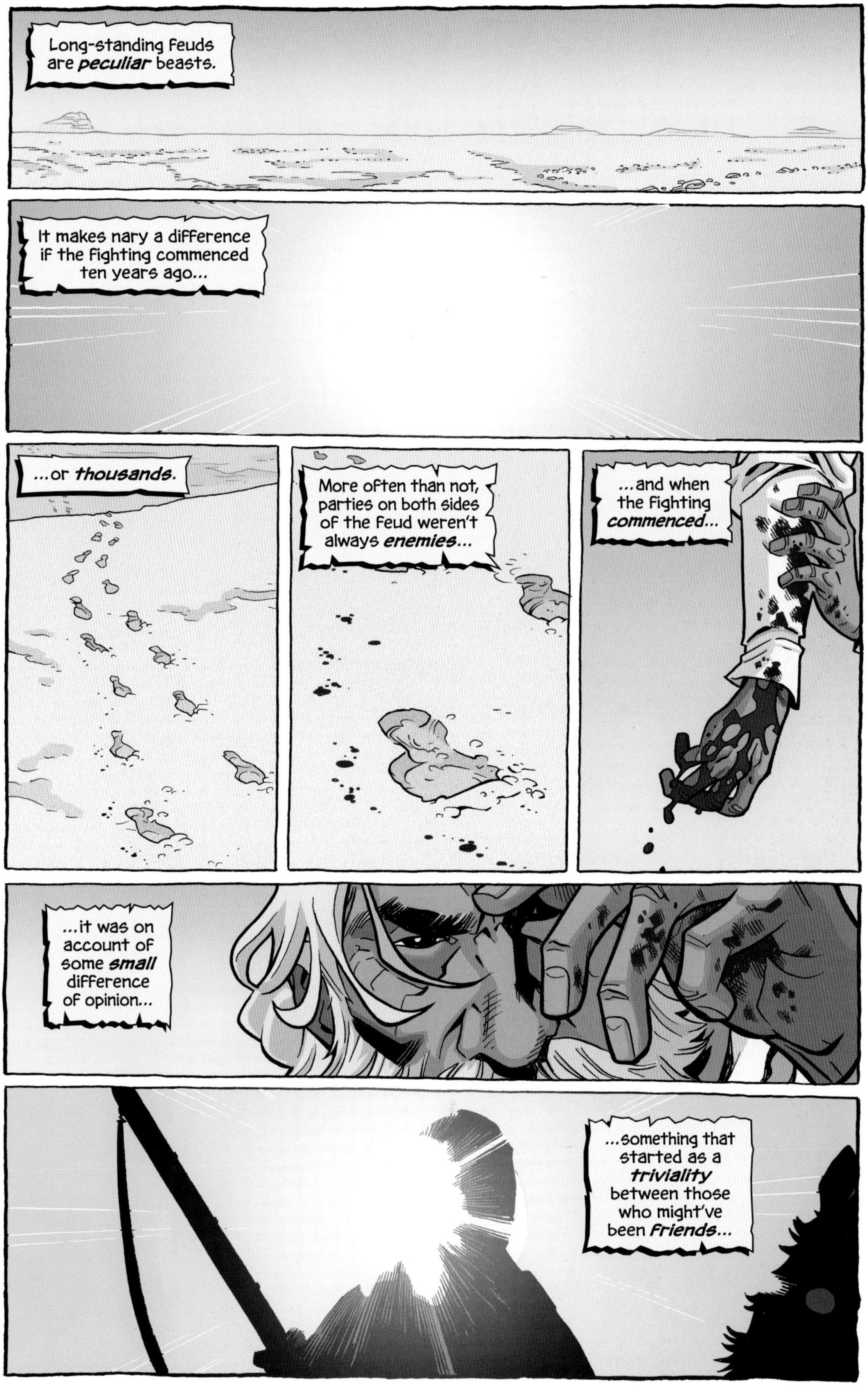
Long-standing feuds are *peculiar* beasts.
It makes nary a difference if the fighting commenced ten years ago...
...or *thousands.*
More often than not, parties on both sides of the feud weren't always *enemies*...
...and when the fighting *commenced*...
...it was on account of some *small* difference of opinion...
...something that started as a *triviality* between those who might've been *friends*...

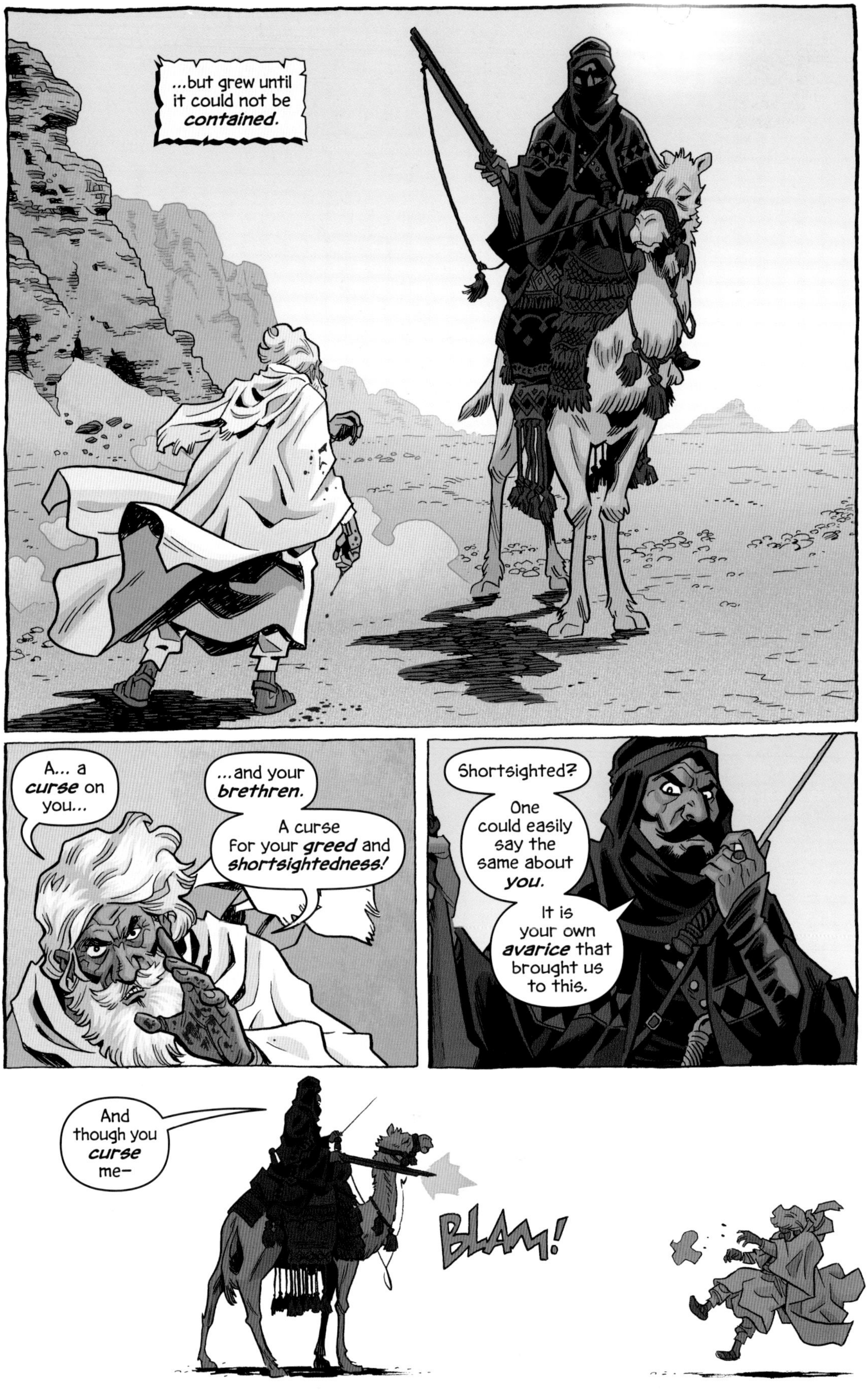
...but grew until it could not be contained.
A... a curse on you...
...and your brethren.
A curse for your greed and shortsightedness!
Shortsighted?
One could easily say the same about you.
It is your own avarice that brought us to this.
And though you curse me—
BLAM!

—I take *no pleasure* in your death.

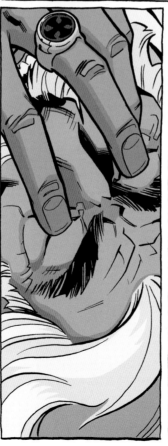

No pleasure at all.

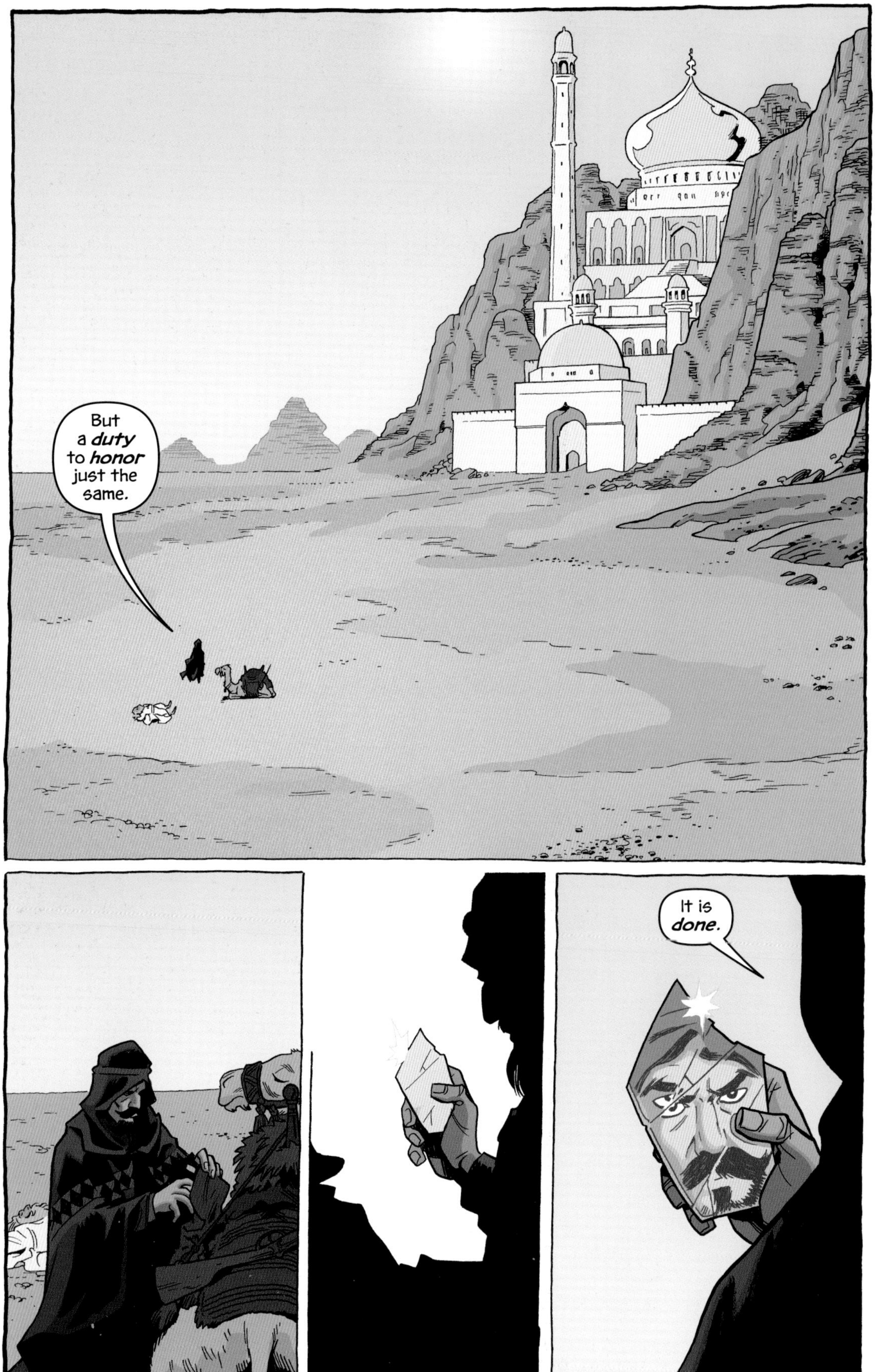
But a *duty* to *honor* just the same.
It is *done*.

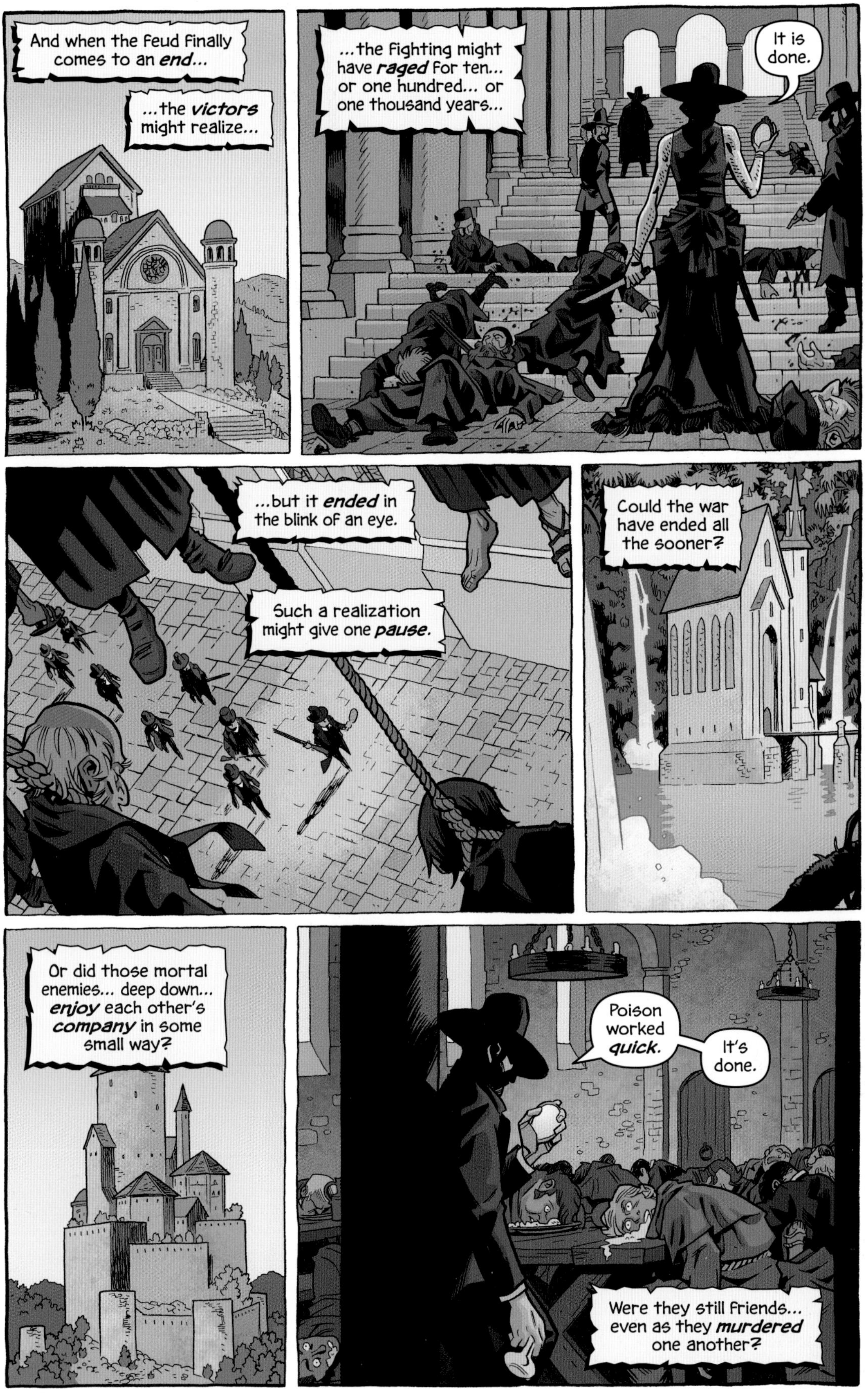
And when the feud finally comes to an *end*...
...the *victors* might realize...
...the fighting might have *raged* for ten... or one hundred... or one thousand years...
It is done.
...but it *ended* in the blink of an eye.
Such a realization might give one *pause*.
Could the war have ended all the sooner?
Or did those mortal enemies... deep down... *enjoy* each other's *company* in some small way?
Poison worked *quick*.
It's done.
Were they still friends... even as they *murdered* one another?

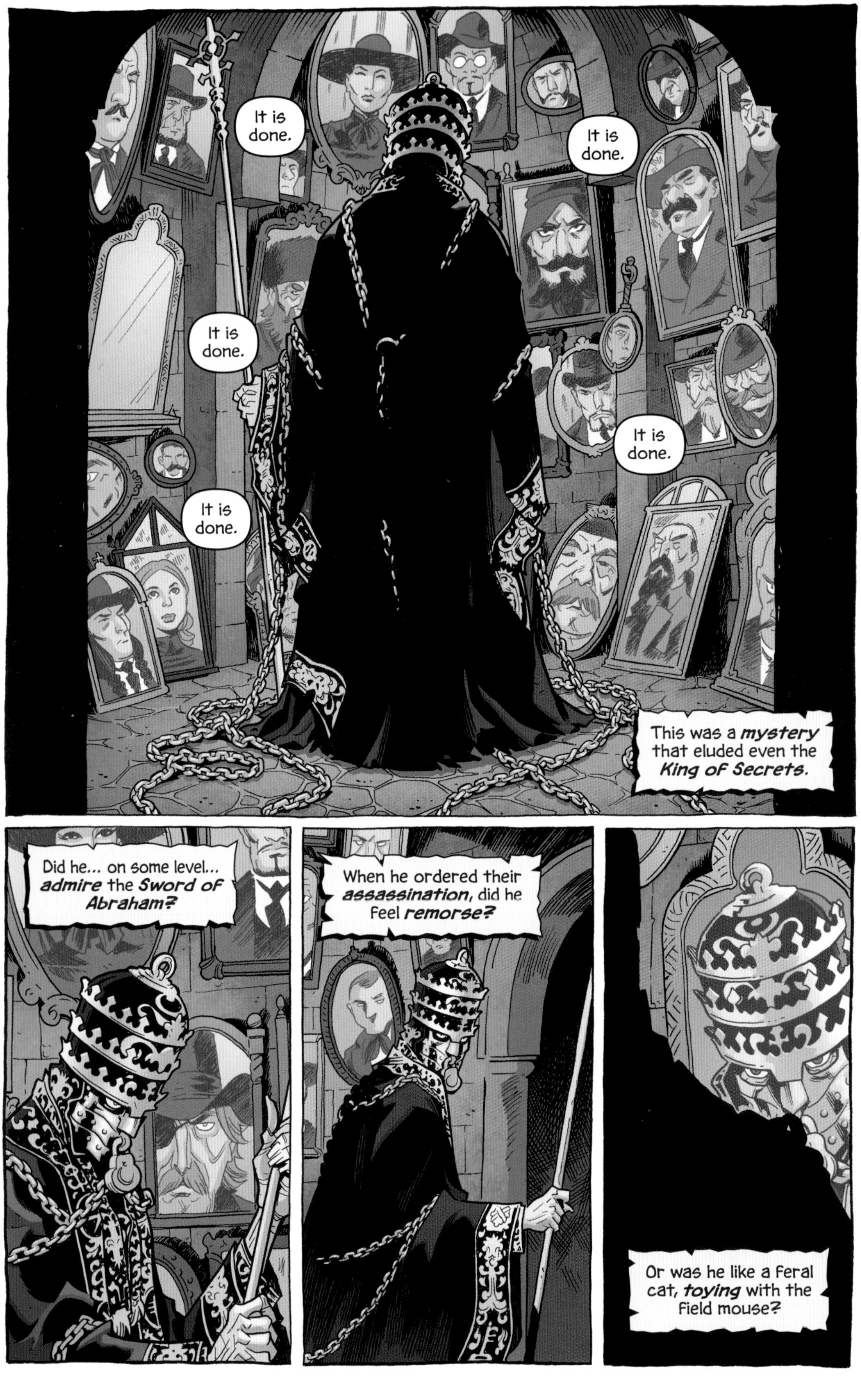
It is done.
It is done.
It is done.
It is done.
It is done.
This was a mystery that eluded even the King of Secrets.
Did he... on some level... admire the Sword of Abraham?
When he ordered their assassination, did he feel remorse?
Or was he like a feral cat, toying with the field mouse?

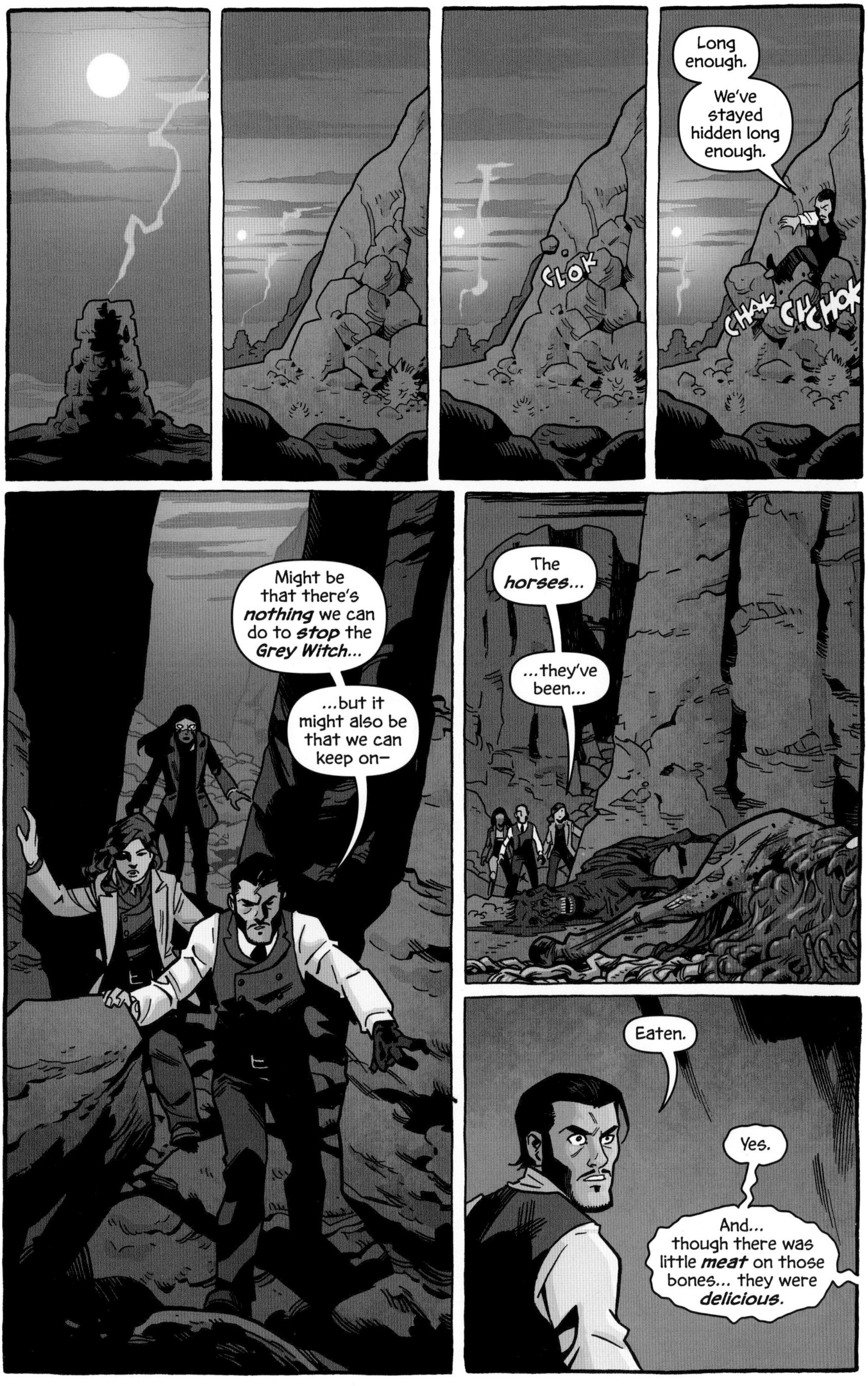
CLOK
Long enough.
We've stayed hidden long enough.
CHAK CHCHOK
Might be that there's *nothing* we can do to *stop* the *Grey Witch*...
...but it might also be that we can keep on–
The *horses*...
...they've been...
Eaten.
Yes.
And... though there was little *meat* on those bones... they were *delicious*.

You didn't expect us to go *hungry*, did you?

When you trespassed upon our lands...

...we considered eating *you*.

But one of you is more *ghost* than *flesh*.

One of you is so *old* the flesh would taste of *dust*.

And one of you does not *belong* here at all.

What are they talking about?

Is that what you wish to know?

We'll answer *one* question.

To bid you *farewell* and to *thank* you for the food.

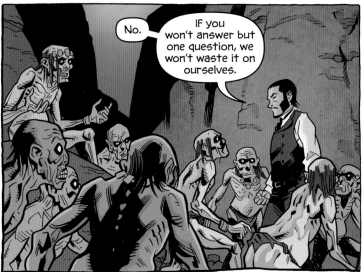

No.

If you won't answer but one question, we won't waste it on ourselves.

If you're going to tell us anything...

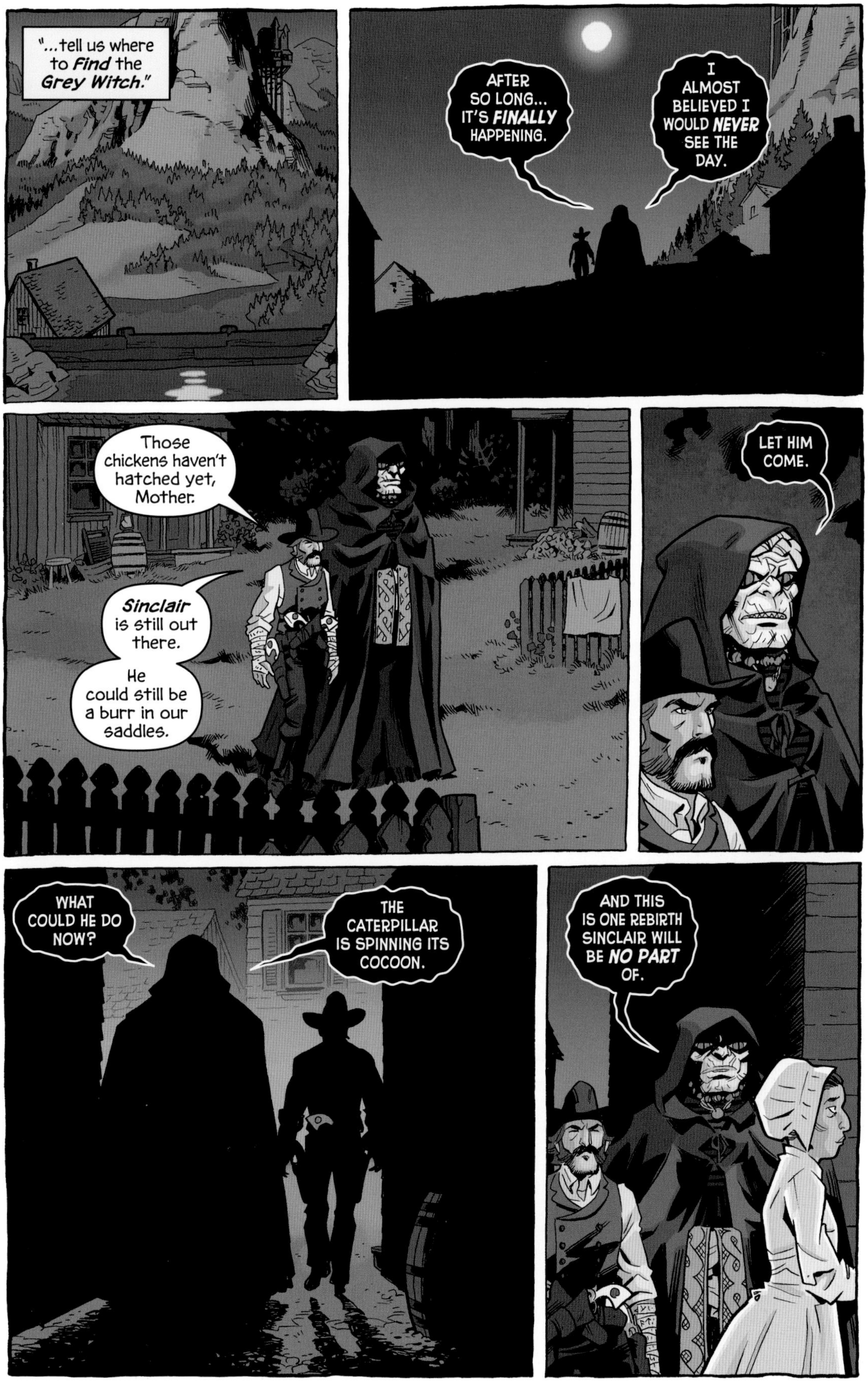
"...tell us where to Find the Grey Witch."
AFTER SO LONG... IT'S FINALLY HAPPENING.
I ALMOST BELIEVED I WOULD NEVER SEE THE DAY.
Those chickens haven't hatched yet, Mother.
Sinclair is still out there.
He could still be a burr in our saddles.
LET HIM COME.
WHAT COULD HE DO NOW?
THE CATERPILLAR IS SPINNING ITS COCOON.
AND THIS IS ONE REBIRTH SINCLAIR WILL BE NO PART OF.

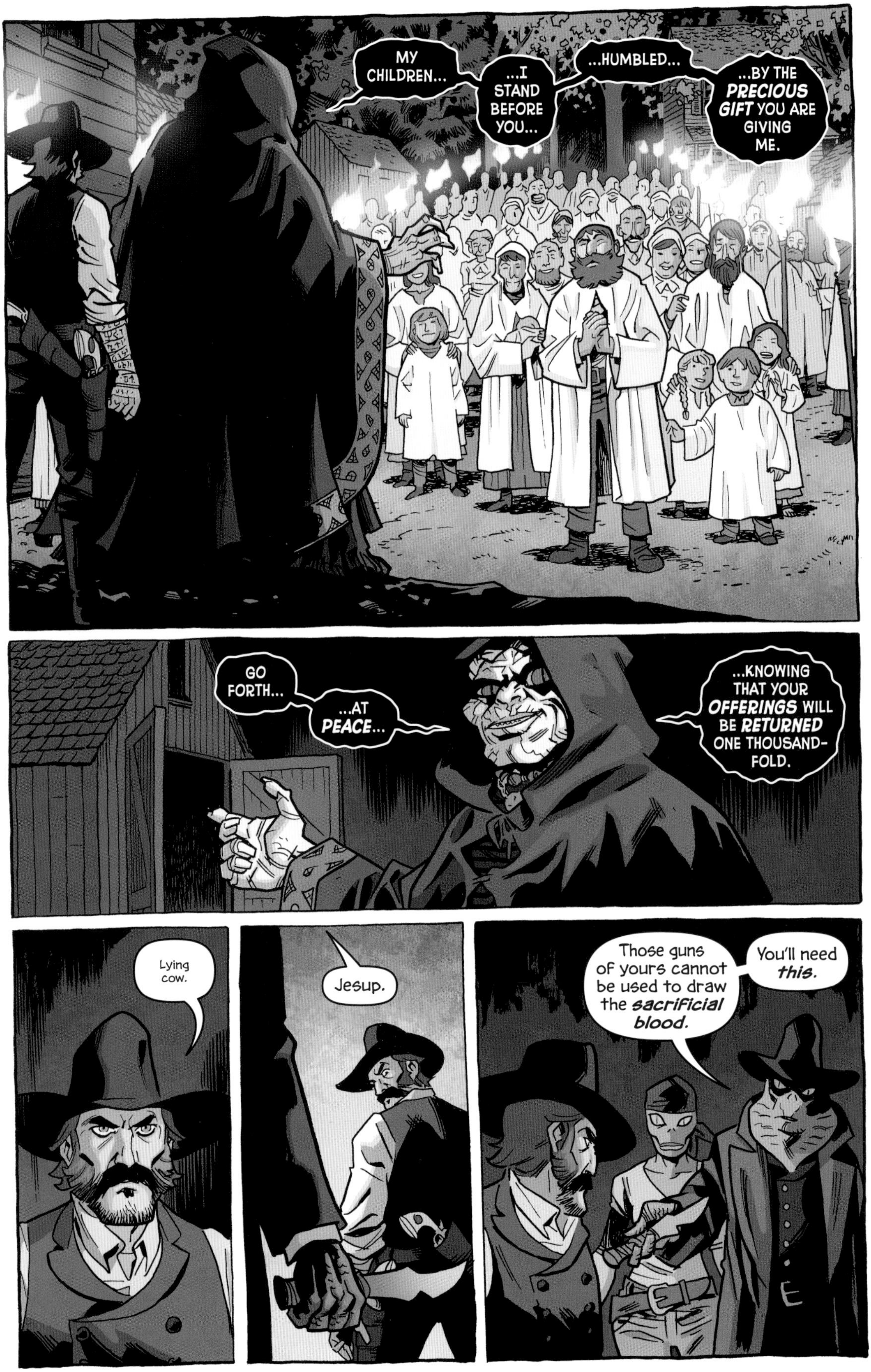
MY CHILDREN...
...I STAND BEFORE YOU...
...HUMBLED...
...BY THE **PRECIOUS GIFT** YOU ARE GIVING ME.
GO FORTH...
...AT **PEACE**...
...KNOWING THAT YOUR **OFFERINGS** WILL BE **RETURNED** ONE THOUSAND-FOLD.
Lying cow.
Jesup.
Those guns of yours cannot be used to draw the ***sacrificial blood***.
You'll need ***this***.

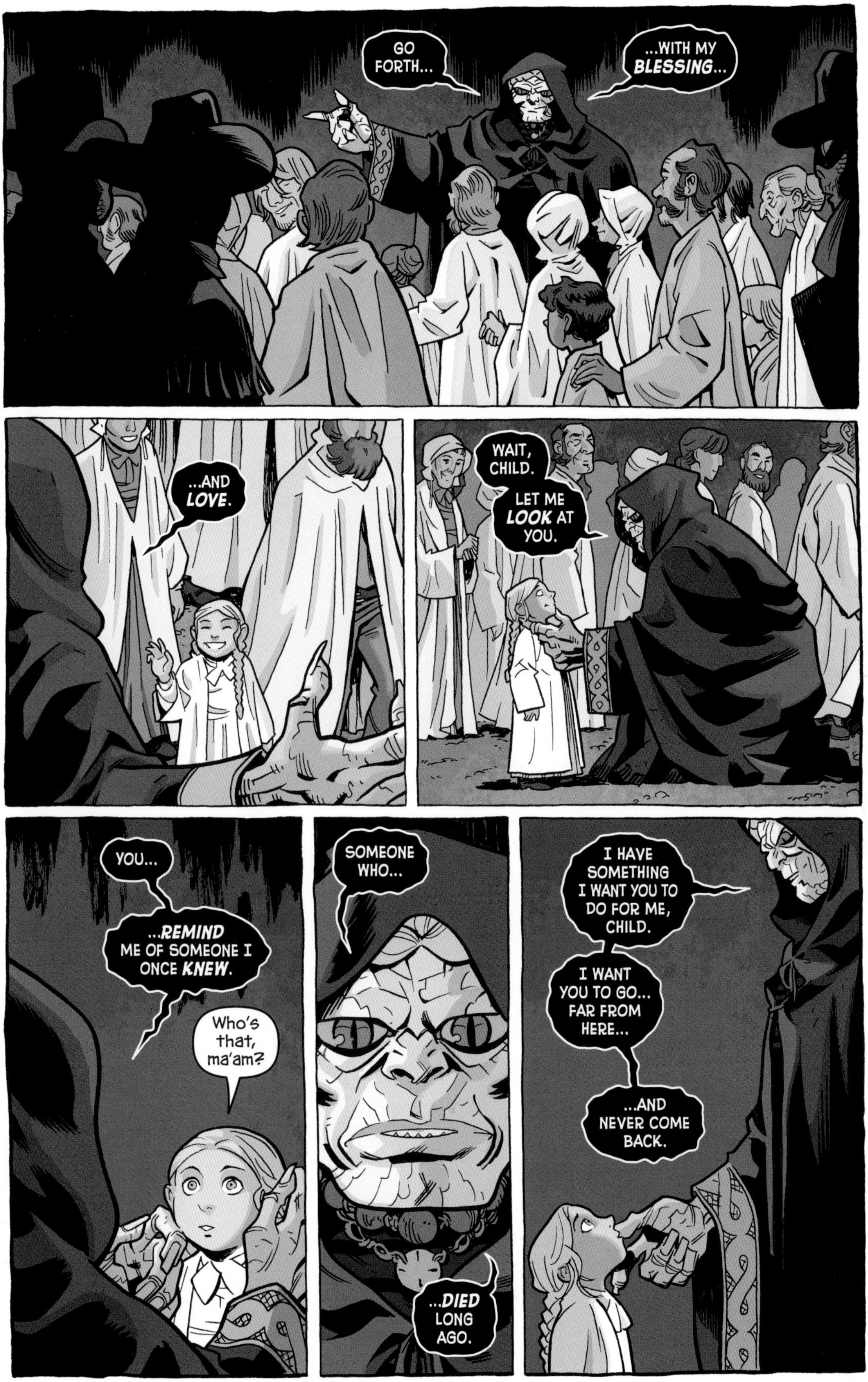
GO FORTH...
...WITH MY BLESSING...
...AND LOVE.
WAIT, CHILD.
LET ME LOOK AT YOU.
YOU...
...REMIND ME OF SOMEONE I ONCE KNEW.
Who's that, ma'am?
SOMEONE WHO...
...DIED LONG AGO.
I HAVE SOMETHING I WANT YOU TO DO FOR ME, CHILD.
I WANT YOU TO GO... FAR FROM HERE...
...AND NEVER COME BACK.

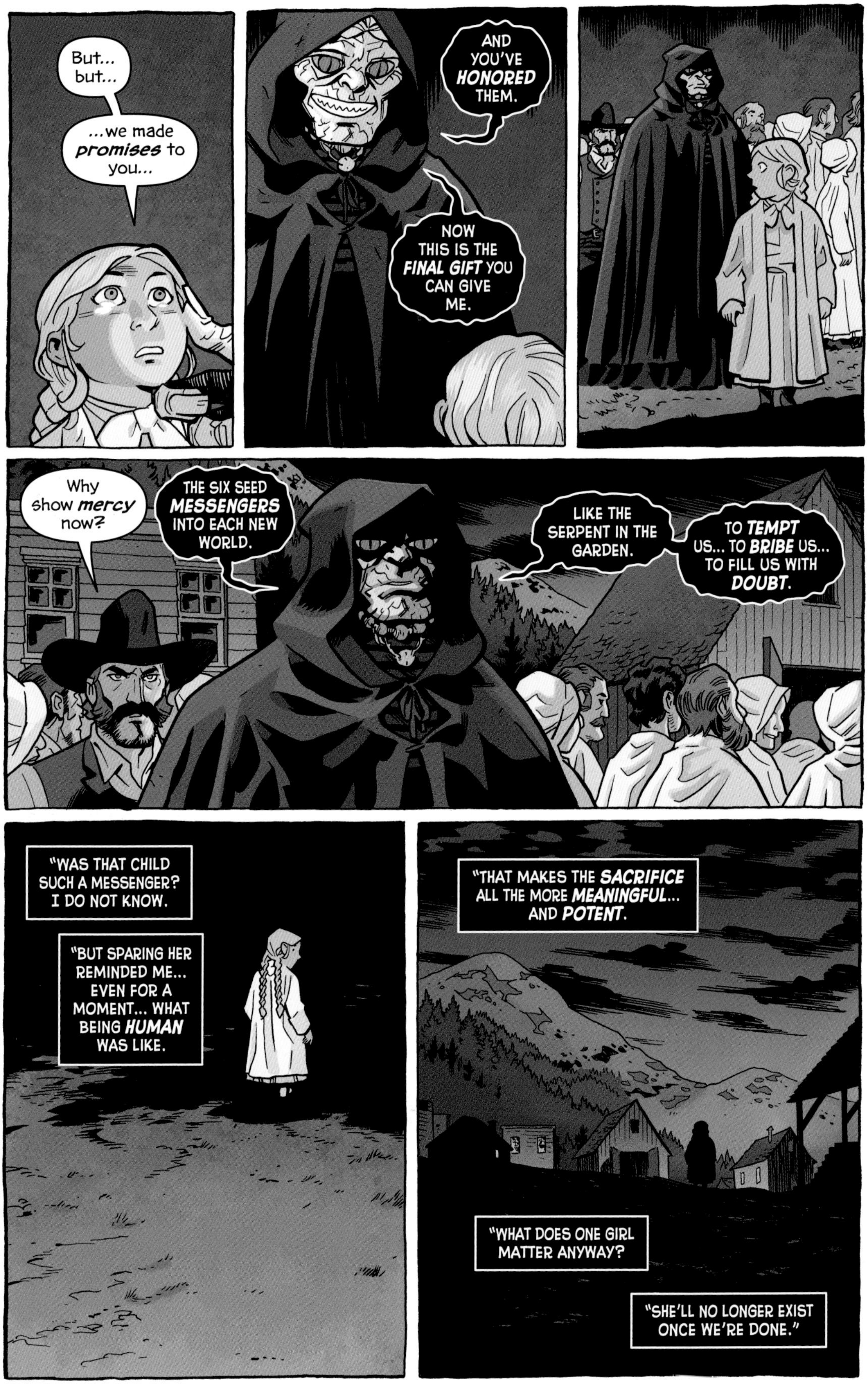

But... but...
...we made *promises* to you...
AND YOU'VE *HONORED* THEM.
NOW THIS IS THE *FINAL GIFT* YOU CAN GIVE ME.
Why show *mercy* now?
THE SIX SEED *MESSENGERS* INTO EACH NEW WORLD.
LIKE THE SERPENT IN THE GARDEN.
TO *TEMPT* US... TO *BRIBE* US... TO FILL US WITH *DOUBT*.
"WAS THAT CHILD SUCH A MESSENGER? I DO NOT KNOW.
"BUT SPARING HER REMINDED ME... EVEN FOR A MOMENT... WHAT BEING *HUMAN* WAS LIKE.
"THAT MAKES THE *SACRIFICE* ALL THE MORE *MEANINGFUL*... AND *POTENT*.
"WHAT DOES ONE GIRL MATTER ANYWAY?
"SHE'LL NO LONGER EXIST ONCE WE'RE DONE."

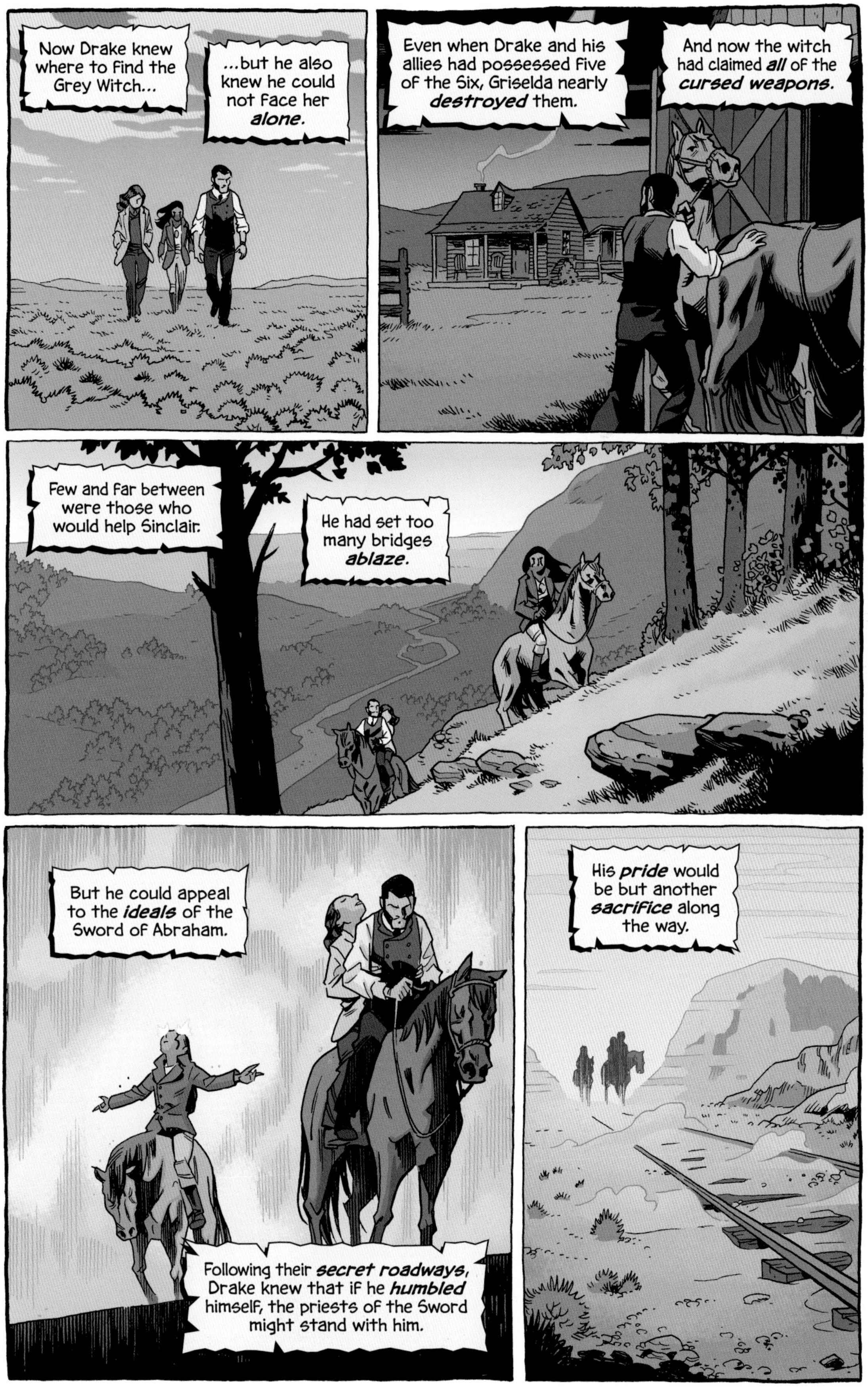
Now Drake knew where to find the Grey Witch...
...but he also knew he could not face her *alone*.
Even when Drake and his allies had possessed five of the Six, Griselda nearly *destroyed* them.
And now the witch had claimed *all* of the *cursed weapons*.
Few and far between were those who would help Sinclair.
He had set too many bridges *ablaze*.
But he could appeal to the *ideals* of the Sword of Abraham.
Following their *secret roadways*, Drake knew that if he *humbled* himself, the priests of the Sword might stand with him.
His *pride* would be but another *sacrifice* along the way.

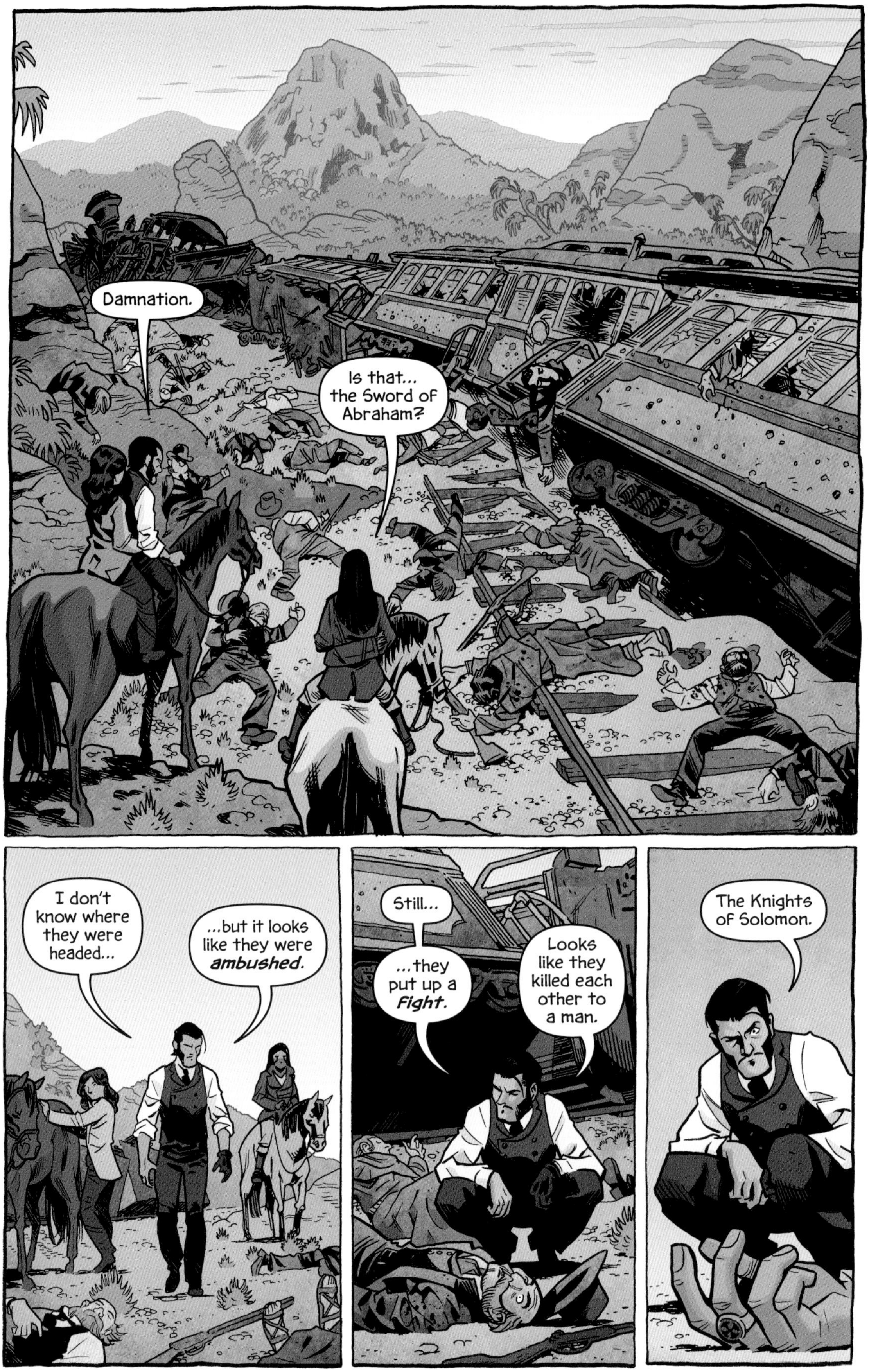

Damnation.
Is that... the Sword of Abraham?
I don't know where they were headed...
...but it looks like they were *ambushed*.
Still...
...they put up a *fight*.
Looks like they killed each other to a man.
The Knights of Solomon.

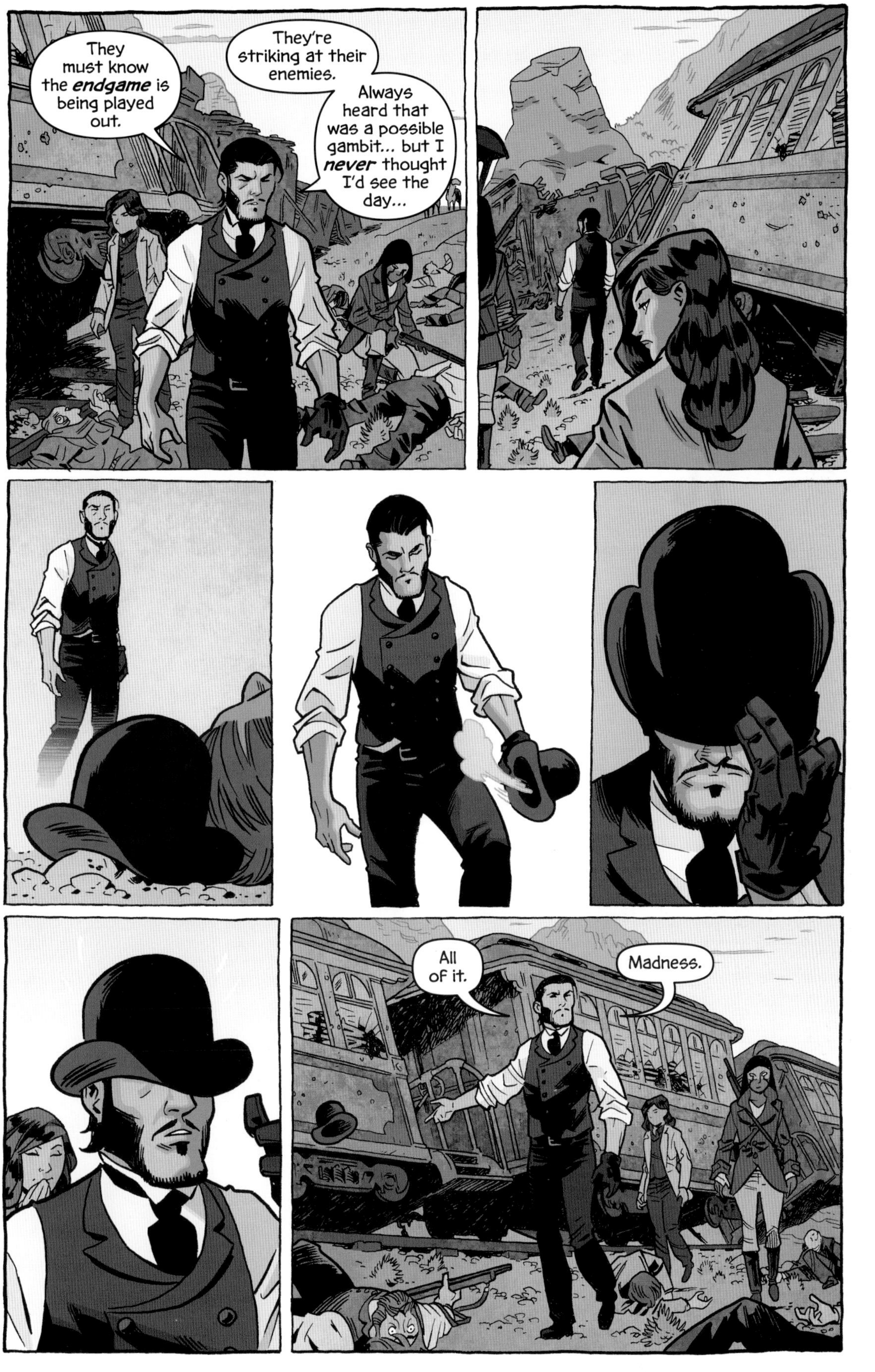
They must know the *endgame* is being played out.
They're striking at their enemies.
Always heard that was a possible gambit... but I *never* thought I'd see the day...
All of it.
Madness.

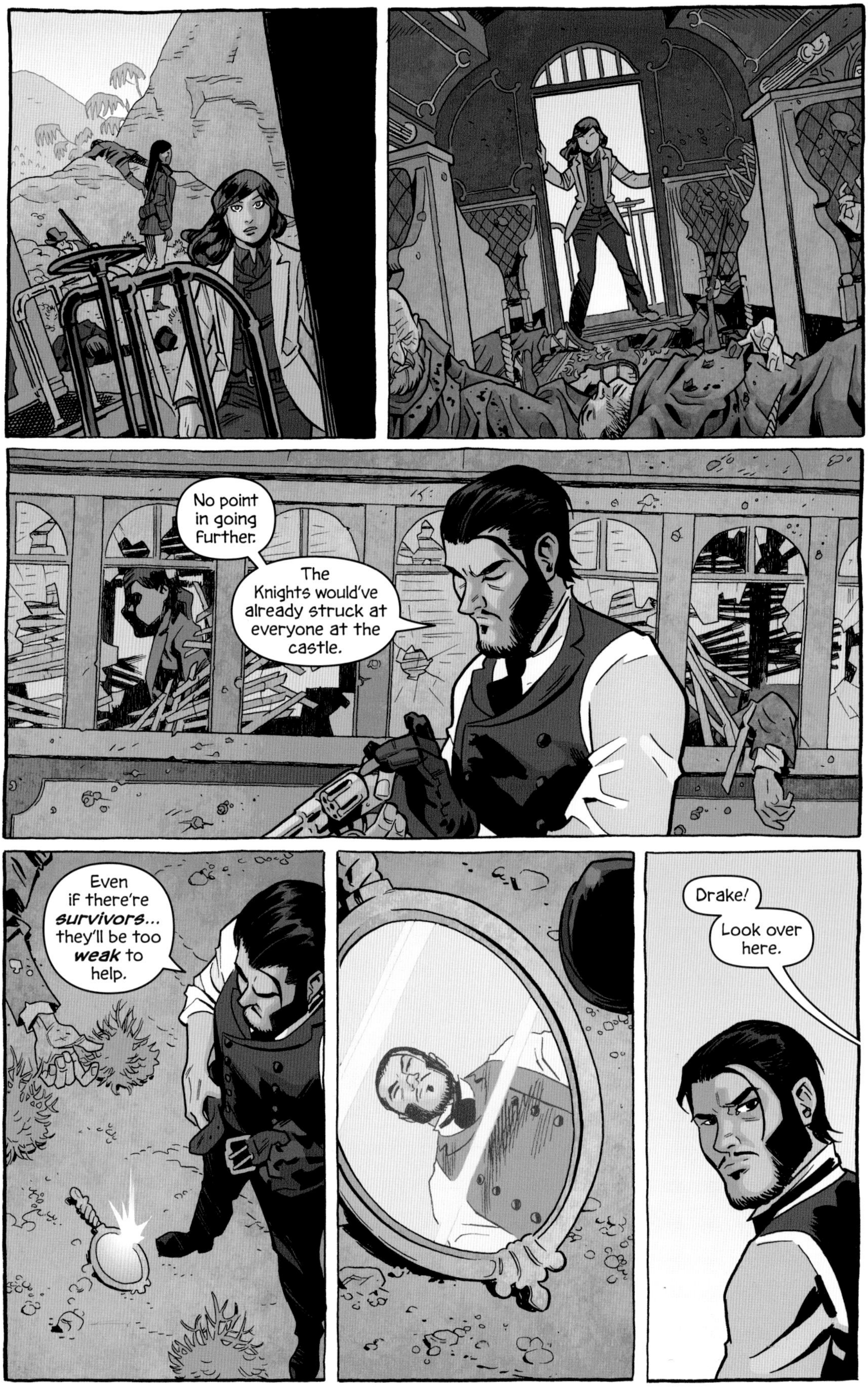
No point in going further.
The Knights would've already struck at everyone at the castle.
Even if there're *survivors*... they'll be too *weak* to help.
Drake!
Look over here.

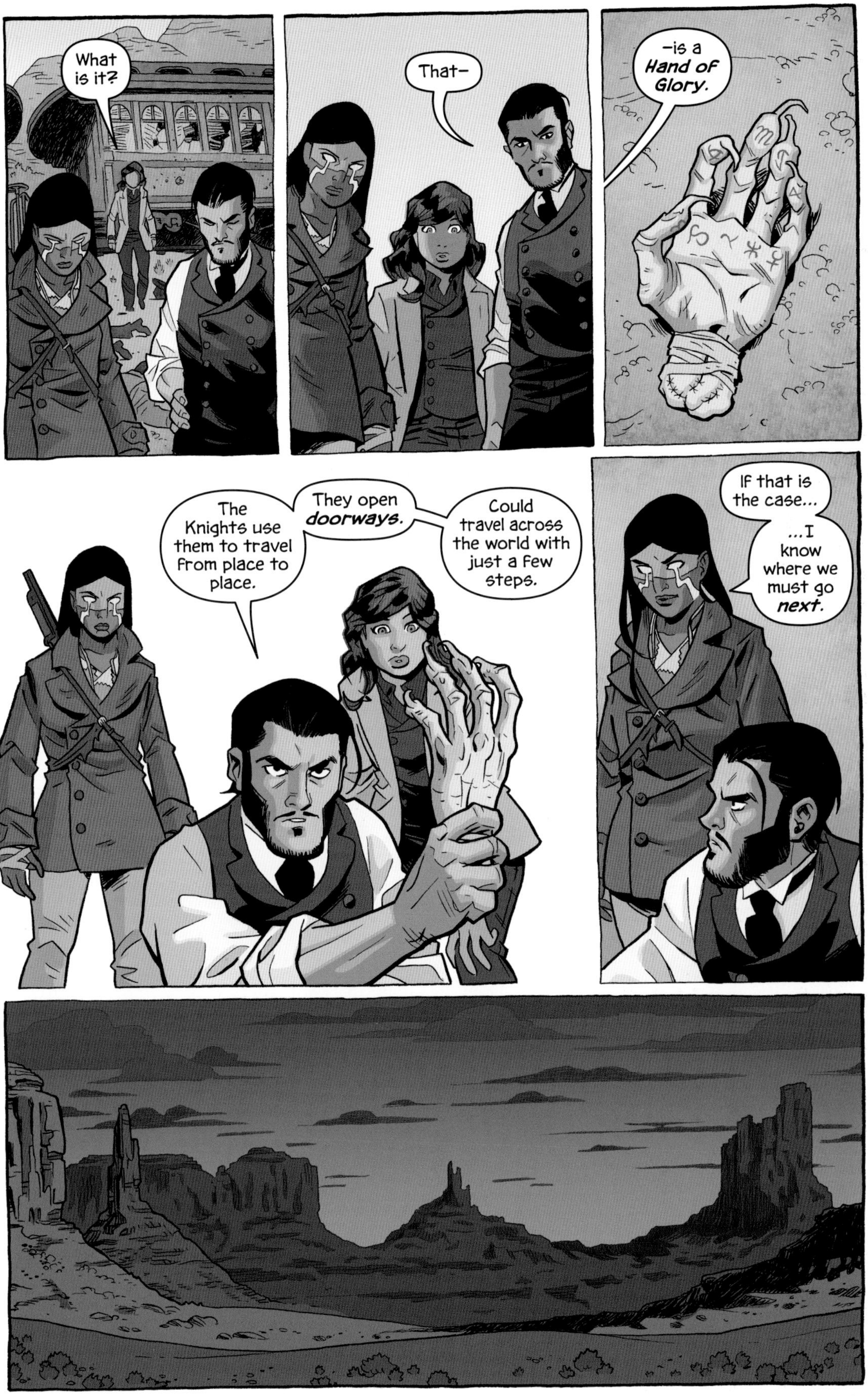

What is it?
That–
–is a *Hand of Glory*.
The Knights use them to travel from place to place.
They open *doorways*.
Could travel across the world with just a few steps.
If that is the case...
...I know where we must go *next*.

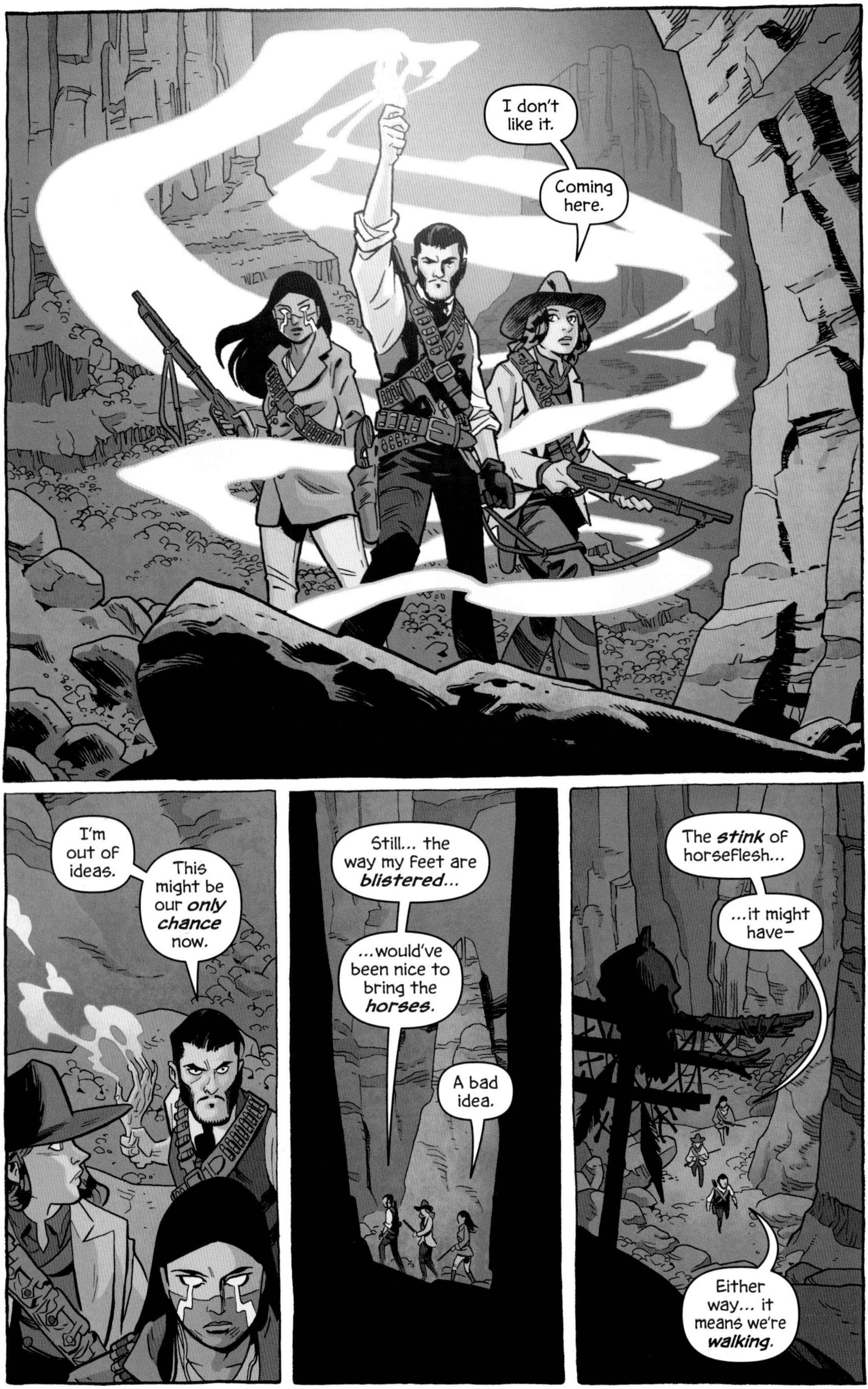
I don't like it.
Coming here.
I'm out of ideas.
This might be our *only chance* now.
Still... the way my feet are *blistered*...
...would've been nice to bring the *horses*.
A bad idea.
The *stink* of horseflesh...
...it might have—
Either way... it means we're *walking*.

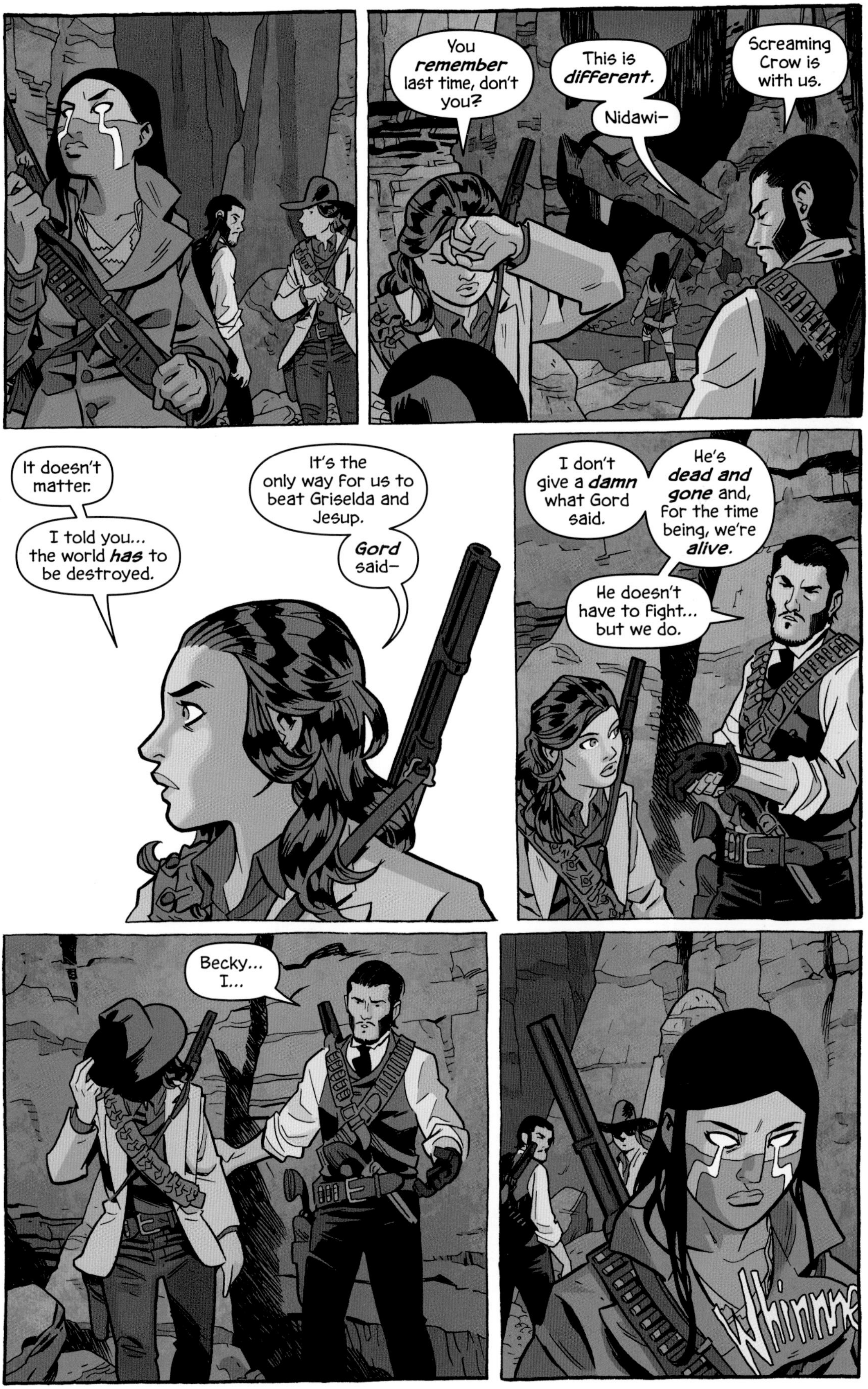
You *remember* last time, don't you?
This is *different*.
Nidawi–
Screaming Crow is with us.
It doesn't matter.
I told you... the world *has* to be destroyed.
It's the only way for us to beat Griselda and Jesup.
Gord said–
I don't give a *damn* what Gord said.
He's *dead and gone* and, for the time being, we're *alive*.
He doesn't have to fight... but we do.
Becky... I...
Whinnne

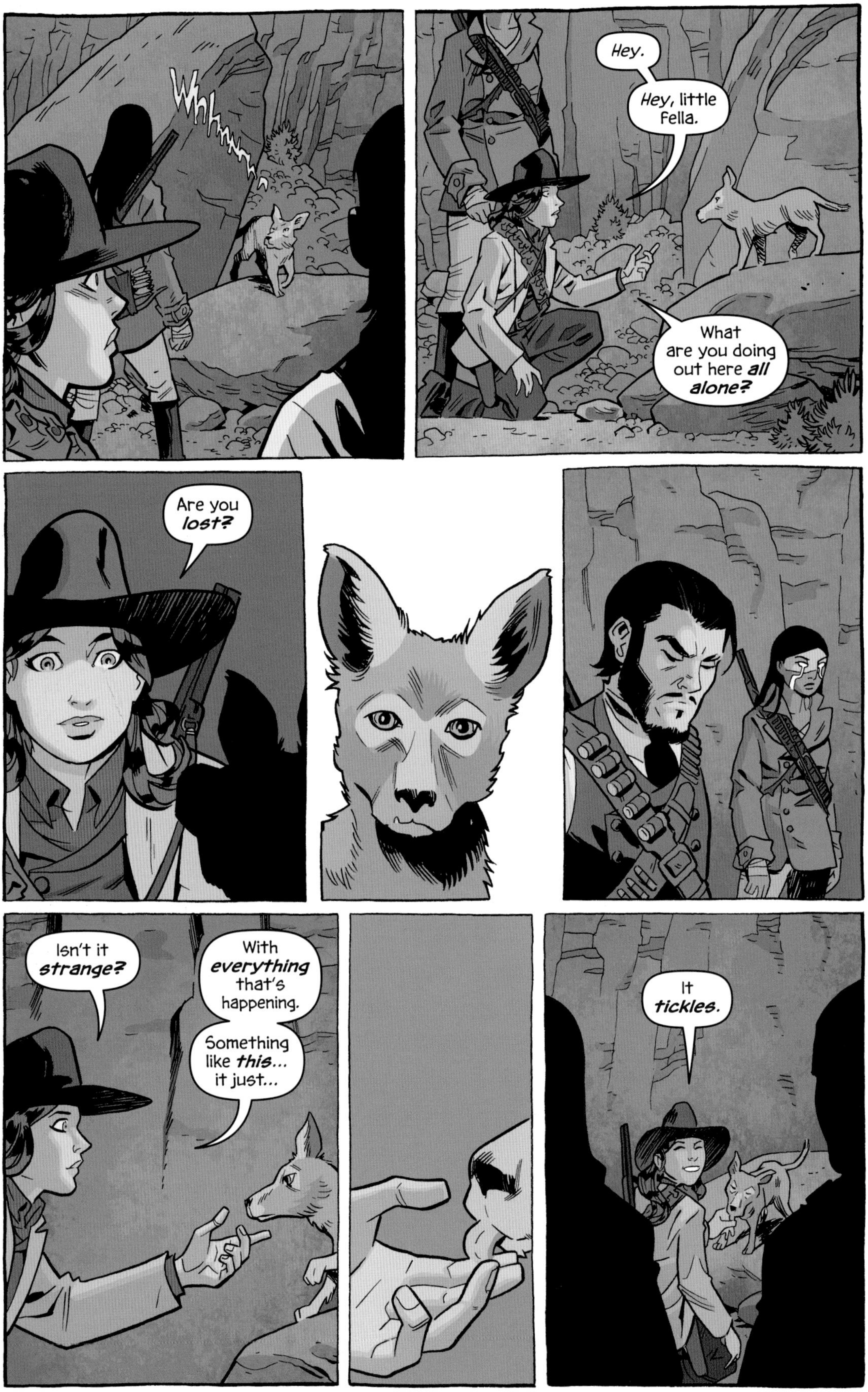
Whhnnnnnn
Hey.
Hey, little fella.
What are you doing out here *all alone?*
Are you *lost?*
Isn't it *strange?*
With *everything* that's happening.
Something like *this*... it just...
It *tickles.*

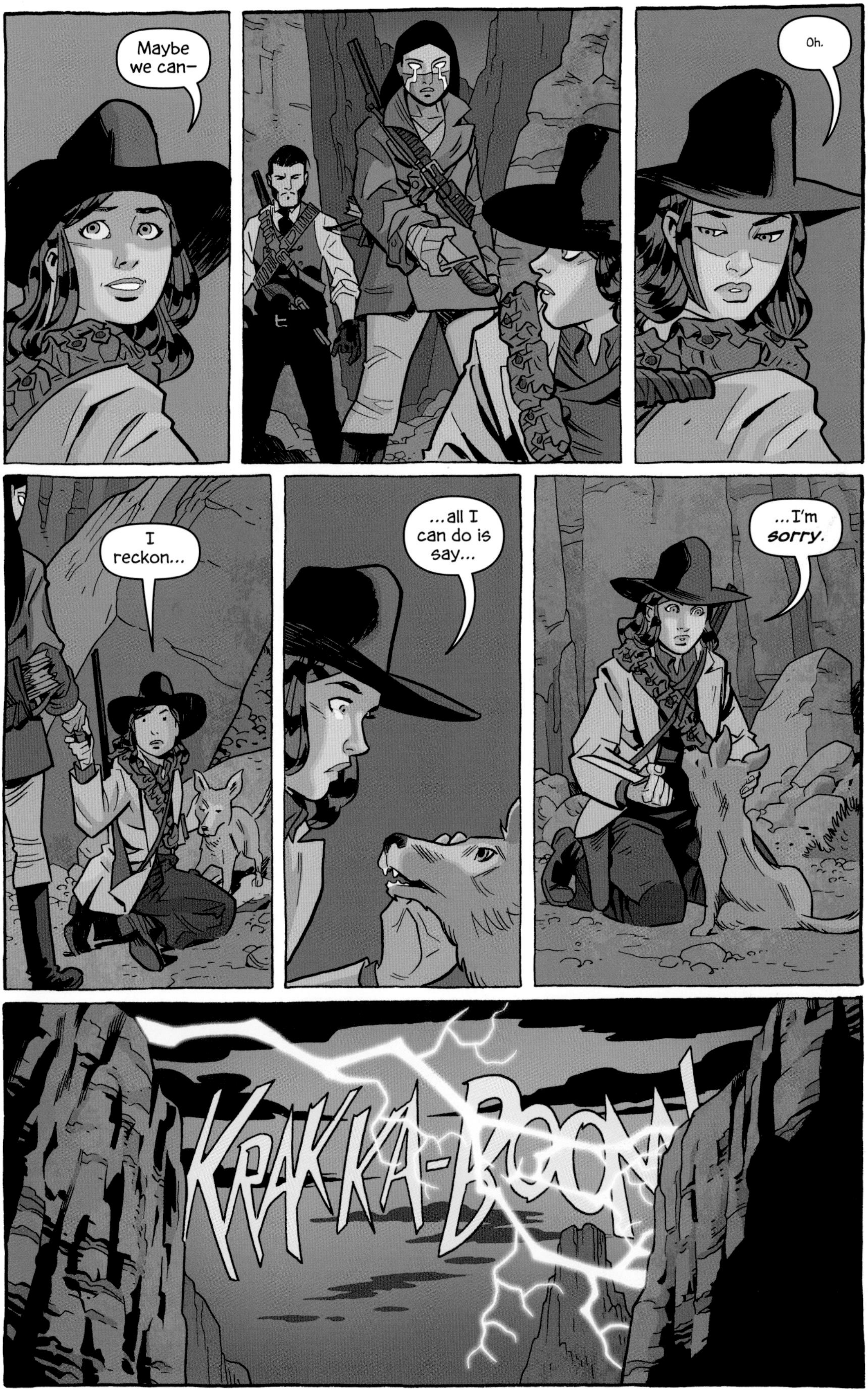
Maybe we can–
Oh.
I reckon...
...all I can do is say...
...I'm *sorry*.
KRAK KA-BOOM!

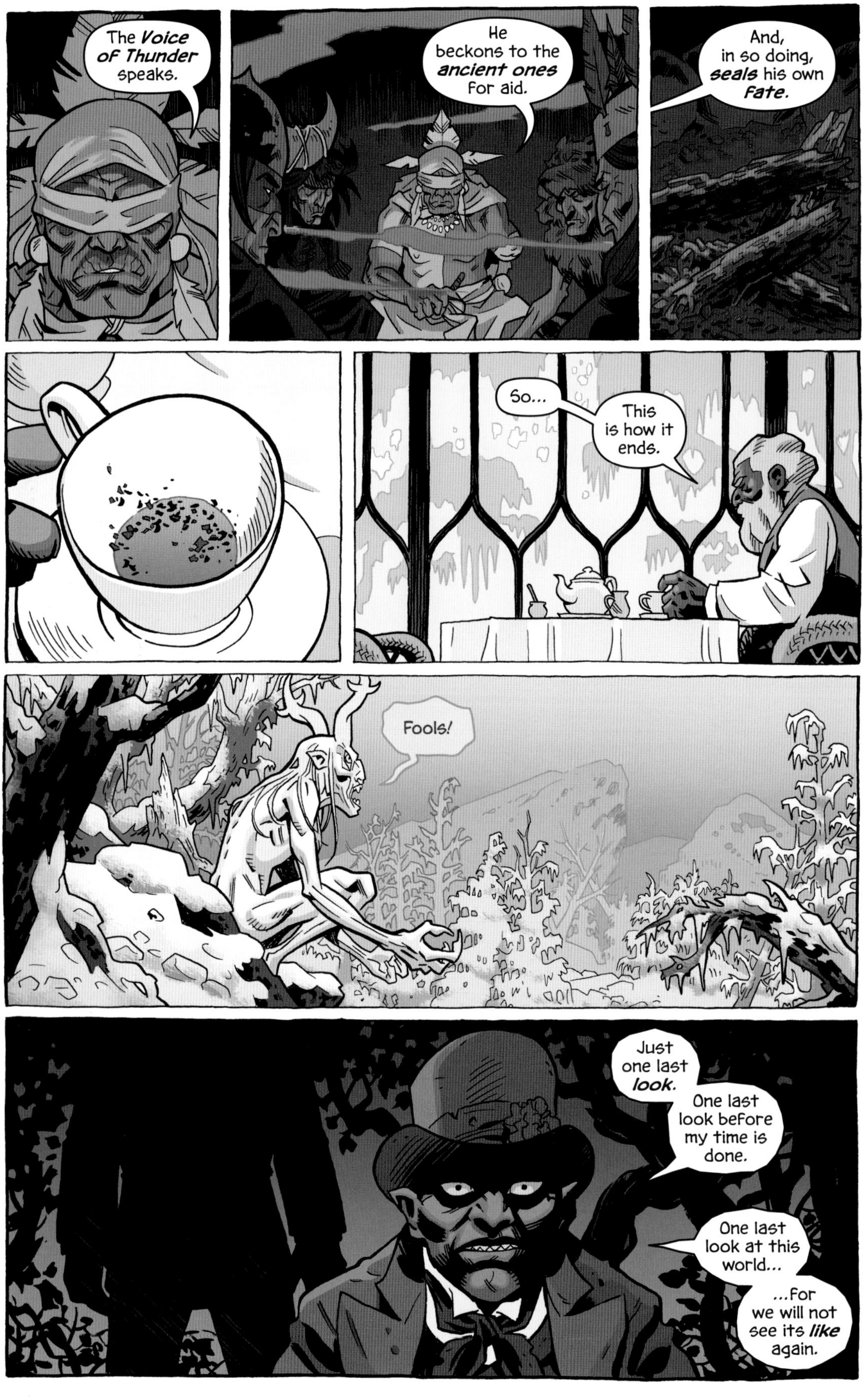
The *Voice of Thunder* speaks.
He beckons to the *ancient ones* for aid.
And, in so doing, *seals* his own *fate.*
So...
This is how it ends.
Fools!
Just one last *look.*
One last look before my time is done.
One last look at this world...
...For we will not see its *like* again.

CHAPTER THREE

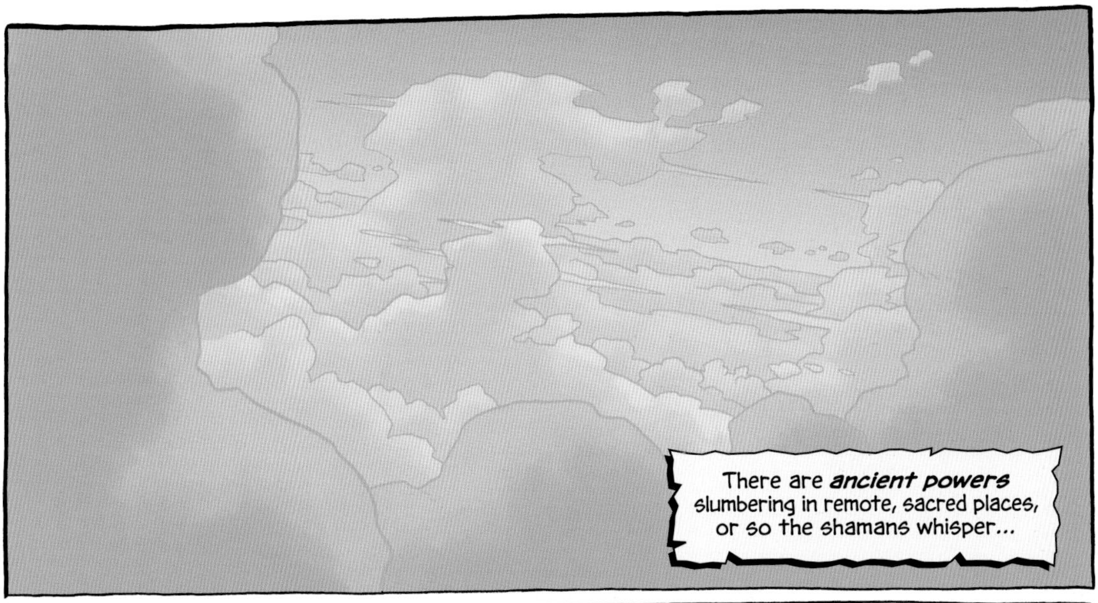
There are ***ancient powers*** slumbering in remote, sacred places, or so the shamans whisper...

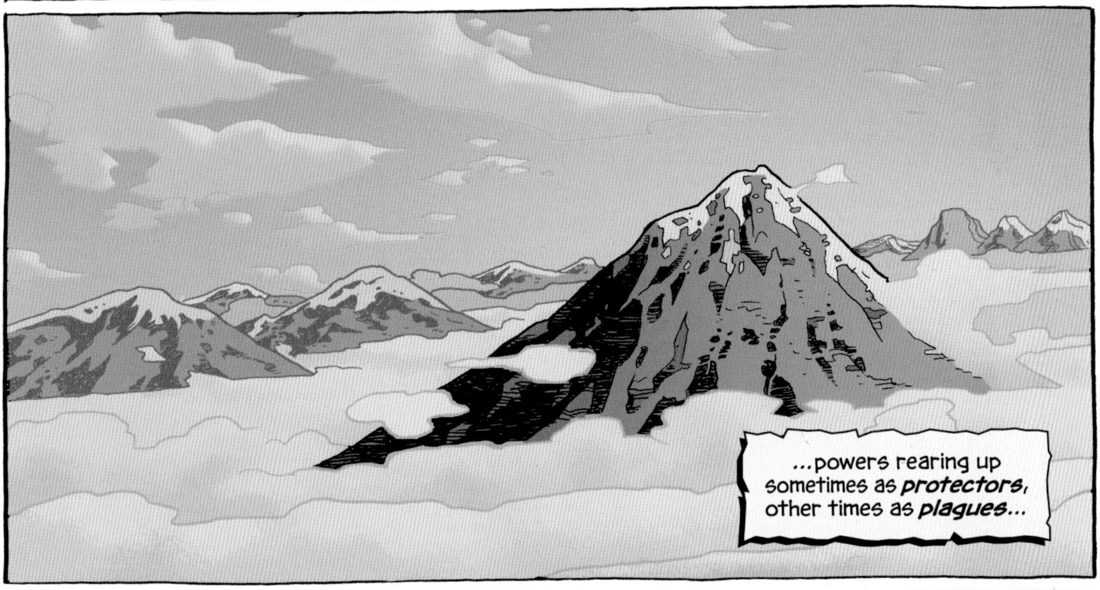
...powers rearing up sometimes as ***protectors***, other times as ***plagues***...

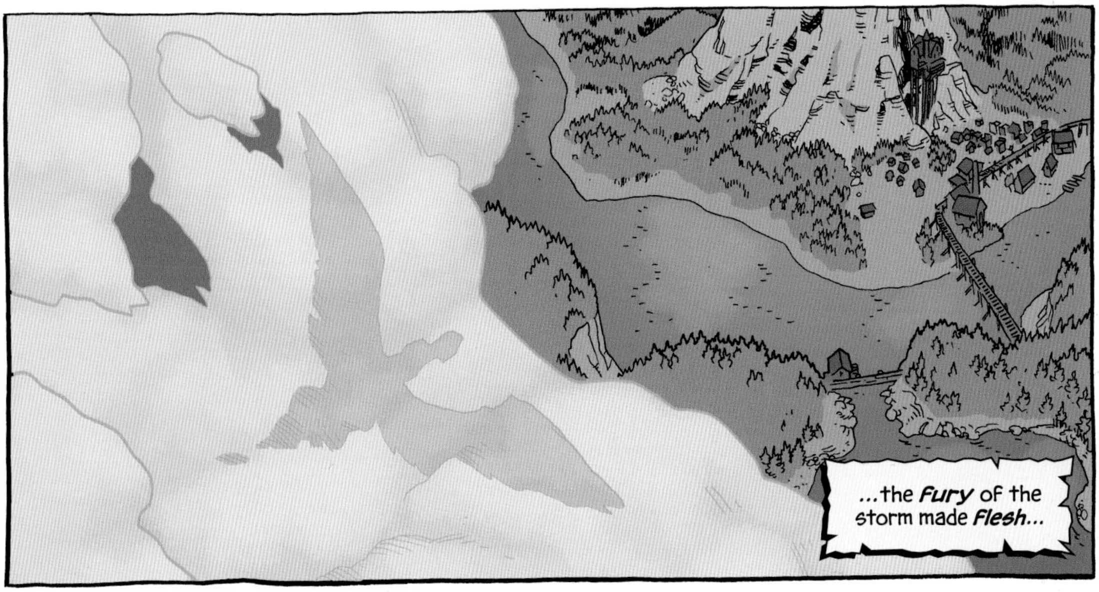
...the ***fury*** of the storm made ***flesh***...

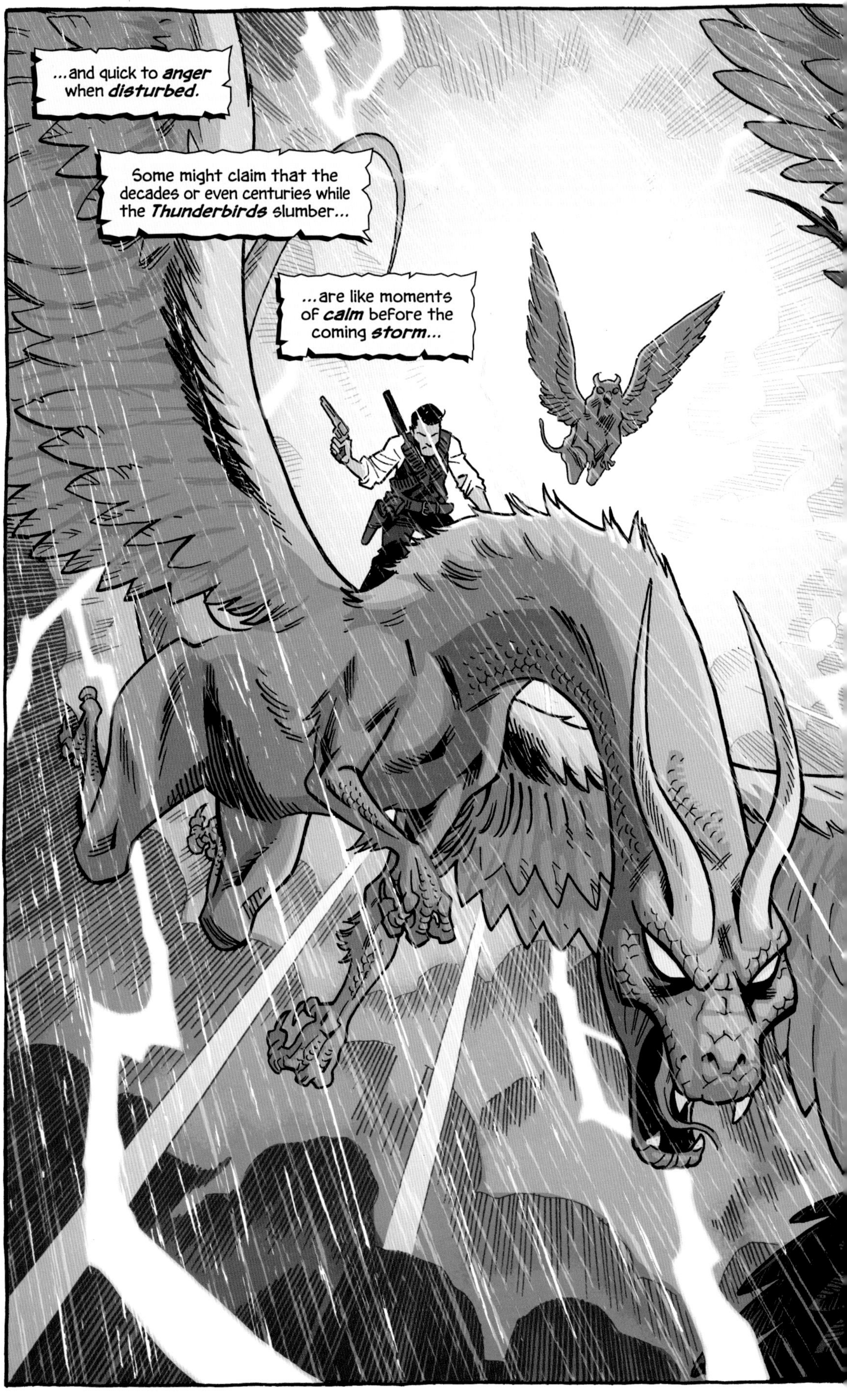
...and quick to *anger* when *disturbed*.
Some might claim that the decades or even centuries while the *Thunderbirds* slumber...
...are like moments of *calm* before the coming *storm*...

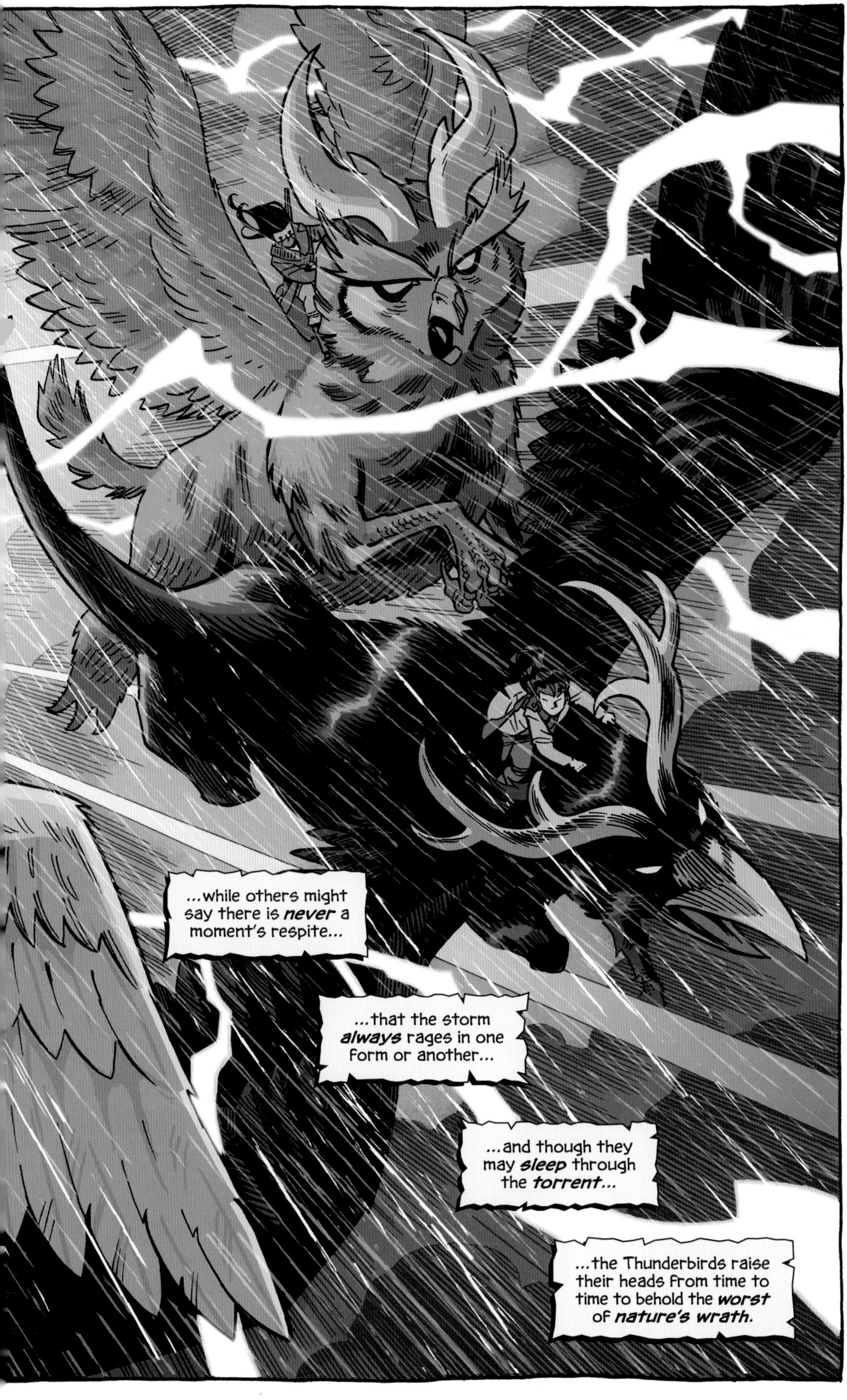
...while others might say there is *never* a moment's respite...
...that the storm *always* rages in one form or another...
...and though they may *sleep* through the *torrent*...
...the Thunderbirds raise their heads from time to time to behold the *worst* of *nature's wrath*.

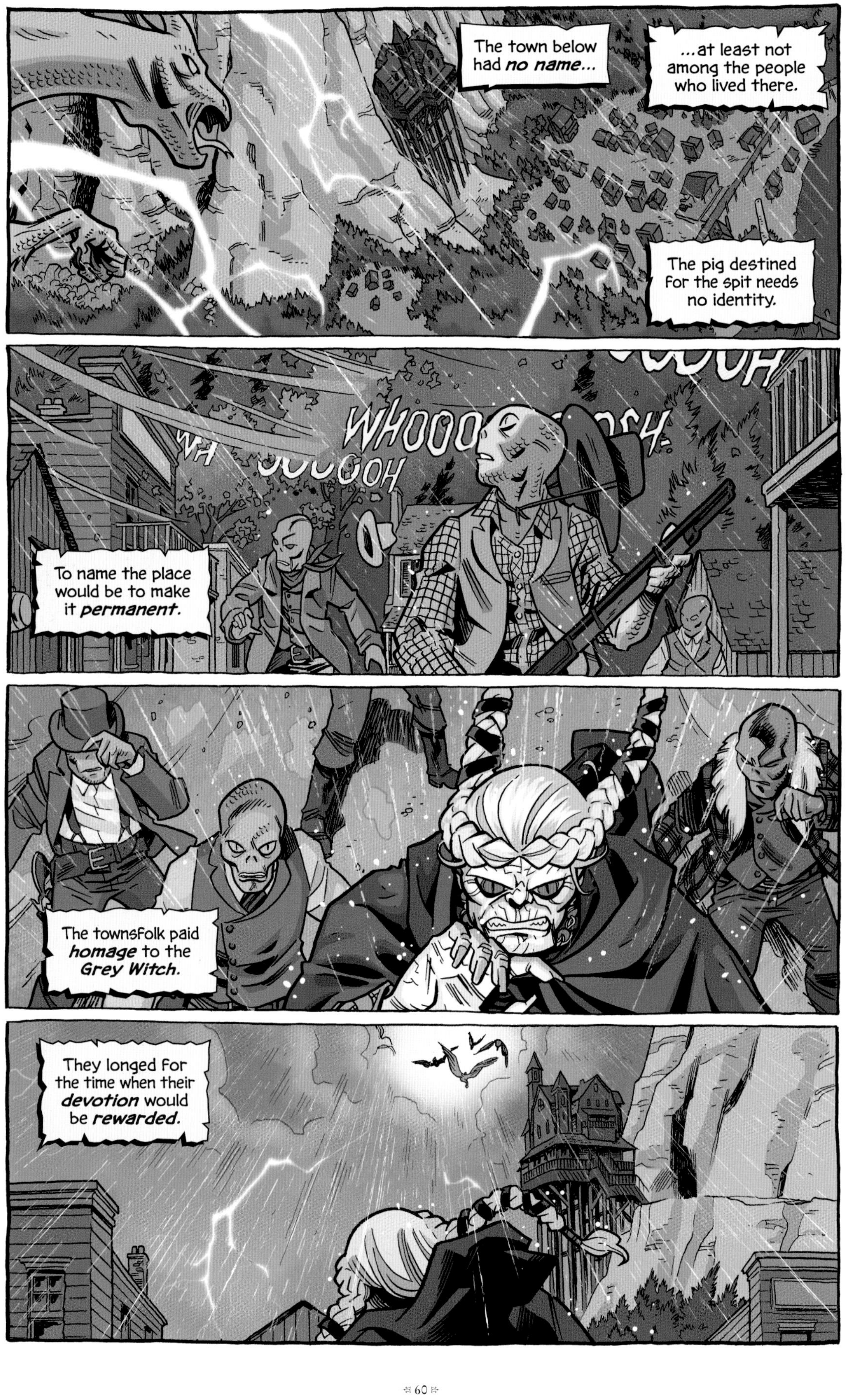
The town below had ***no name***...
...at least not among the people who lived there.
The pig destined for the spit needs no identity.
To name the place would be to make it ***permanent.***
The townsfolk paid ***homage*** to the ***Grey Witch.***
They longed for the time when their ***devotion*** would be ***rewarded.***

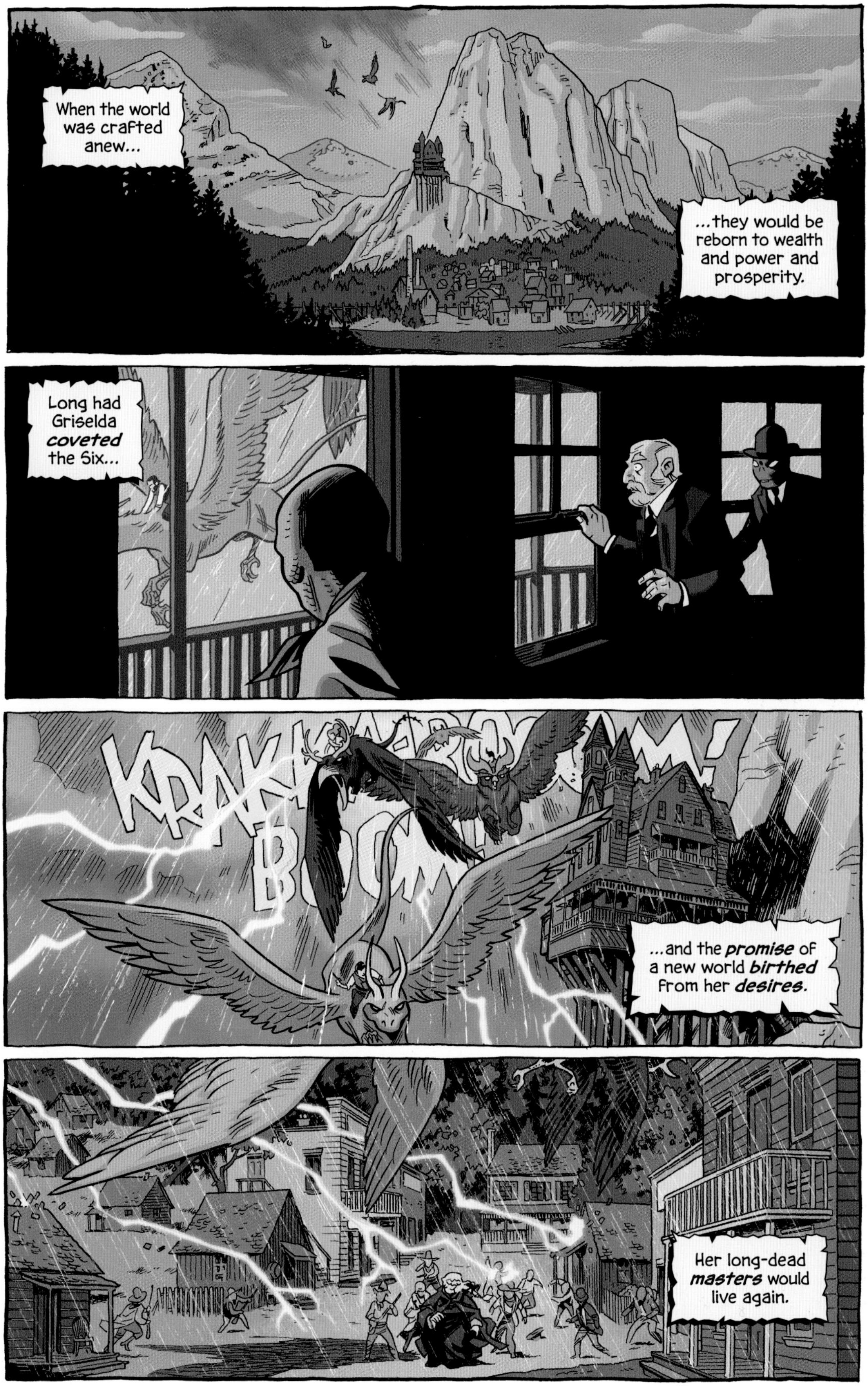
When the world was crafted anew...
...they would be reborn to wealth and power and prosperity.
Long had Griselda *coveted* the Six...
KRAKA-BOOM!
...and the *promise* of a new world *birthed* from her *desires.*
Her long-dead *masters* would live again.

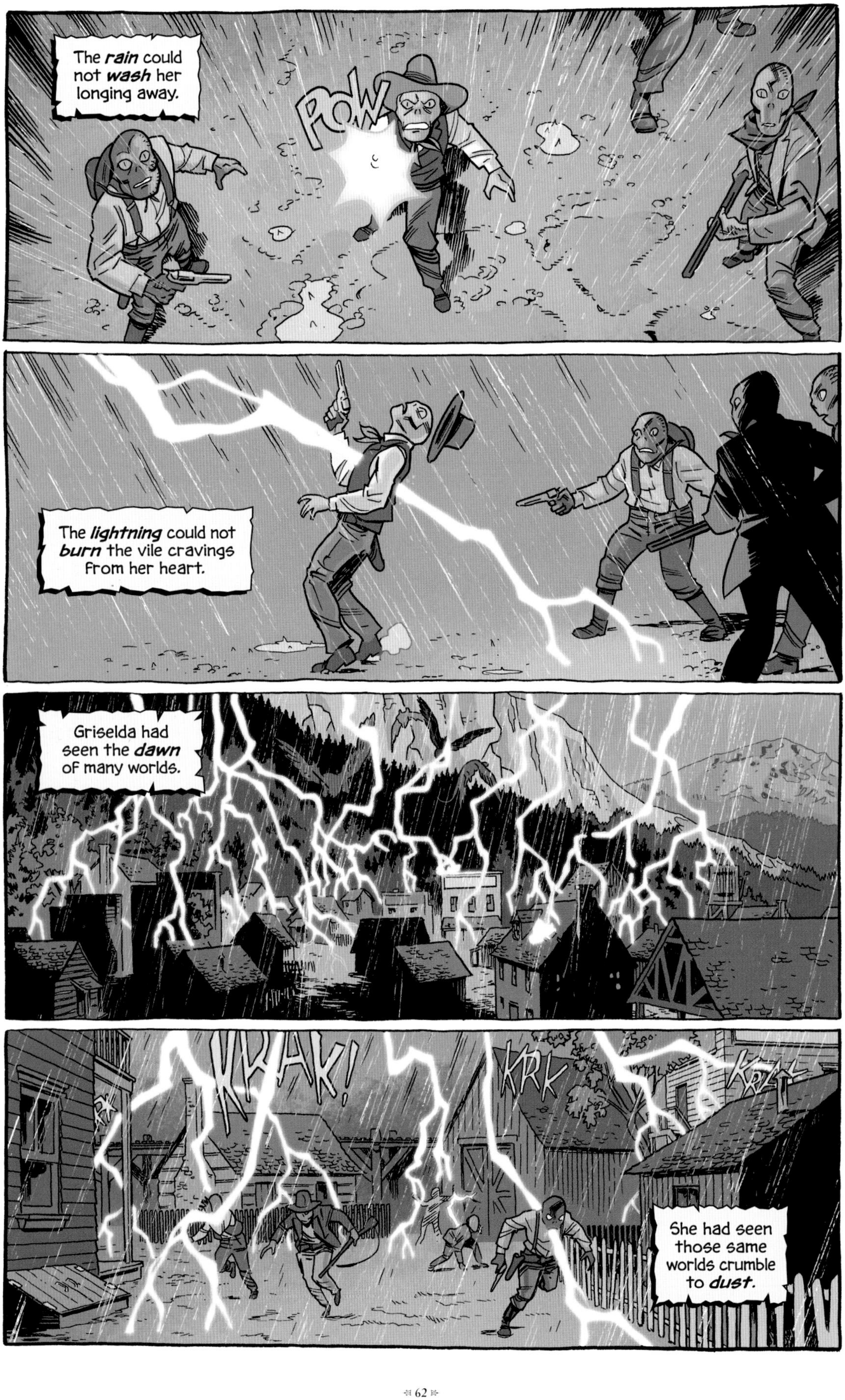
The rain could not wash her longing away.
POW
The lightning could not burn the vile cravings from her heart.
Griselda had seen the dawn of many worlds.
WHAK!
KRK
She had seen those same worlds crumble to dust.

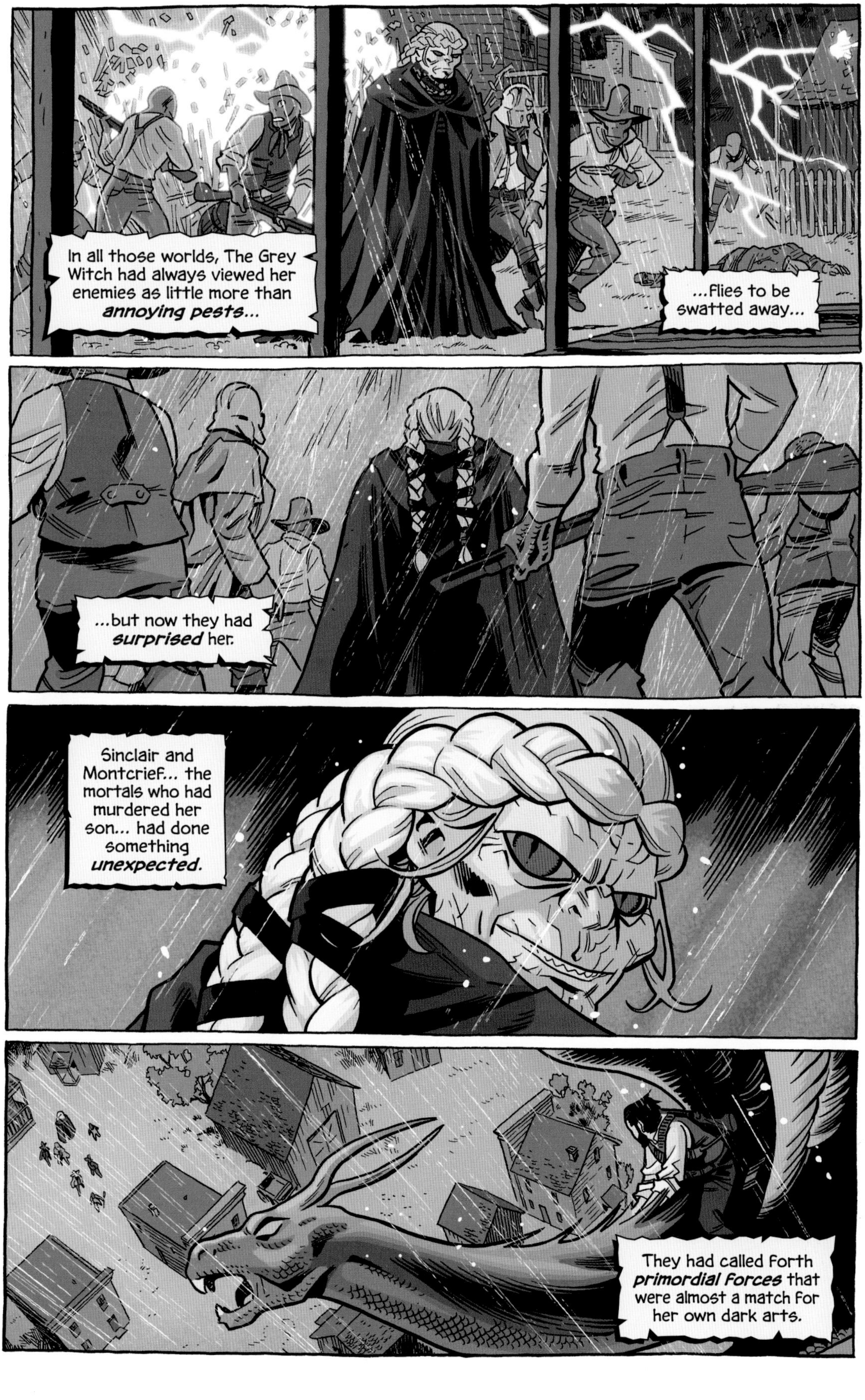
In all those worlds, The Grey Witch had always viewed her enemies as little more than ***annoying pests***...
...Flies to be swatted away...
...but now they had ***surprised*** her.
Sinclair and Montcrief... the mortals who had murdered her son... had done something ***unexpected.***
They had called forth ***primordial forces*** that were almost a match for her own dark arts.

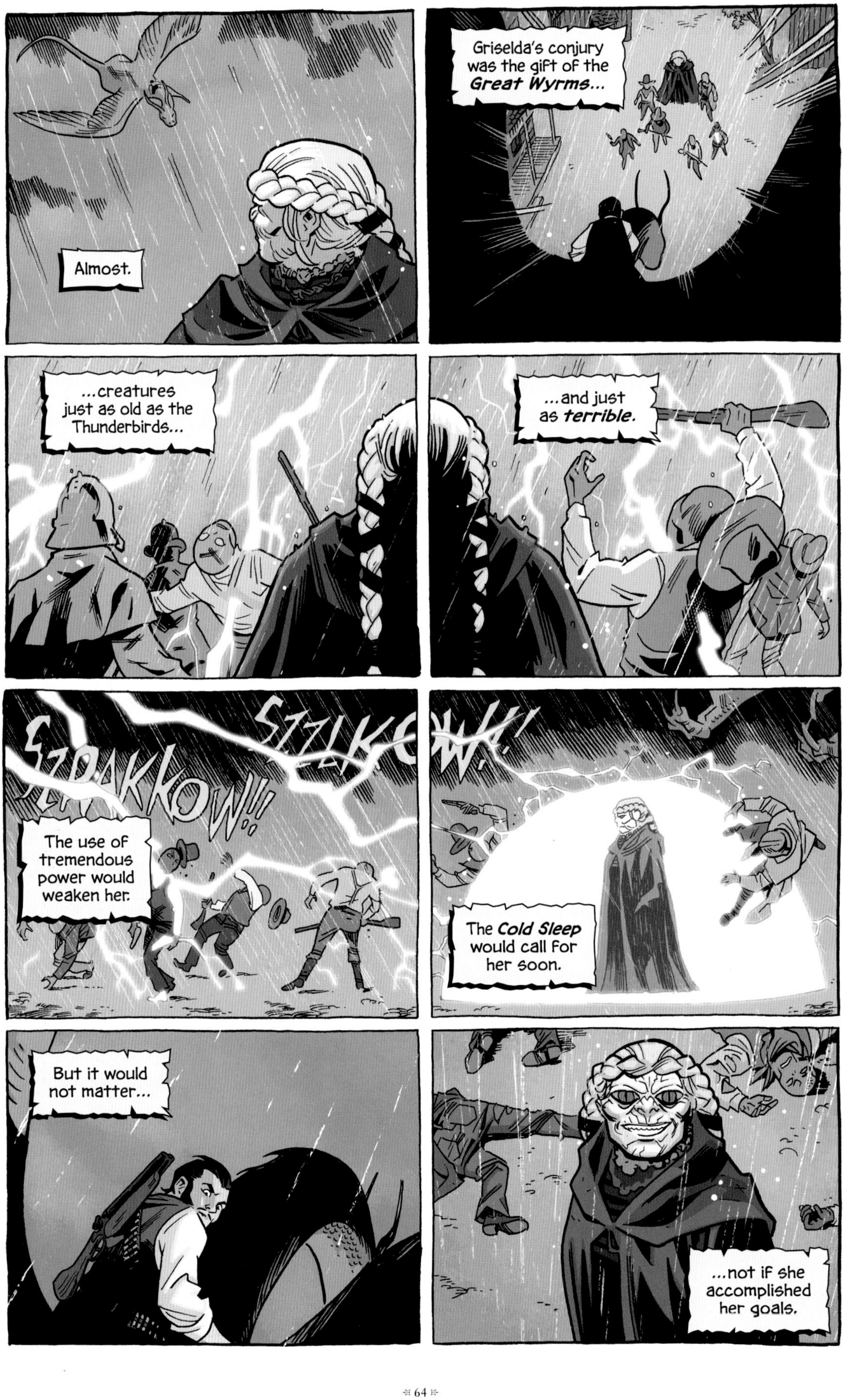
Almost.
Griselda's conjury was the gift of the *Great Wyrms*...
...creatures just as old as the Thunderbirds...
...and just as *terrible*.
SZRAKKOW!!!
SZZKOW!
The use of tremendous power would weaken her.
The *Cold Sleep* would call for her soon.
But it would not matter...
...not if she accomplished her goals.

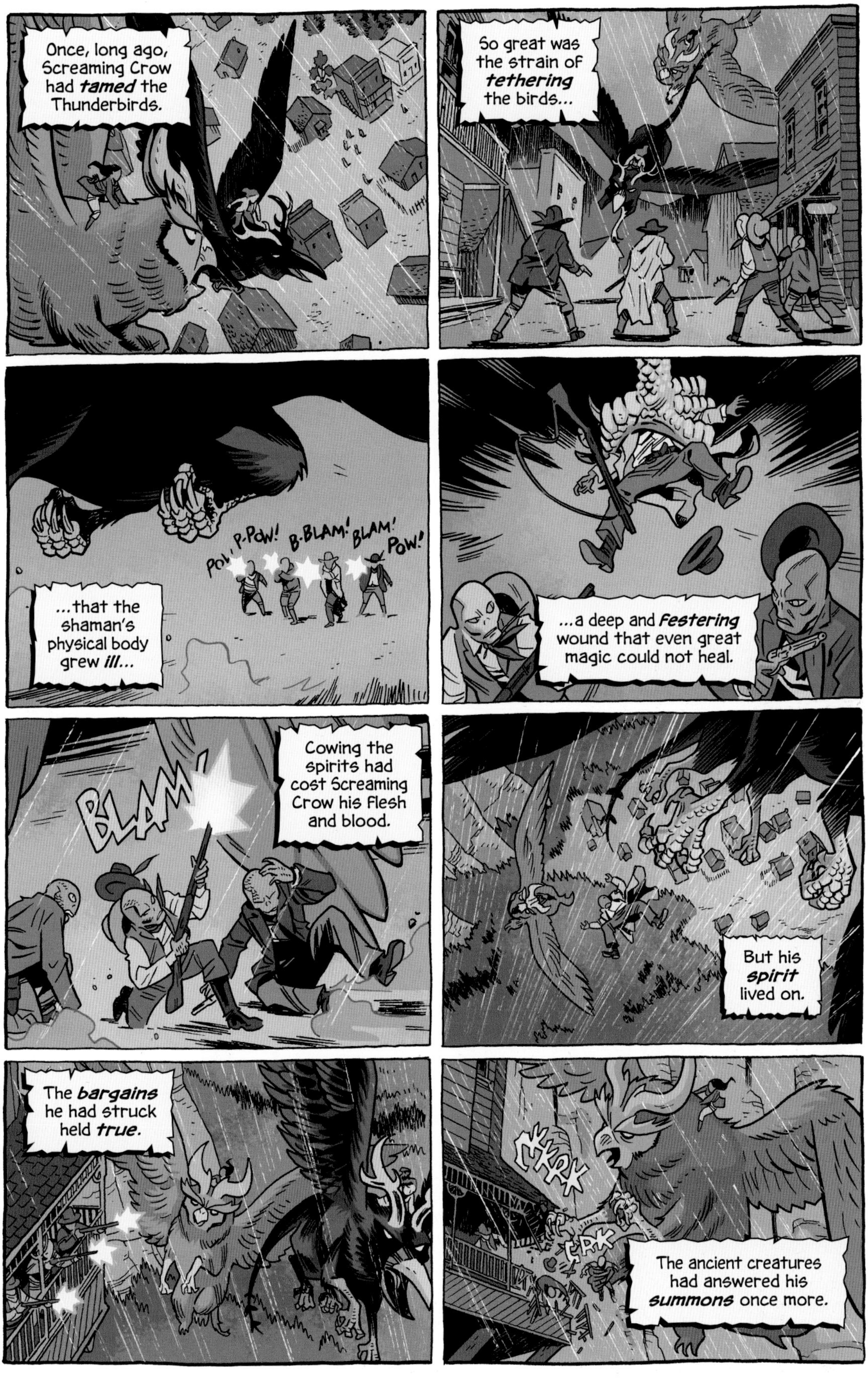

Once, long ago, Screaming Crow had tamed the Thunderbirds.
So great was the strain of tethering the birds...
POW! P-POW! B-BLAM! BLAM! POW!
...that the shaman's physical body grew ill...
...a deep and festering wound that even great magic could not heal.
Cowing the spirits had cost Screaming Crow his flesh and blood.
BLAM!
But his spirit lived on.
The bargains he had struck held true.
CKRK
CRK
The ancient creatures had answered his summons once more.

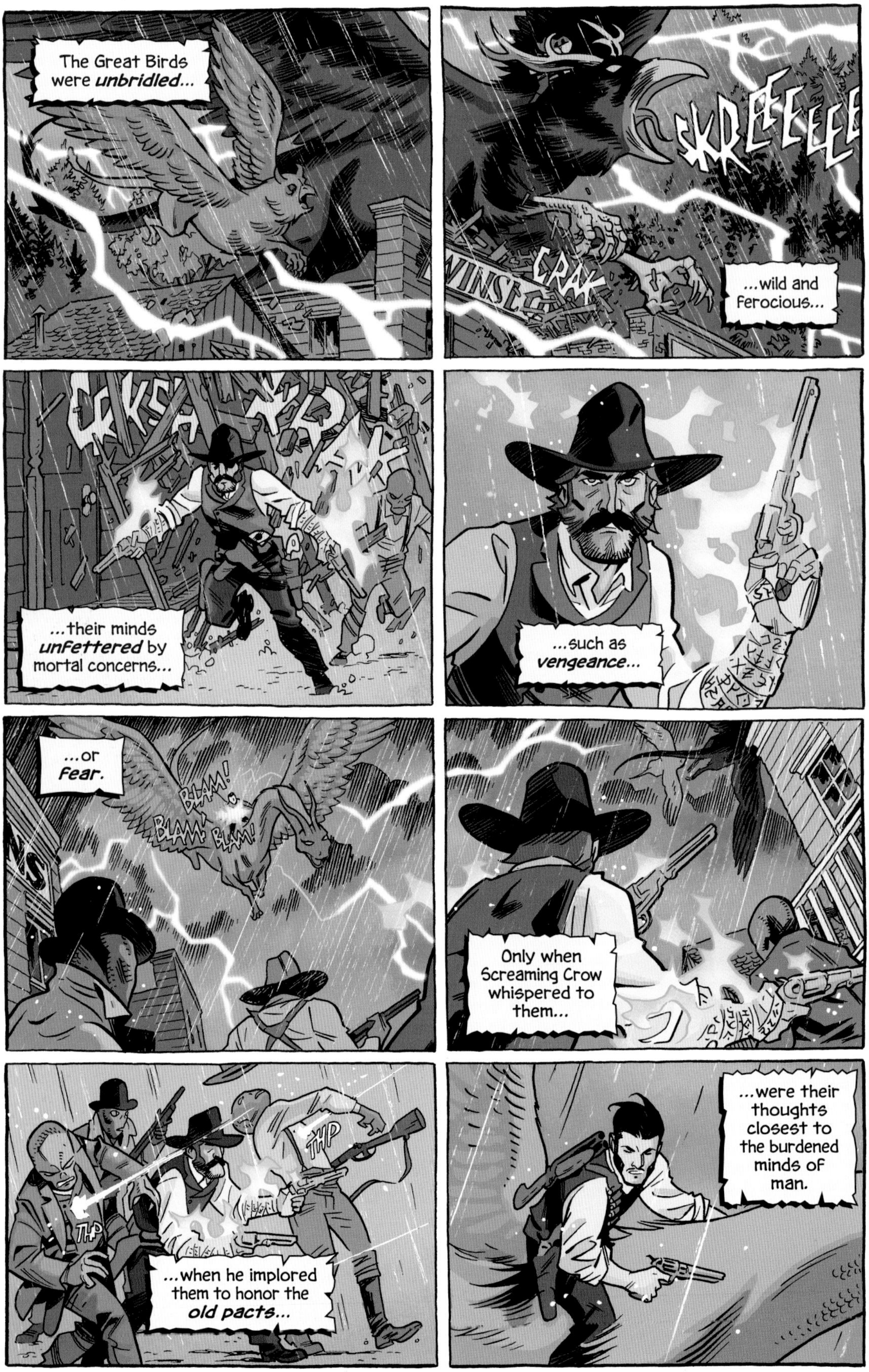
The Great Birds were *unbridled*...
SKREEEEEEE
CRAK
...wild and ferocious...
...their minds *unfettered* by mortal concerns...
...such as *vengeance*...
...or *fear*.
BLAM!
BLAM! BLAM!
Only when Screaming Crow whispered to them...
THP
THP
...when he implored them to honor the *old pacts*...
...were their thoughts closest to the burdened minds of man.

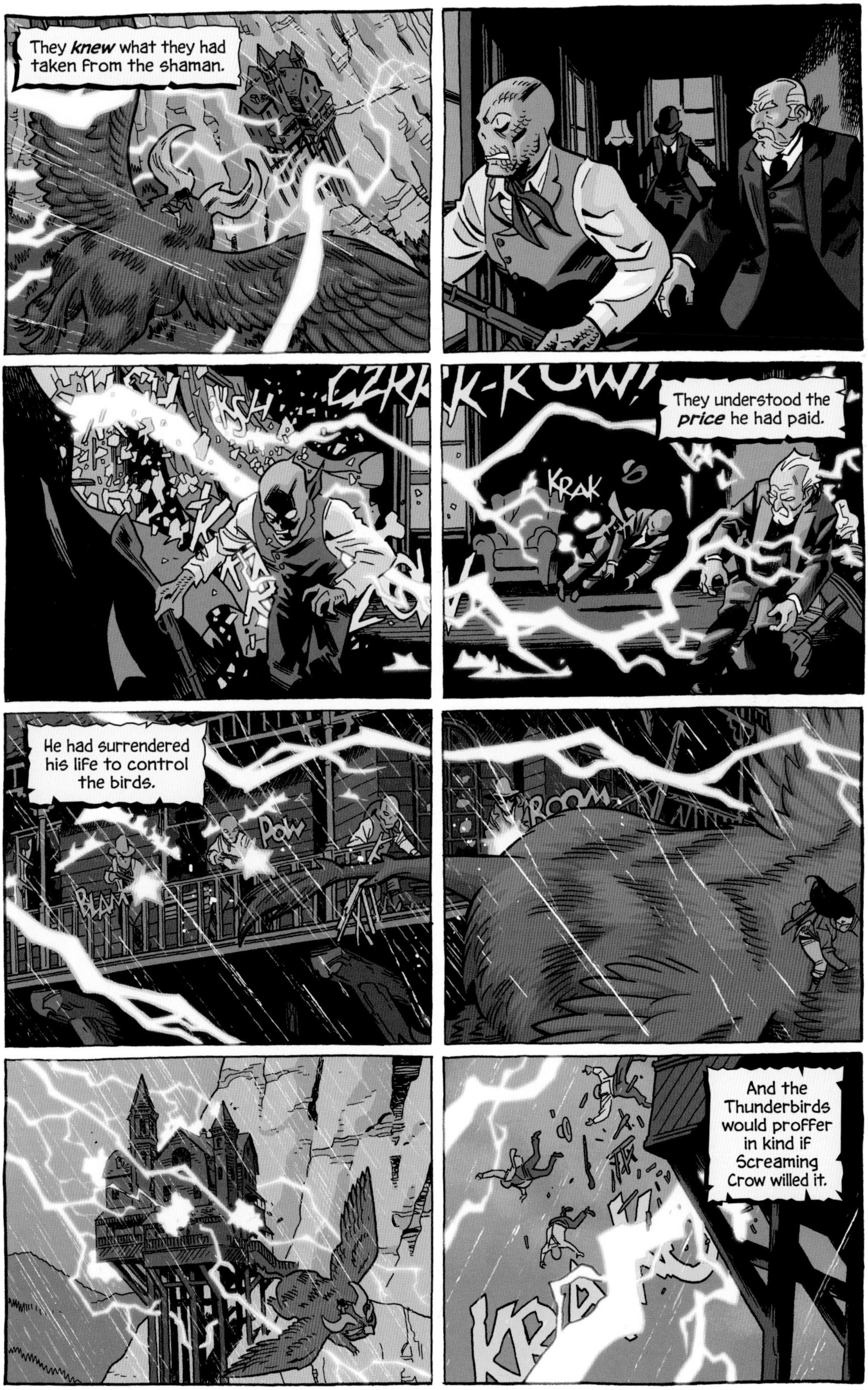
They *knew* what they had taken from the shaman.
CZRKK-KOW!
KRAK
They understood the *price* he had paid.
He had surrendered his life to control the birds.
POW
BLAM
ROOM
And the Thunderbirds would proffer in kind if Screaming Crow willed it.

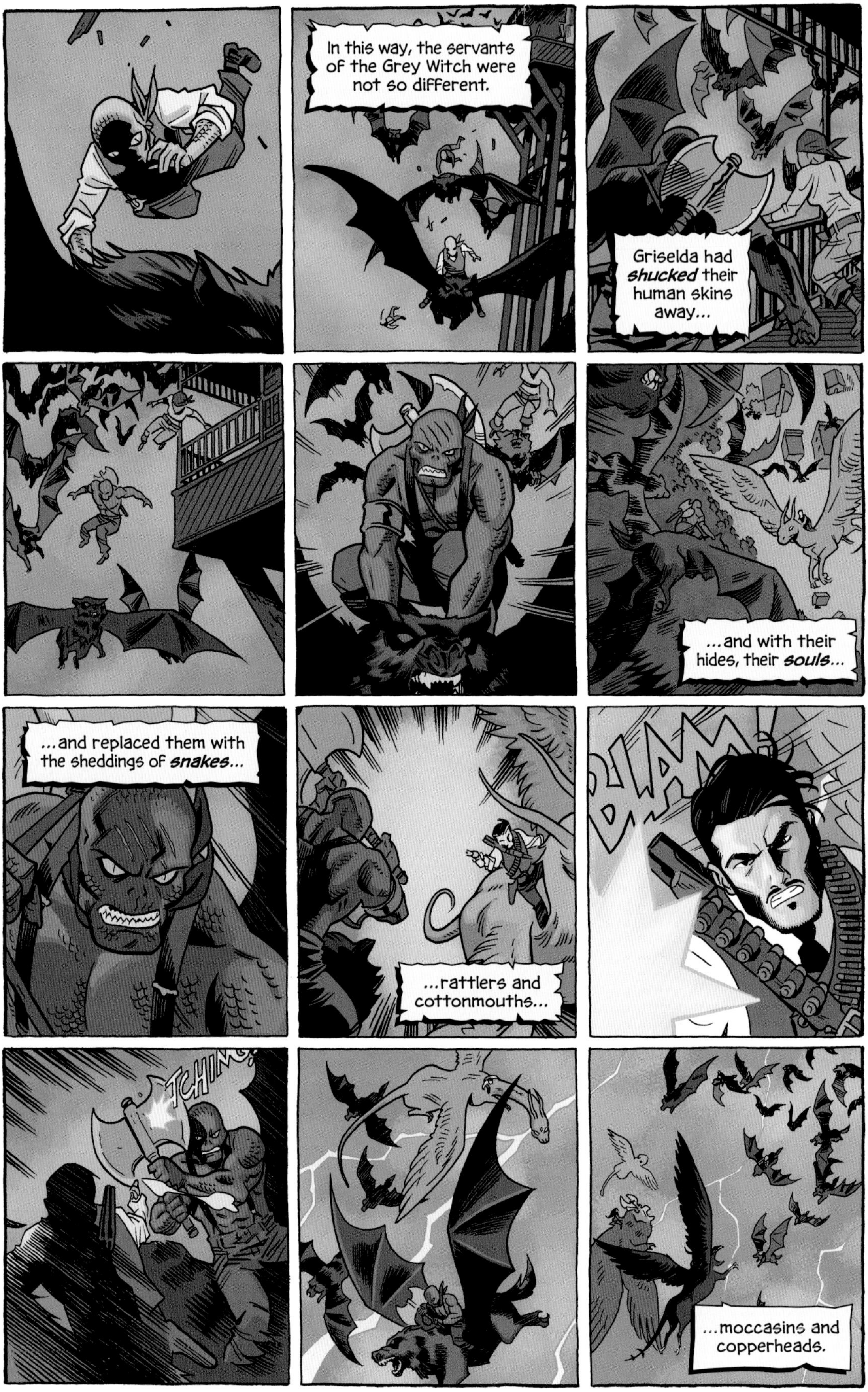

In this way, the servants of the Grey Witch were not so different.
Griselda had *shucked* their human skins away...
...and with their hides, their *souls*...
...and replaced them with the sheddings of *snakes*...
...rattlers and cottonmouths...
BLAM
TCHING
...moccasins and copperheads.

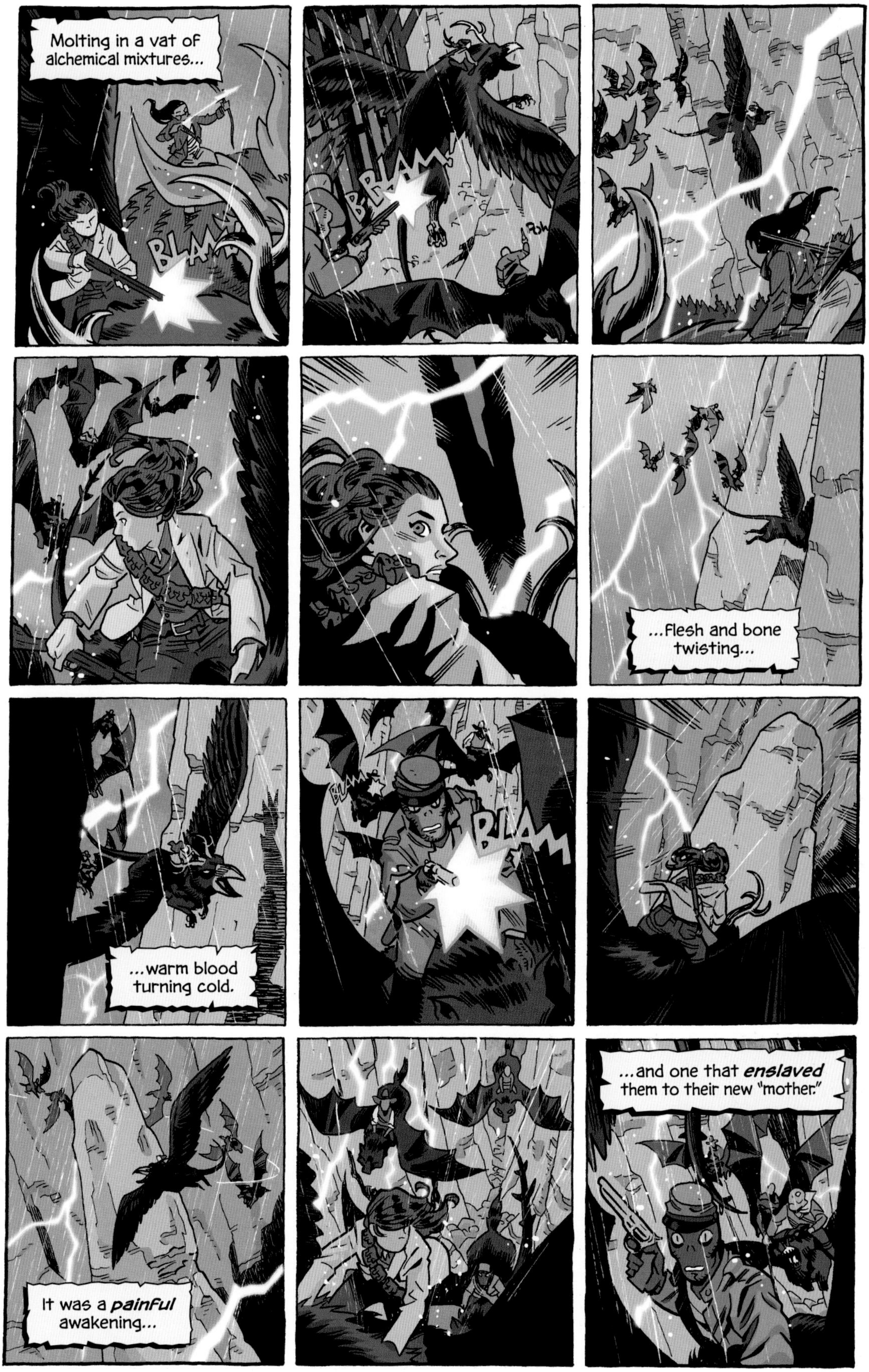
Molting in a vat of alchemical mixtures...
BLAM
BLAM
...flesh and bone twisting...
...warm blood turning cold.
BLAM
BLAM
It was a ***painful*** awakening...
...and one that ***enslaved*** them to their new "mother."

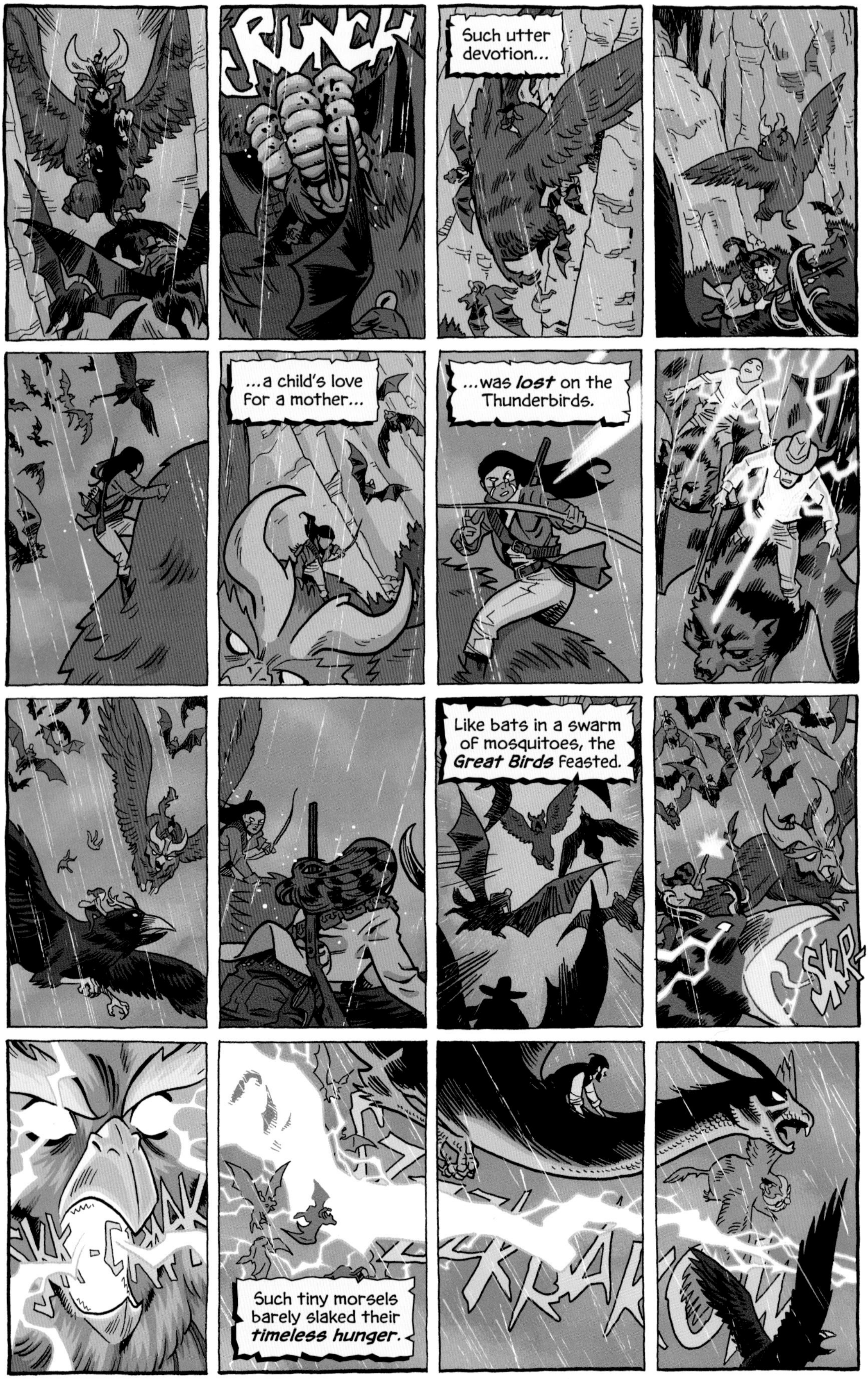
Such utter devotion...
...a child's love for a mother...
...was *lost* on the Thunderbirds.
Like bats in a swarm of mosquitoes, the ***Great Birds*** feasted.
Such tiny morsels barely slaked their ***timeless hunger***.

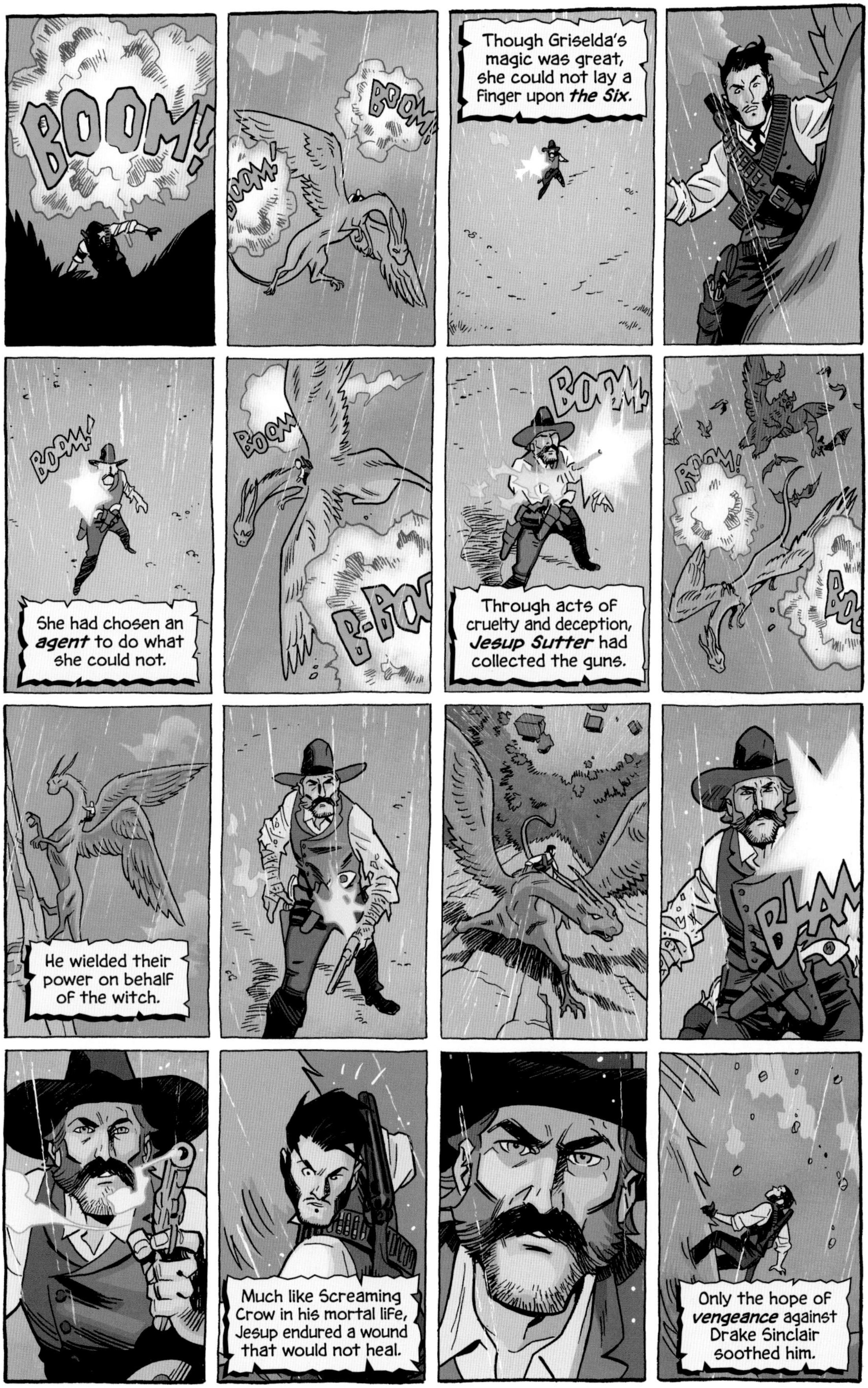
BOOM!
BOOM!
BOOM!
Though Griselda's magic was great, she could not lay a finger upon the Six.
BOOM!
She had chosen an agent to do what she could not.
BOOM
B-BOO
BOOM
Through acts of cruelty and deception, Jesup Sutter had collected the guns.
BOOM!
BO
He wielded their power on behalf of the witch.
BLAM
Much like Screaming Crow in his mortal life, Jesup endured a wound that would not heal.
Only the hope of vengeance against Drake Sinclair soothed him.

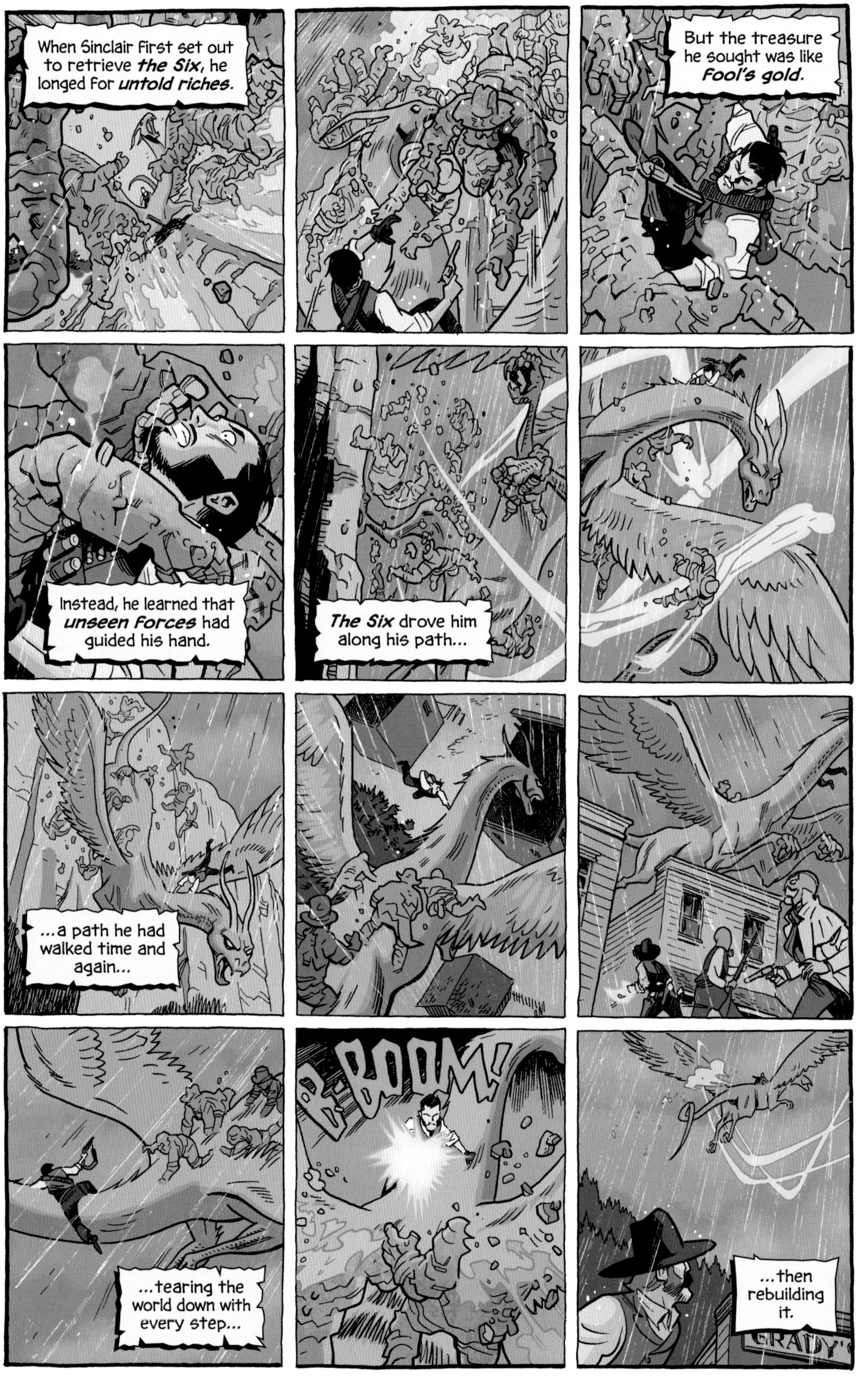
When Sinclair first set out to retrieve the Six, he longed for untold riches.
But the treasure he sought was like Fool's gold.
Instead, he learned that unseen forces had guided his hand.
The Six drove him along his path...
...a path he had walked time and again...
...tearing the world down with every step...
B-BOOM!
...then rebuilding it.
GRADY'

The *truth* of his existence *eluded* him...

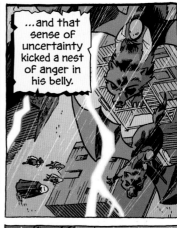

...and that sense of uncertainty kicked a nest of anger in his belly.

He might have been the puppet of *God* or the *Devil.*

Or he might have dreamed up the very notion of the *gods* himself.

Either way, he was *Finished* being a toy soldier.

He would see the guns *destroyed.*

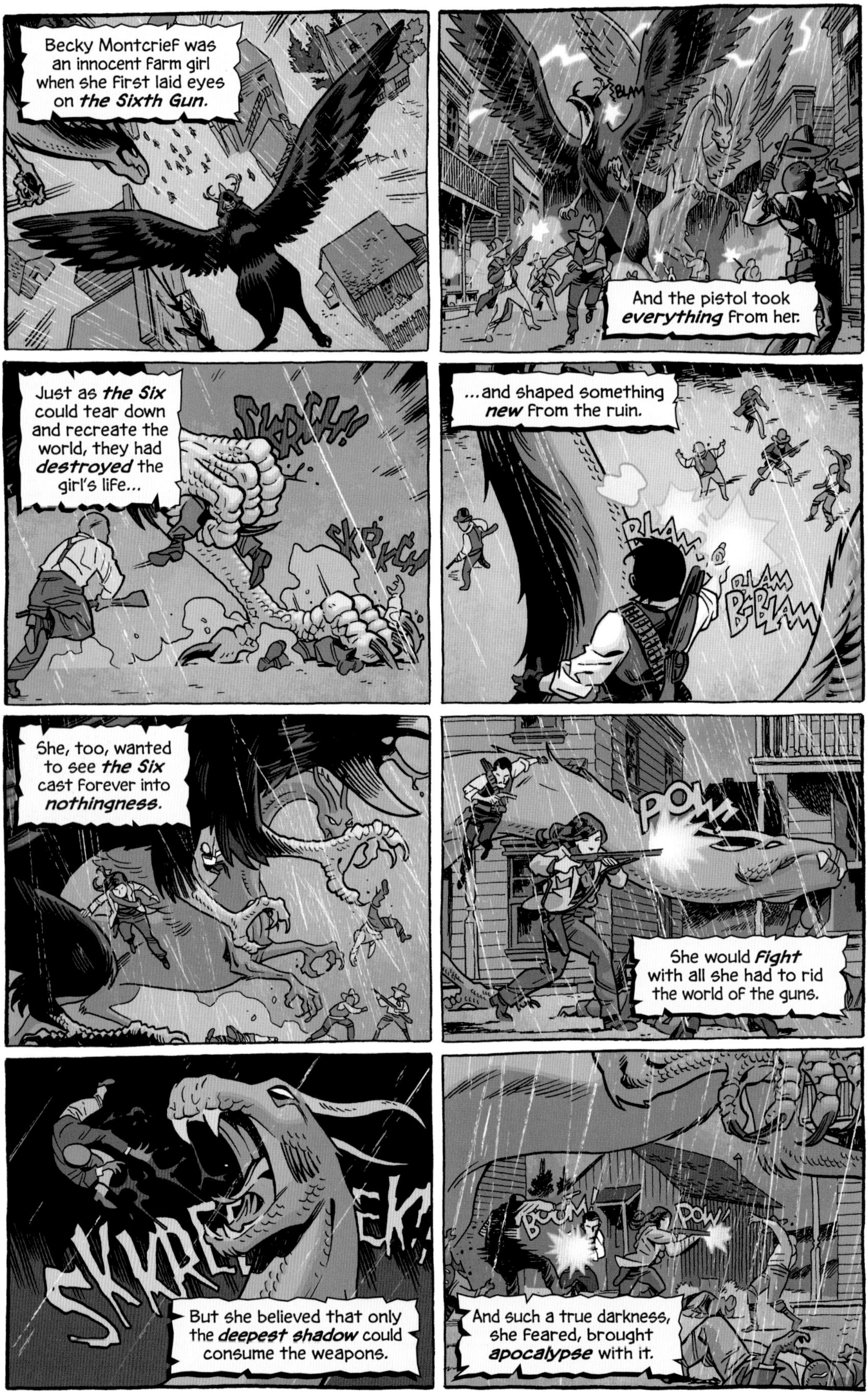
Becky Montcrief was an innocent farm girl when she first laid eyes on *the Sixth Gun*.
BLAM
And the pistol took *everything* from her.
Just as *the Six* could tear down and recreate the world, they had *destroyed* the girl's life...
...and shaped something *new* from the ruin.
BLAM
B-BLAM
She, too, wanted to see *the Six* cast forever into *nothingness*.
POW
She would *fight* with all she had to rid the world of the guns.
But she believed that only the *deepest shadow* could consume the weapons.
BOOM
POW!
And such a true darkness, she feared, brought *apocalypse* with it.

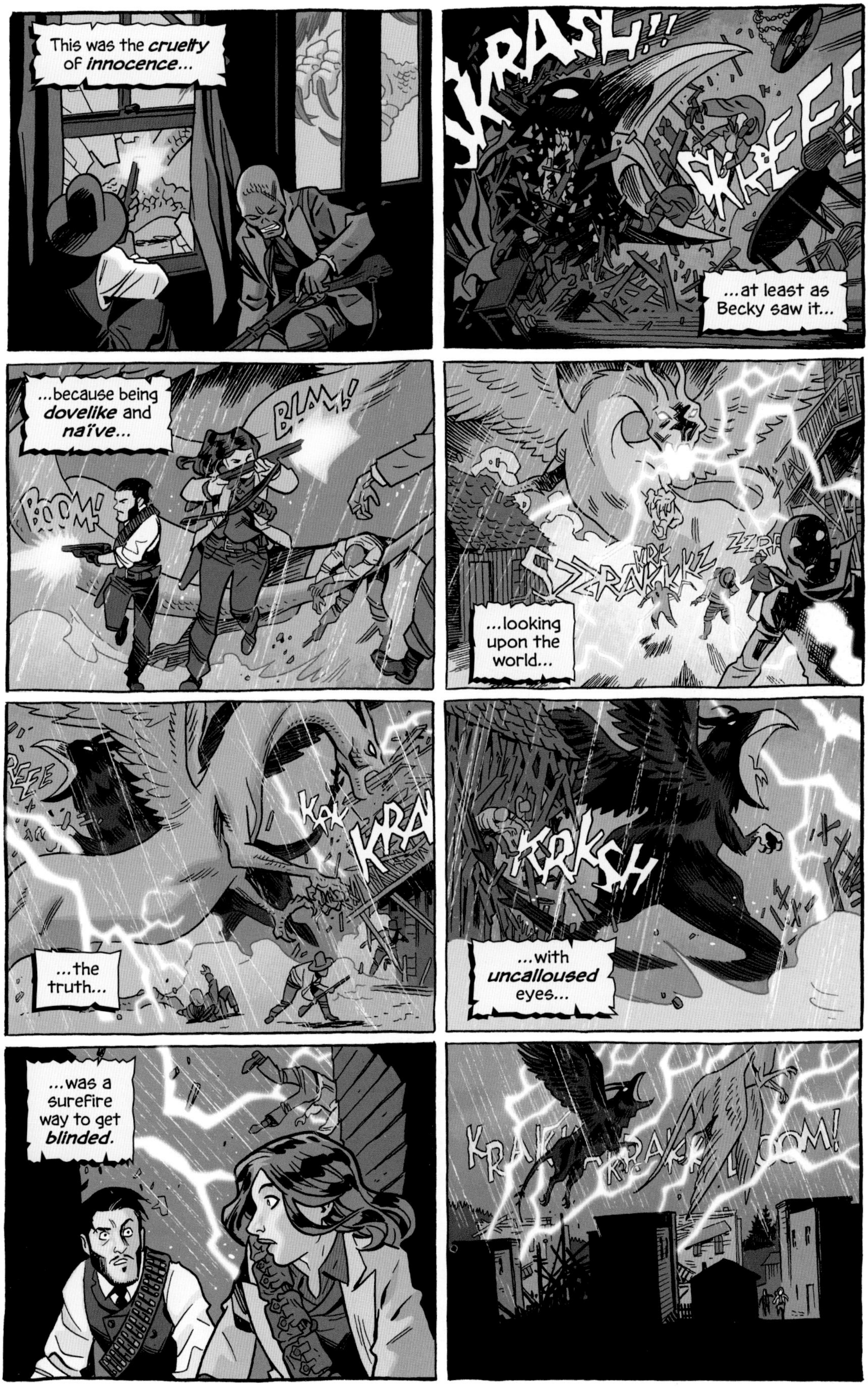
This was the cruelty of innocence...
KRASH!!
SKREEE
...at least as Becky saw it...
...because being dovelike and naïve...
BLAM!
BOOM!
...looking upon the world...
SZZRAKKK
KRK
ZZRR
EEE
...the truth...
KRAK
KRA
KRKSH
...with uncalloused eyes...
...was a surefire way to get blinded.
KRAK
KRAKK
OOM!

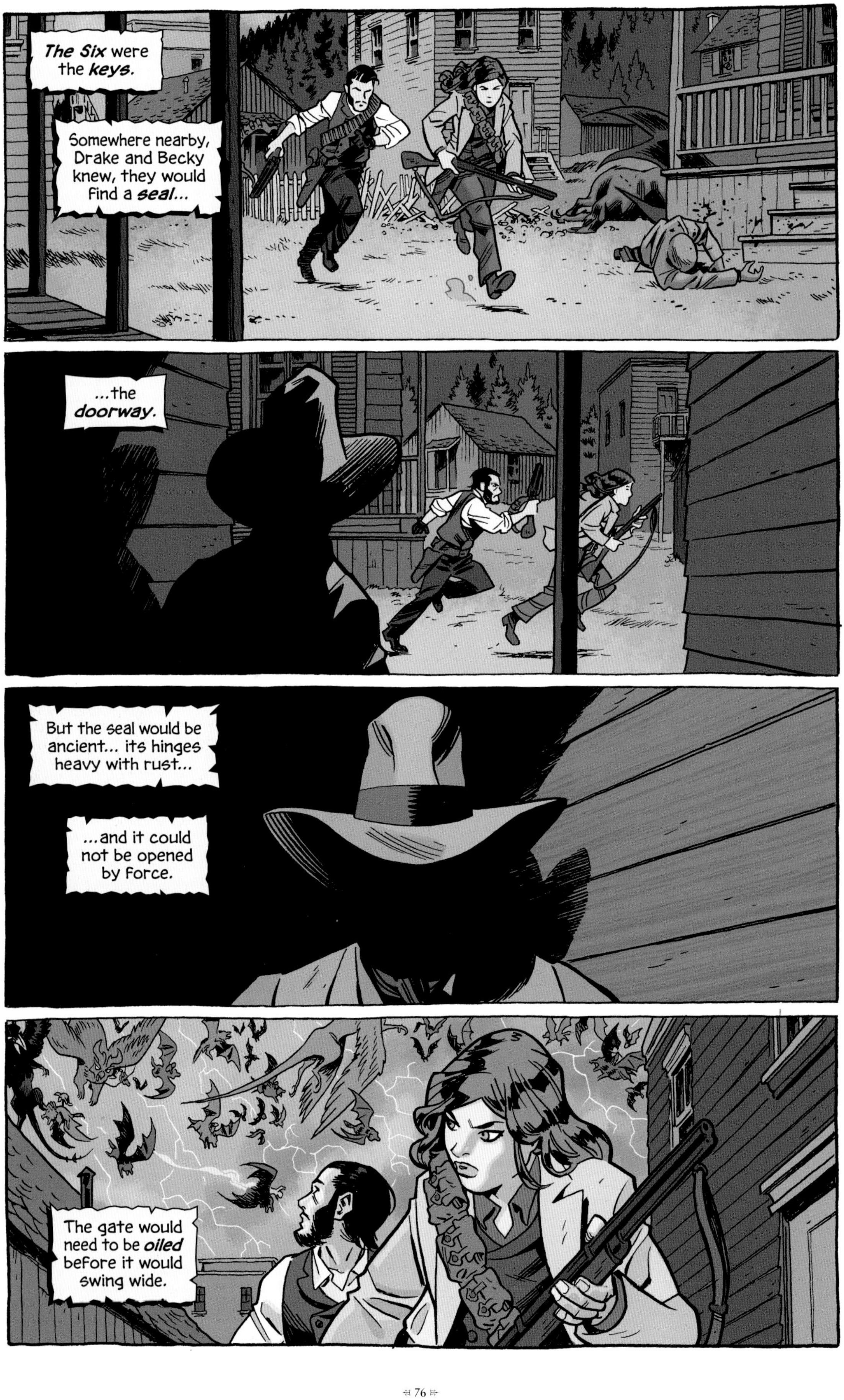
The Six were the keys.
Somewhere nearby, Drake and Becky knew, they would find a seal...
...the doorway.
But the seal would be ancient... its hinges heavy with rust...
...and it could not be opened by force.
The gate would need to be oiled before it would swing wide.

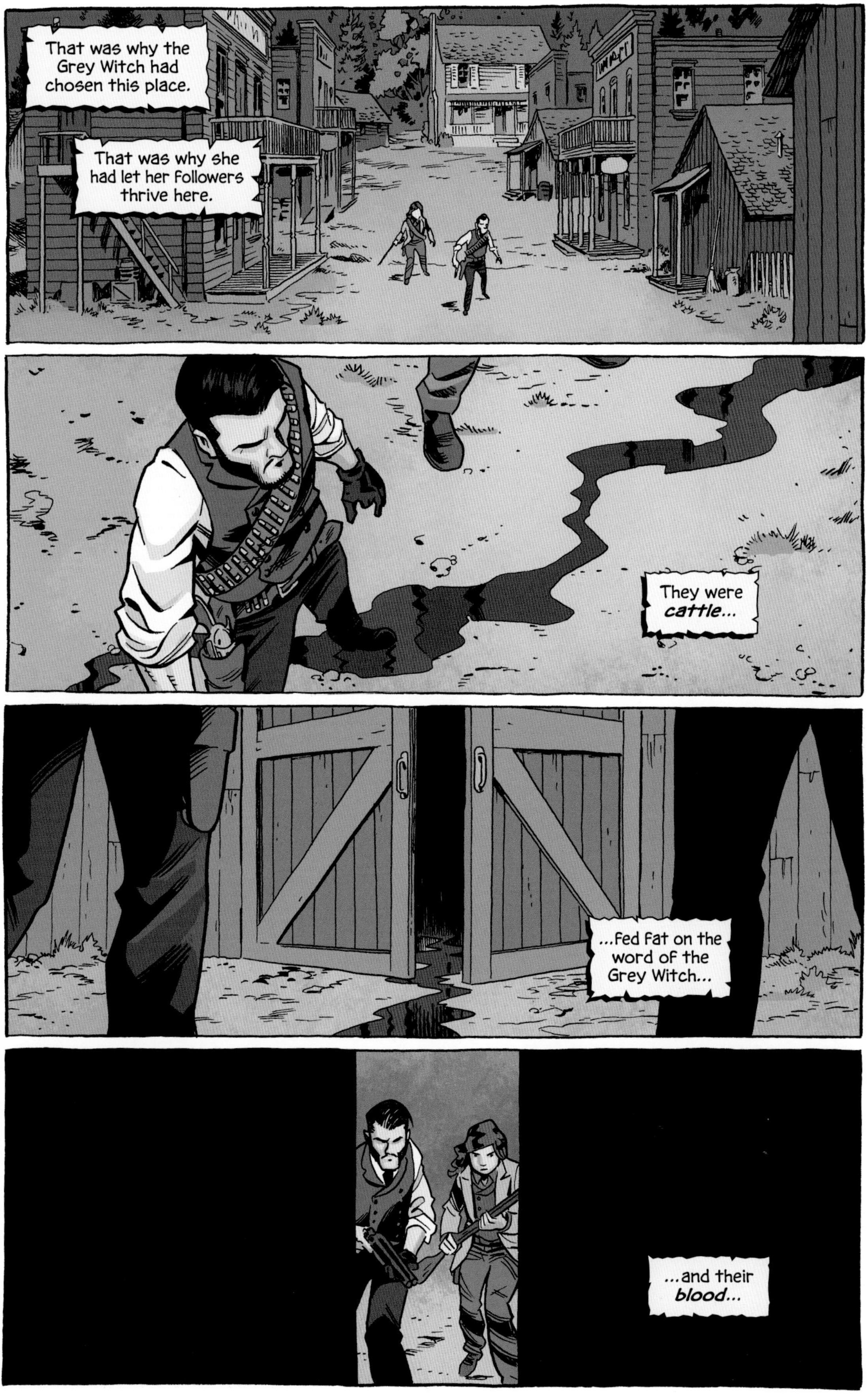
That was why the Grey Witch had chosen this place.
That was why she had let her followers thrive here.
They were *cattle*...
...fed fat on the word of the Grey Witch...
...and their *blood*...

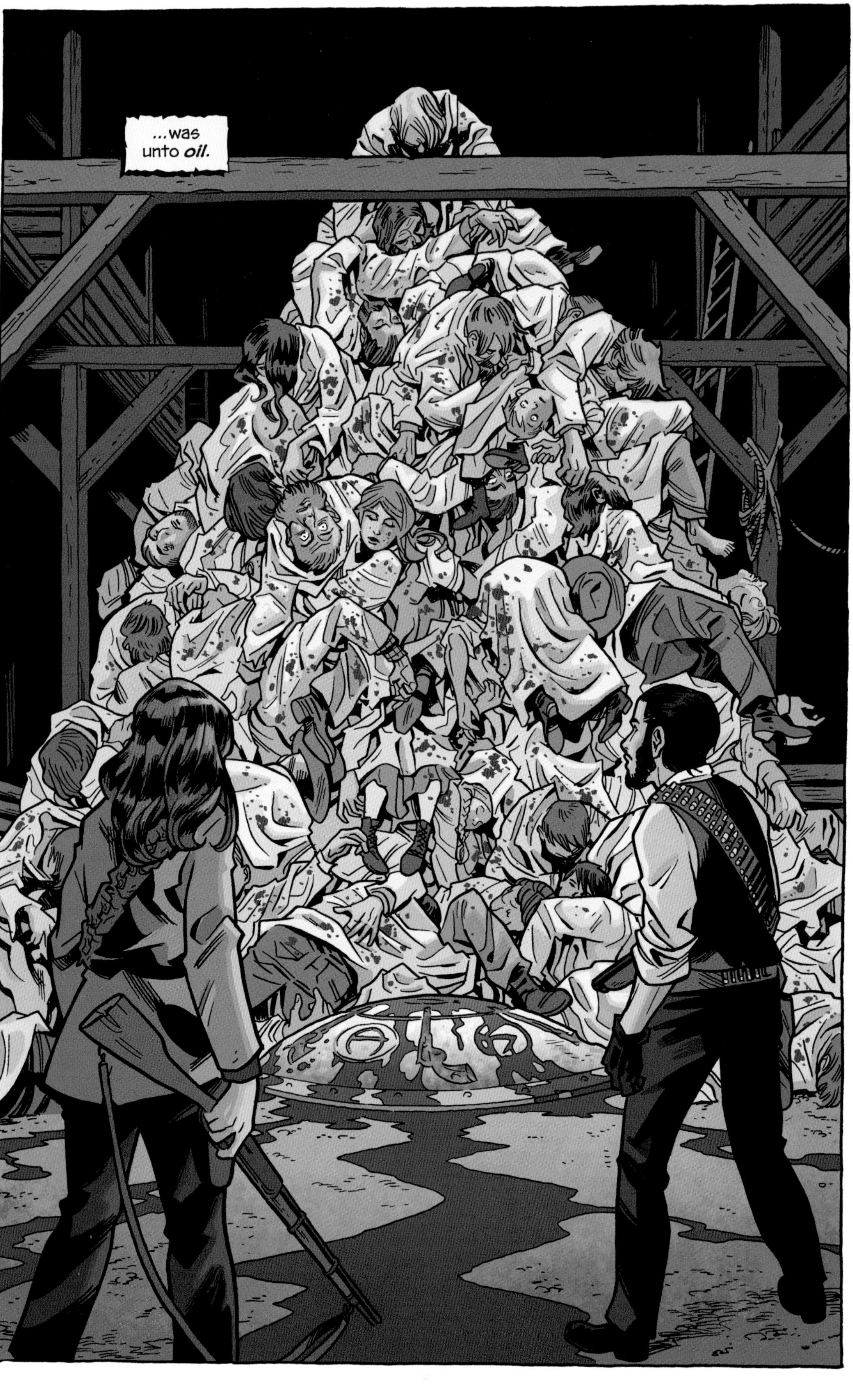
...was unto oil.

CHAPTER FOUR

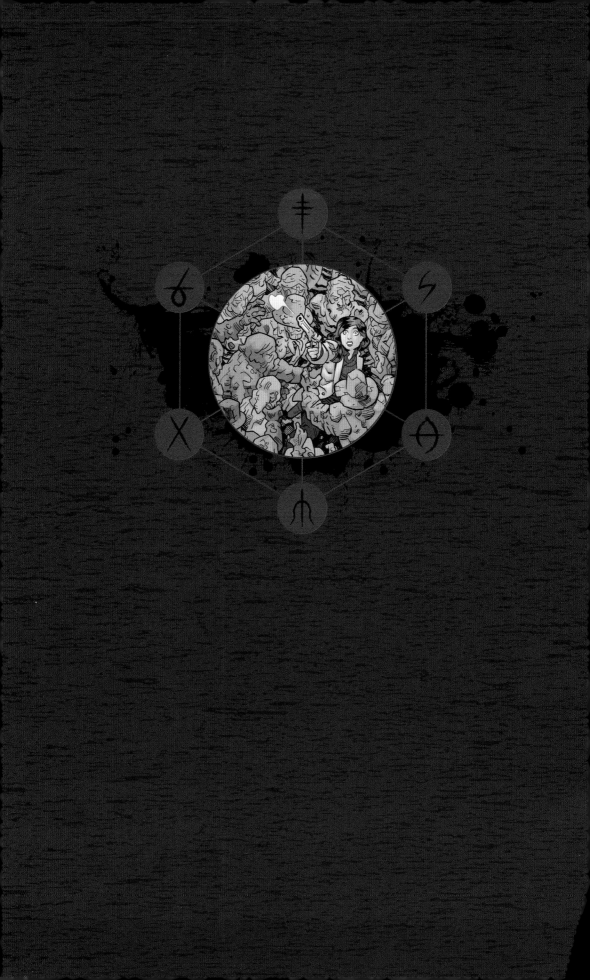

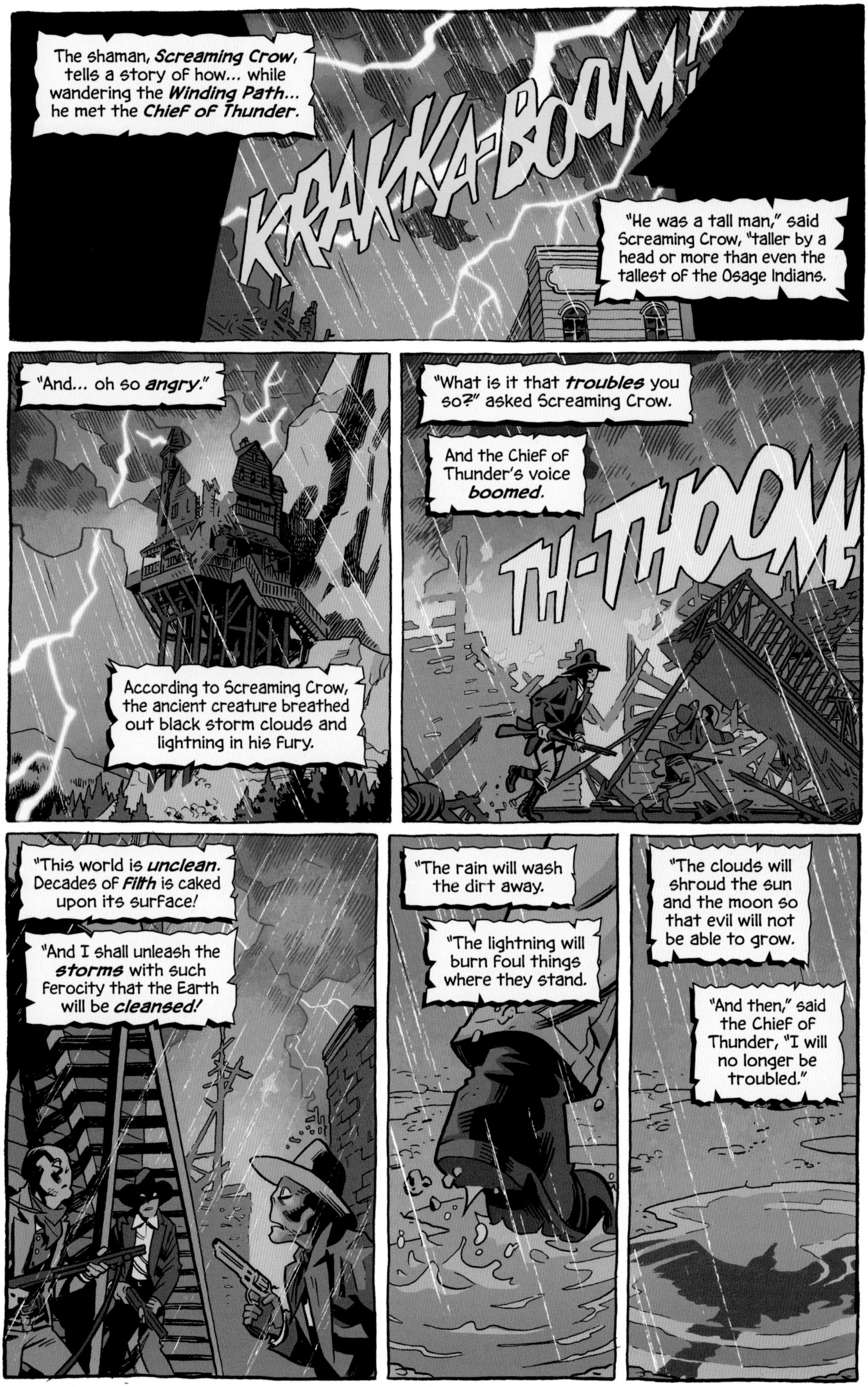
The shaman, Screaming Crow, tells a story of how... while wandering the Winding Path... he met the Chief of Thunder.
KRAKKA-BOOM!
"He was a tall man," said Screaming Crow, "taller by a head or more than even the tallest of the Osage Indians.
"And... oh so angry."
According to Screaming Crow, the ancient creature breathed out black storm clouds and lightning in his fury.
"What is it that troubles you so?" asked Screaming Crow.
And the Chief of Thunder's voice boomed.
TH-THOOM
"This world is unclean. Decades of filth is caked upon its surface!
"And I shall unleash the storms with such ferocity that the Earth will be cleansed!
"The rain will wash the dirt away.
"The lightning will burn foul things where they stand.
"The clouds will shroud the sun and the moon so that evil will not be able to grow.
"And then," said the Chief of Thunder, "I will no longer be troubled."

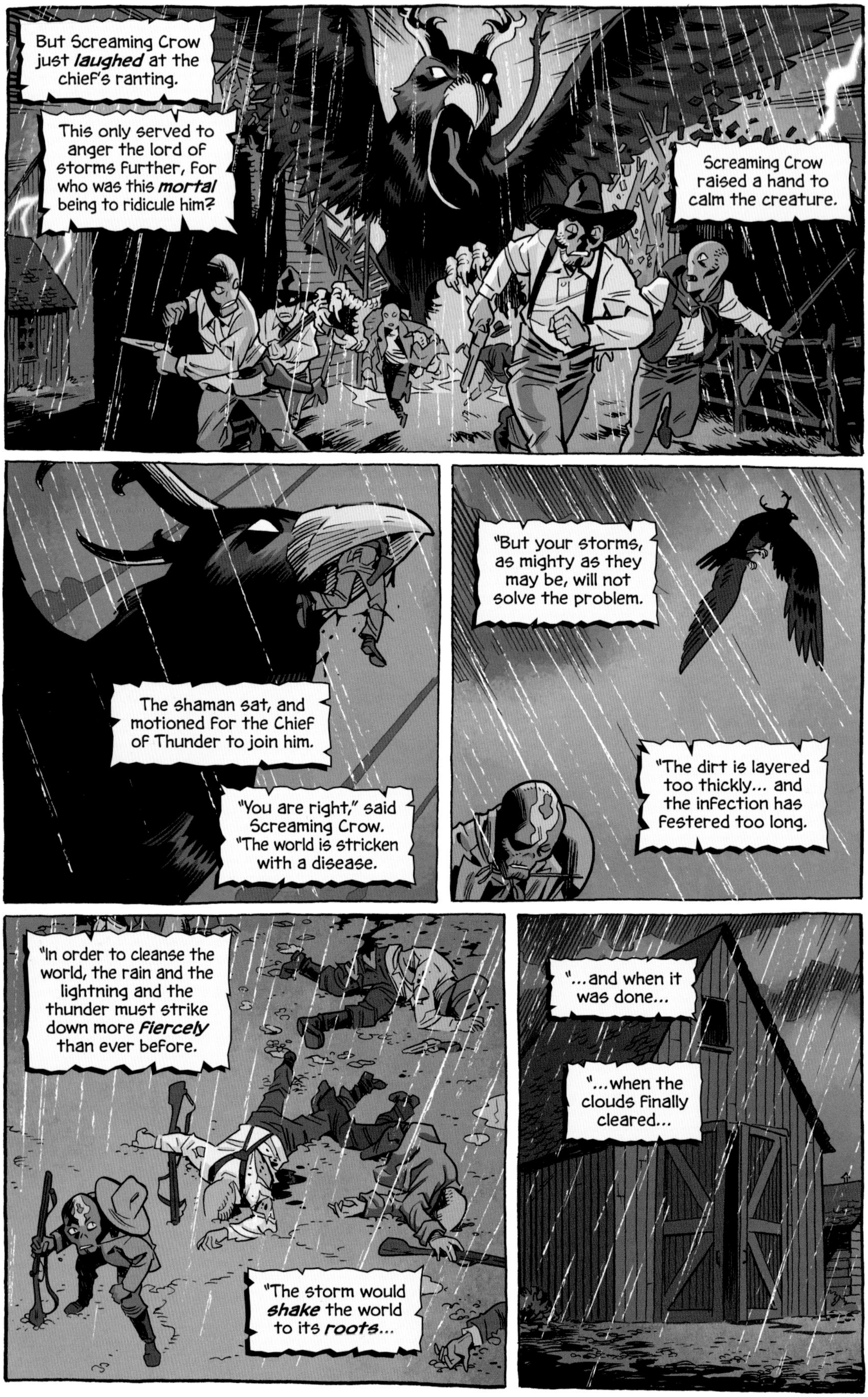
But Screaming Crow just *laughed* at the chief's ranting.
This only served to anger the lord of storms further, for who was this *mortal* being to ridicule him?
Screaming Crow raised a hand to calm the creature.
The shaman sat, and motioned for the Chief of Thunder to join him.
"You are right," said Screaming Crow. "The world is stricken with a disease.
"But your storms, as mighty as they may be, will not solve the problem.
"The dirt is layered too thickly... and the infection has festered too long.
"In order to cleanse the world, the rain and the lightning and the thunder must strike down more *fiercely* than ever before.
"The storm would *shake* the world to its *roots*...
"...and when it was done...
"...when the clouds finally cleared...

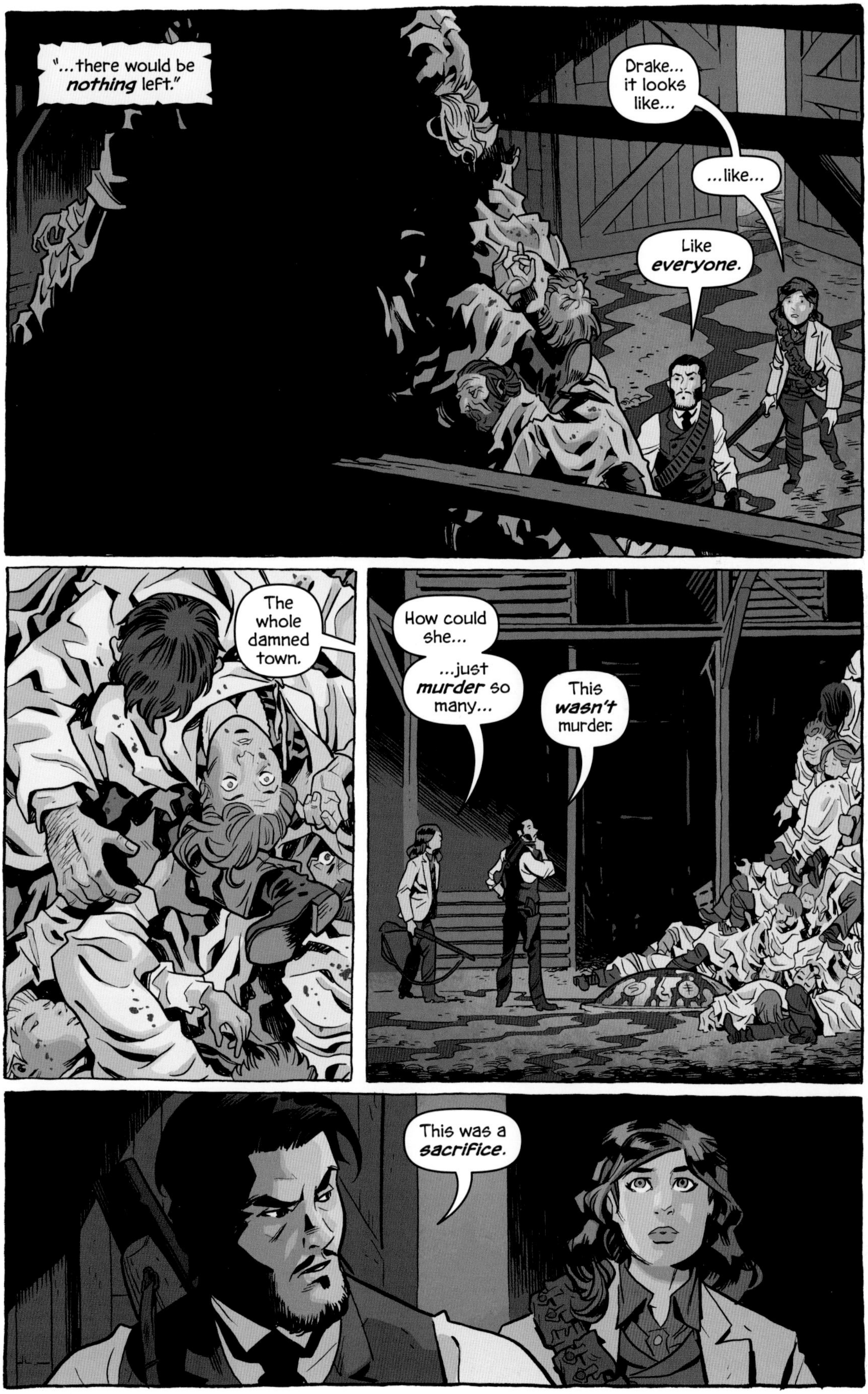
"...there would be *nothing* left."
Drake... it looks like...
...like...
Like *everyone*.
The whole damned town.
How could she...
...just *murder* so many...
This *wasn't* murder.
This was a *sacrifice*.

Look at how they're dressed.

There's no sign of struggle.

Lambs for the slaughter.

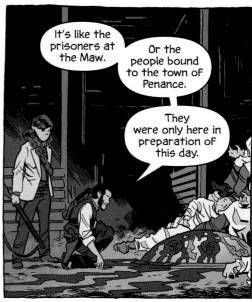

It's like the prisoners at the Maw.

Or the people bound to the town of Penance.

They were only here in preparation of this day.

Only, I think these people let themselves be killed *willingly.*

I don't understand.

Why would anyone *do* that?

Might be they died for what they *believed* in...

...or maybe because they didn't have anything left *deserving* of *faith.*

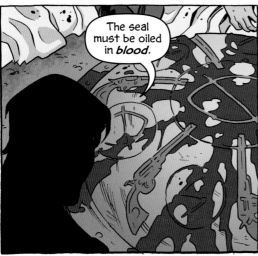

The seal must be oiled in *blood.*

So... why isn't it *opened?*

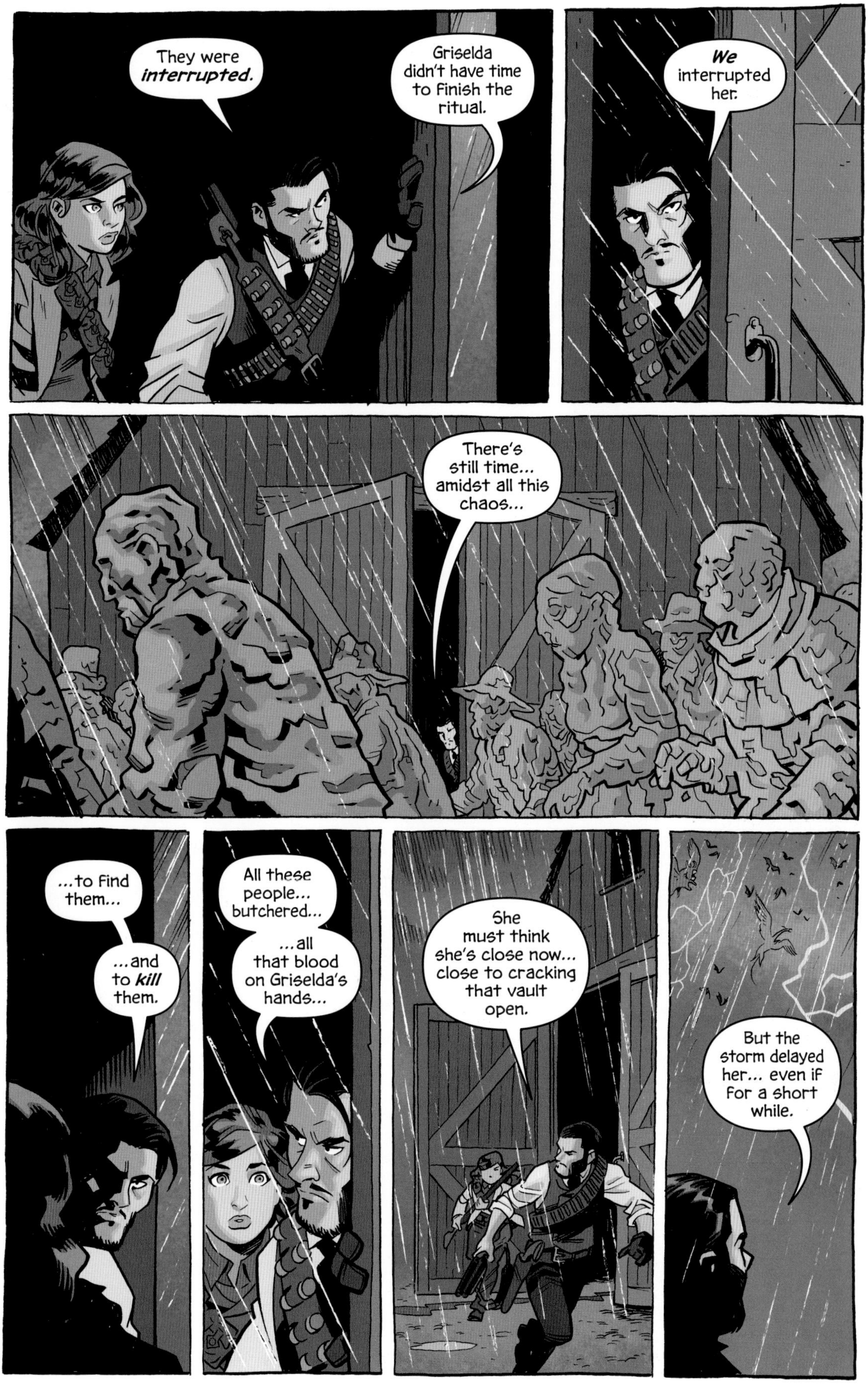
They were *interrupted.*
Griselda didn't have time to finish the ritual.
We interrupted her.
There's still time... amidst all this chaos...
...to find them...
...and to *kill* them.
All these people... butchered...
...all that blood on Griselda's hands...
She must think she's close now... close to cracking that vault open.
But the storm delayed her... even if for a short while.

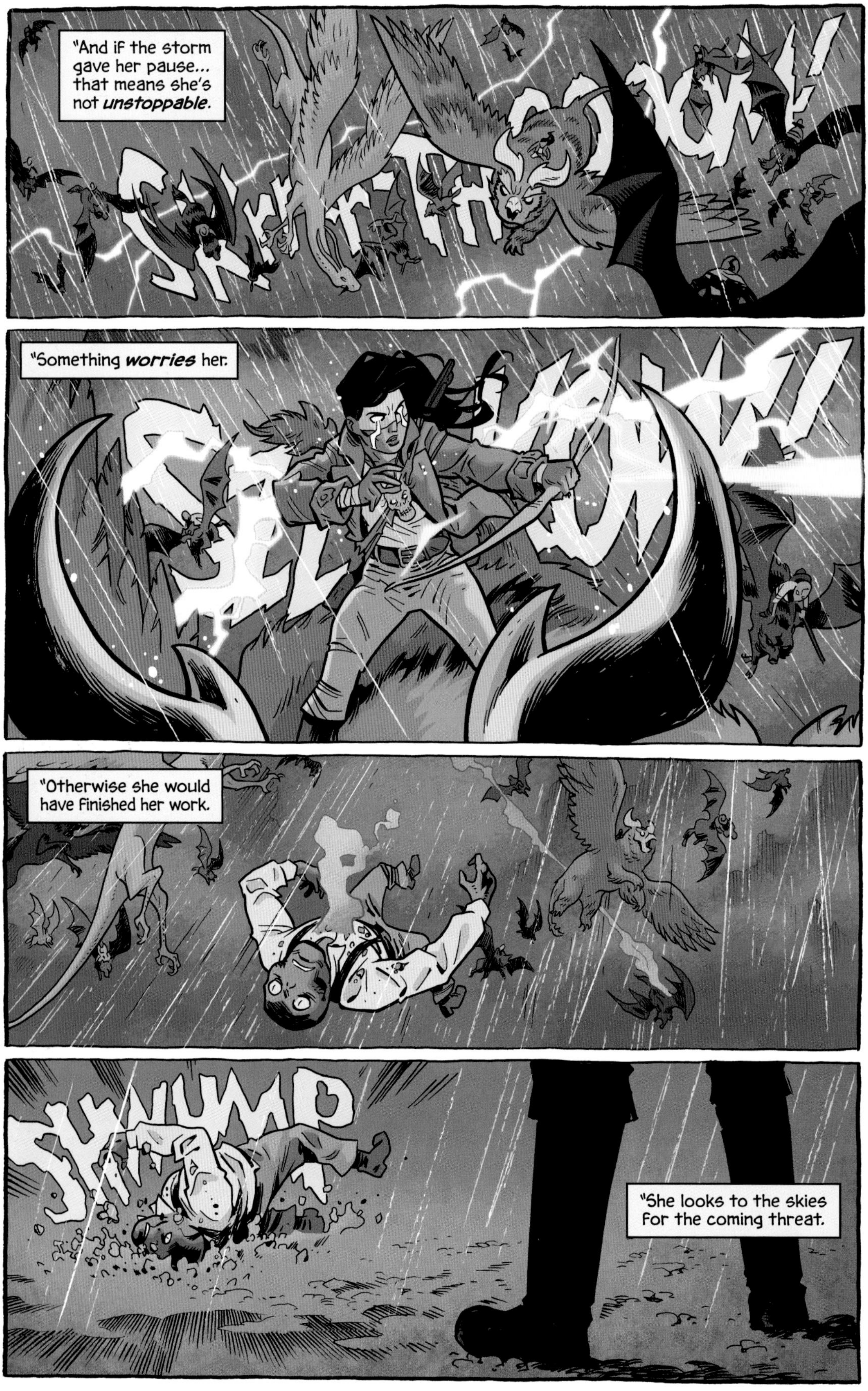
"And if the storm gave her pause... that means she's not *unstoppable*.
"Something *worries* her.
"Otherwise she would have finished her work.
"She looks to the skies for the coming threat.

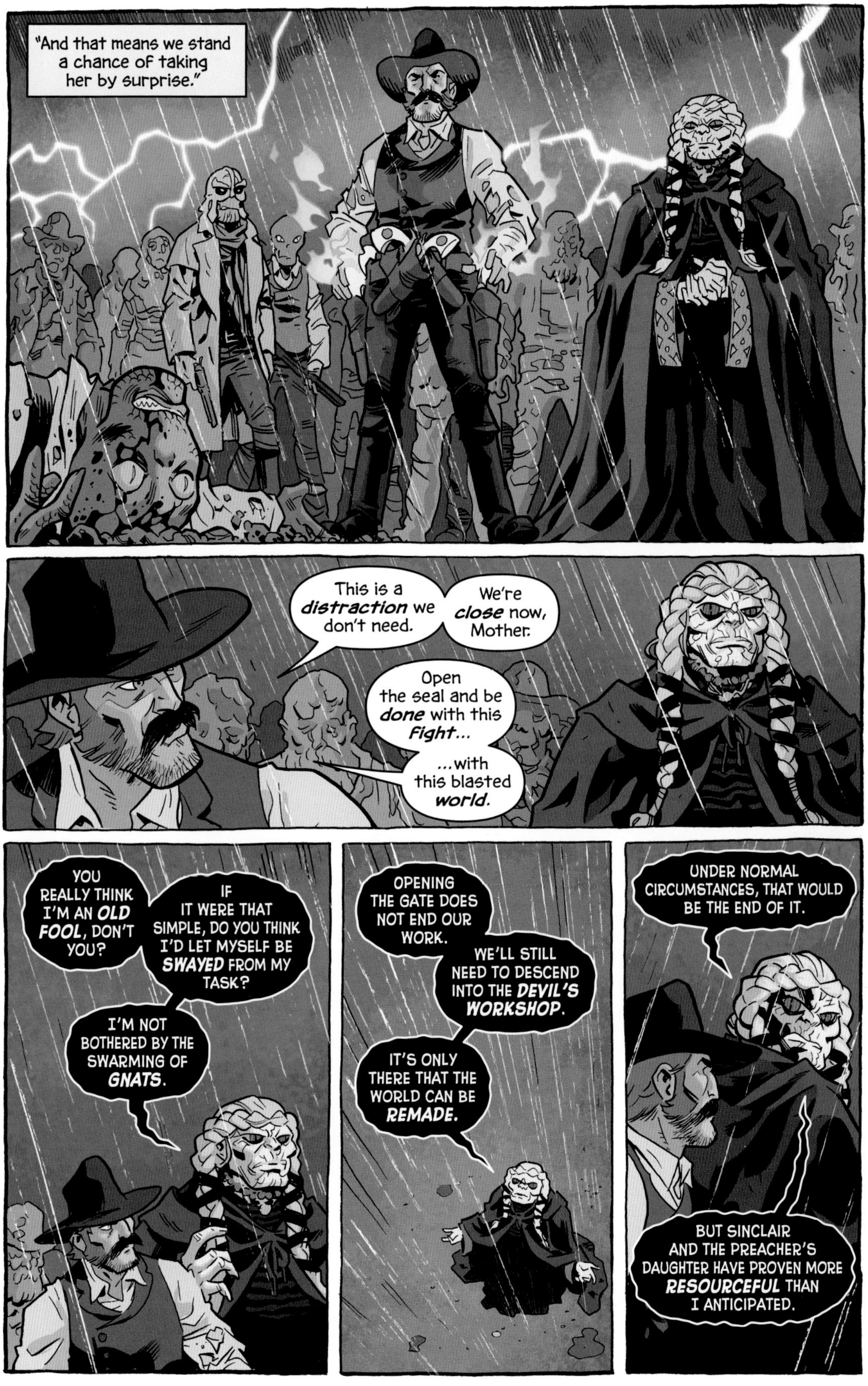

"And that means we stand a chance of taking her by surprise."
This is a *distraction* we don't need.
We're *close* now, Mother.
Open the seal and be *done* with this *fight*...
...with this blasted *world*.
YOU REALLY THINK I'M AN *OLD FOOL*, DON'T YOU?
IF IT WERE THAT SIMPLE, DO YOU THINK I'D LET MYSELF BE *SWAYED* FROM MY TASK?
I'M NOT BOTHERED BY THE SWARMING OF *GNATS*.
OPENING THE GATE DOES NOT END OUR WORK.
WE'LL STILL NEED TO DESCEND INTO THE *DEVIL'S WORKSHOP*.
IT'S ONLY THERE THAT THE WORLD CAN BE *REMADE*.
UNDER NORMAL CIRCUMSTANCES, THAT WOULD BE THE END OF IT.
BUT SINCLAIR AND THE PREACHER'S DAUGHTER HAVE PROVEN MORE *RESOURCEFUL* THAN I ANTICIPATED.

"THEY'VE GOT THEMSELVES A *SPIRIT-TALKER*...

"...A *SHAMAN*.

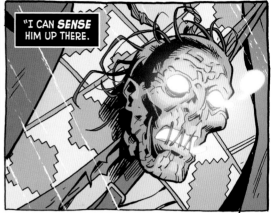

"I CAN *SENSE* HIM UP THERE.

"HE'S *POWERFUL*.

"STRONG ENOUGH TO *MASTER* THOSE ABHORRENT THUNDERBIRDS.

"PERHAPS *WISE* ENOUGH, TOO, TO KNOW HOW TO *FOLLOW* US."

HE PRESENTS TOO MUCH OF A *RISK*... A *DANGER* TO WHAT WE MUST DO.

THIS IS A GNAT THAT WE MUST *SWAT*.

A SMALL MATTER... BUT BEST DEALT WITH *BEFORE* IT RANKLES.

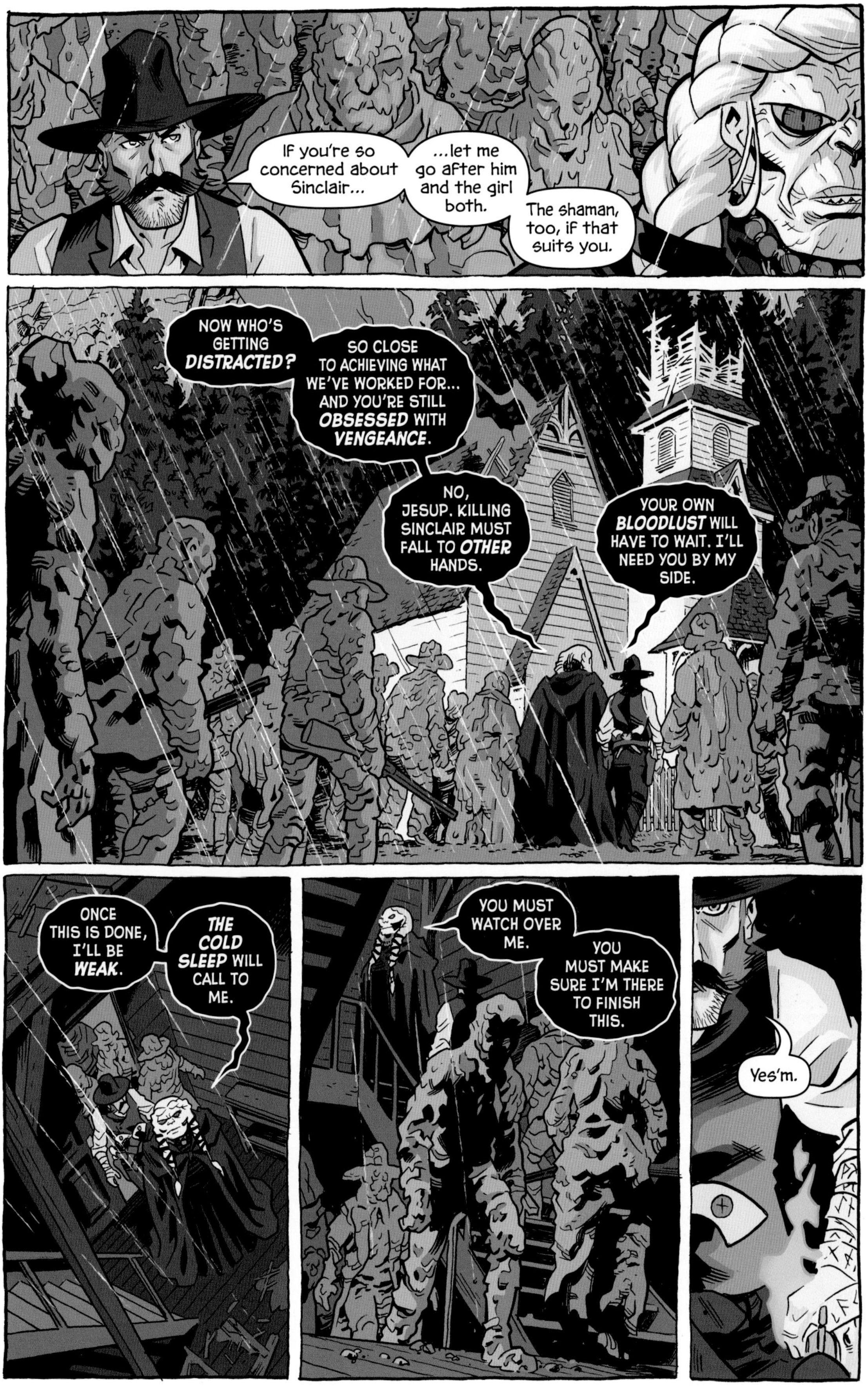

If you're so concerned about Sinclair...
...let me go after him and the girl both.
The shaman, too, if that suits you.
NOW WHO'S GETTING DISTRACTED?
SO CLOSE TO ACHIEVING WHAT WE'VE WORKED FOR... AND YOU'RE STILL OBSESSED WITH VENGEANCE.
NO, JESUP. KILLING SINCLAIR MUST FALL TO OTHER HANDS.
YOUR OWN BLOODLUST WILL HAVE TO WAIT. I'LL NEED YOU BY MY SIDE.
ONCE THIS IS DONE, I'LL BE WEAK.
THE COLD SLEEP WILL CALL TO ME.
YOU MUST WATCH OVER ME.
YOU MUST MAKE SURE I'M THERE TO FINISH THIS.
Yes'm.

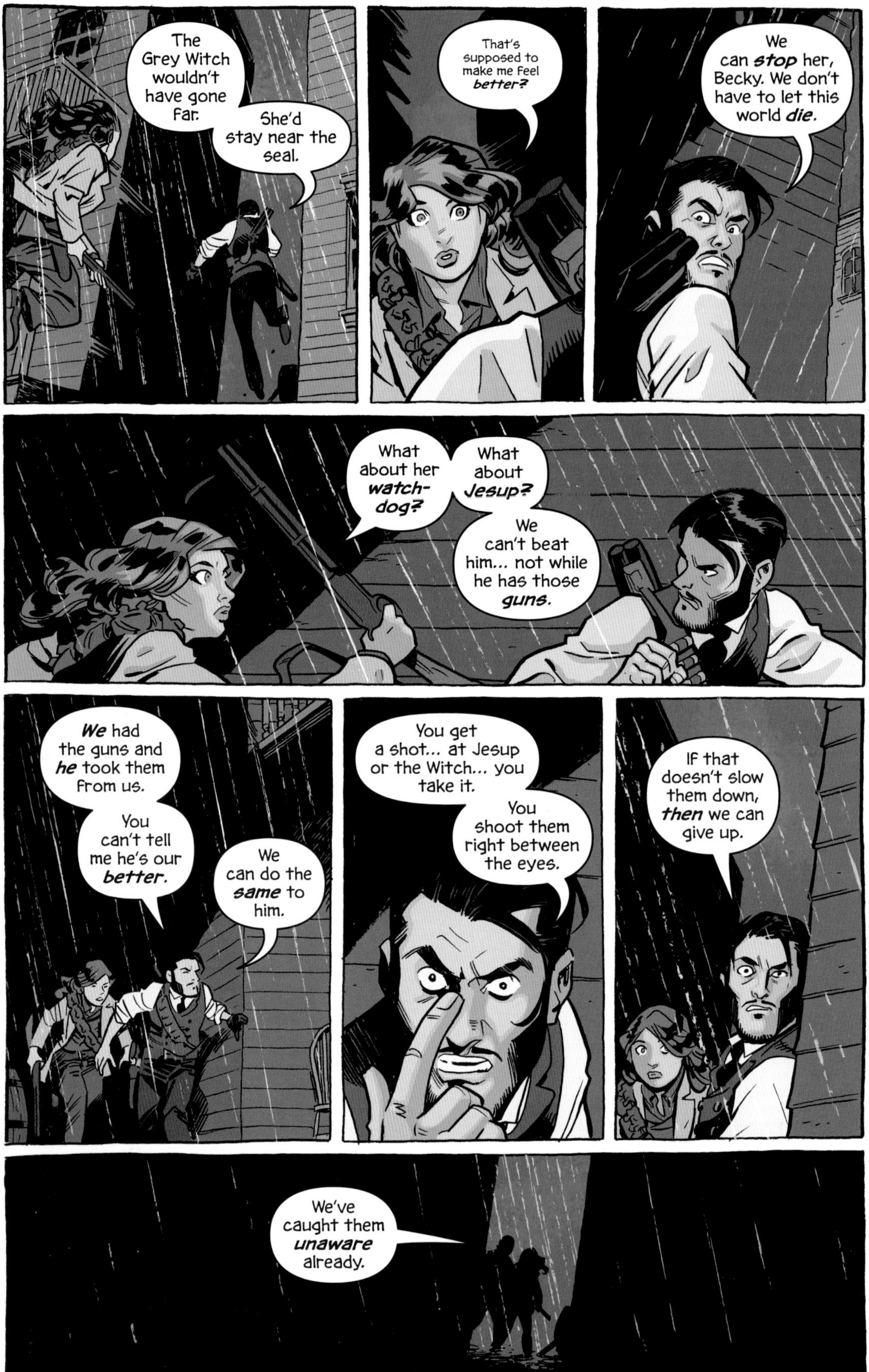
The Grey Witch wouldn't have gone far.
She'd stay near the seal.
That's supposed to make me feel better?
We can stop her, Becky. We don't have to let this world die.
What about her watch-dog?
What about Jesup?
We can't beat him... not while he has those guns.
We had the guns and he took them from us.
You can't tell me he's our better.
We can do the same to him.
You get a shot... at Jesup or the Witch... you take it.
You shoot them right between the eyes.
If that doesn't slow them down, then we can give up.
We've caught them unaware already.

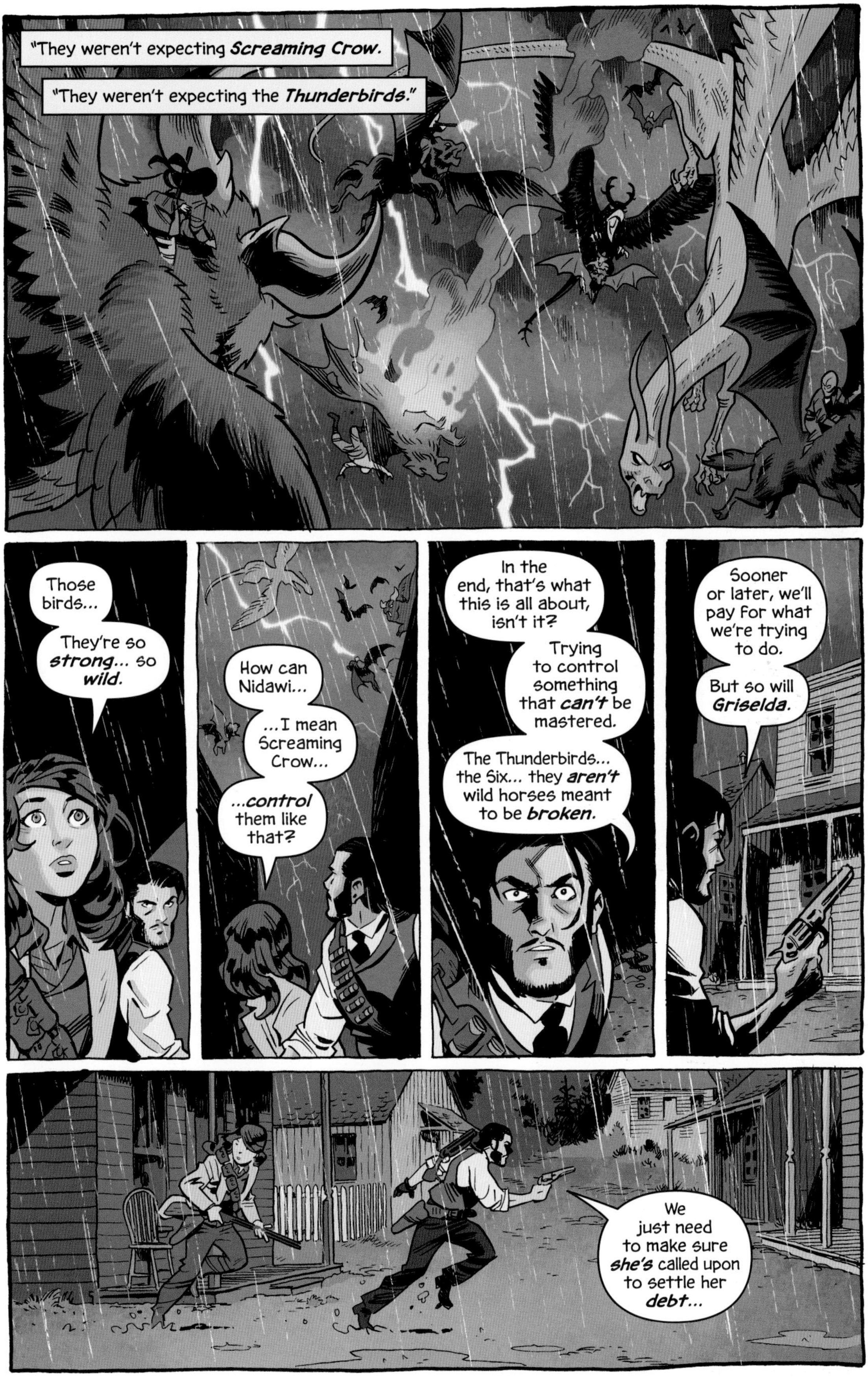
"They weren't expecting *Screaming Crow*.
"They weren't expecting the *Thunderbirds*."
Those birds...
They're so *strong*... so *wild*.
How can Nidawi...
...I mean Screaming Crow...
...*control* them like that?
In the end, that's what this is all about, isn't it?
Trying to control something that *can't* be mastered.
The Thunderbirds... the Six... they *aren't* wild horses meant to be *broken*.
Sooner or later, we'll pay for what we're trying to do.
But so will *Griselda*.
We just need to make sure *she's* called upon to settle her *debt*...

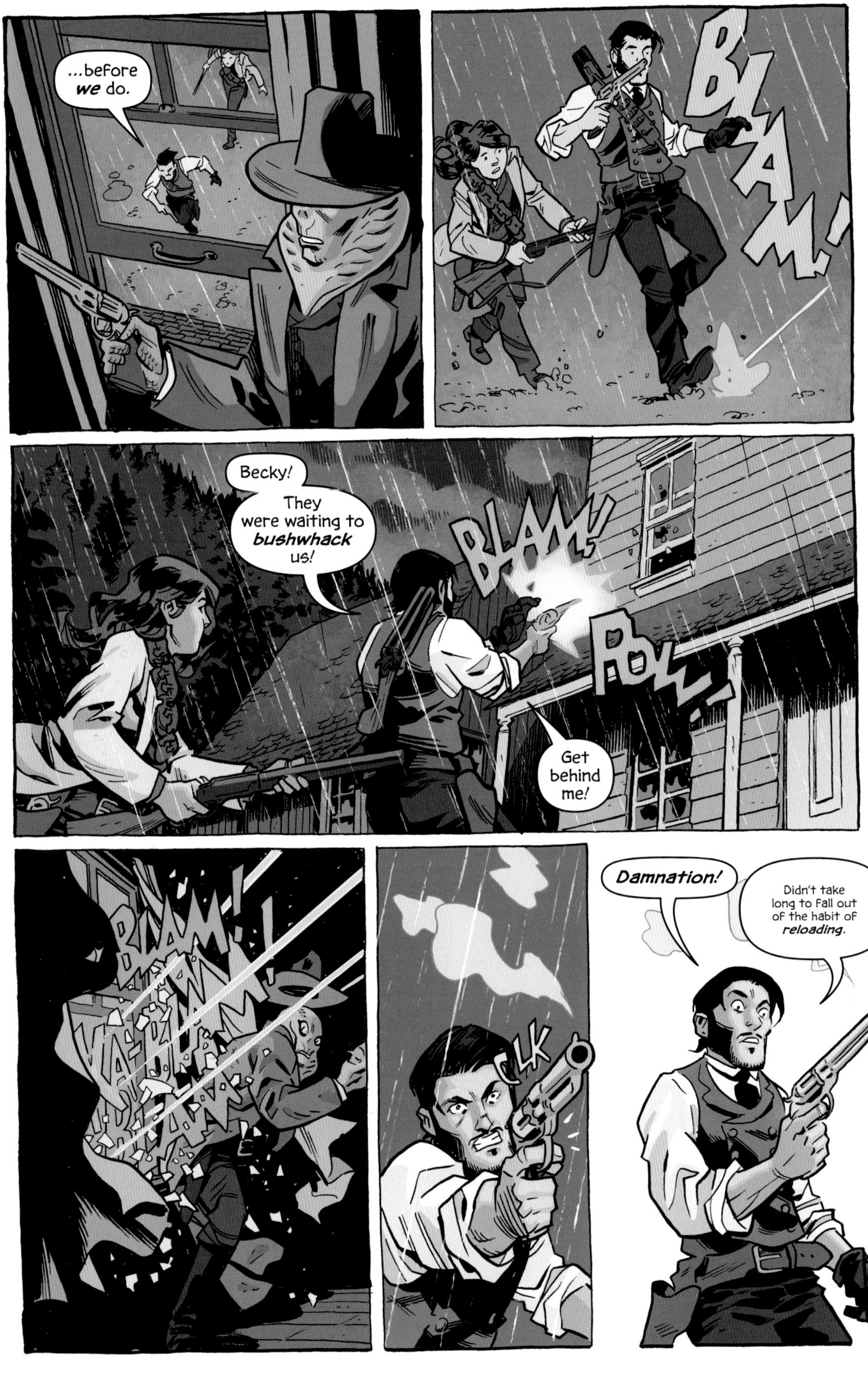
...before *we* do.
BLAM!
Becky!
They were waiting to *bushwhack* us!
BLAM!
POW
Get behind me!
BLAM!
CLK
Damnation!
Didn't take long to fall out of the habit of *reloading*.

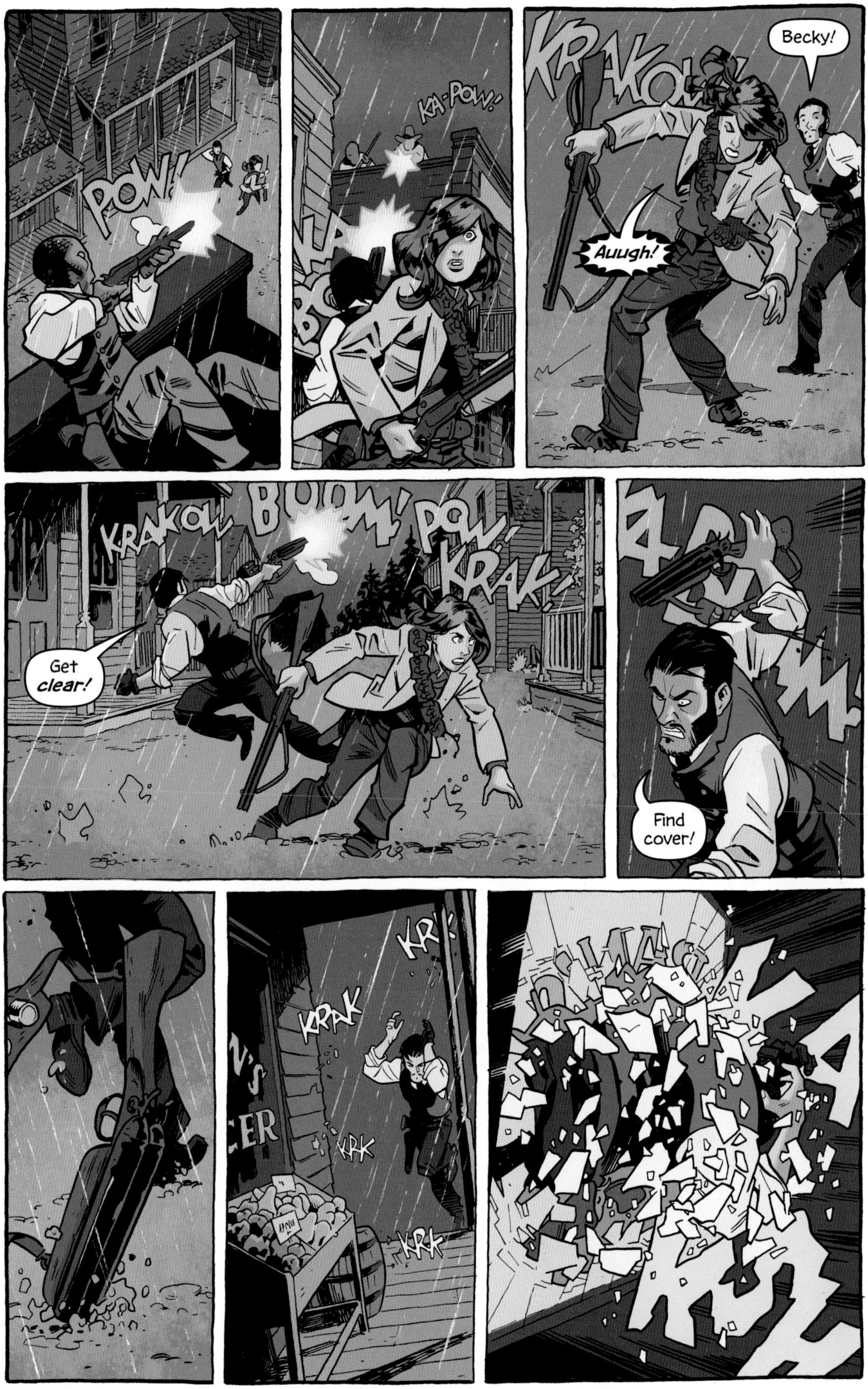
POW!
KA-POW!
Becky!
Auugh!
KRAKOW
BOOM!
POW!
KRAK!
Get clear!
Find cover!
KRAK
KRK
KRK

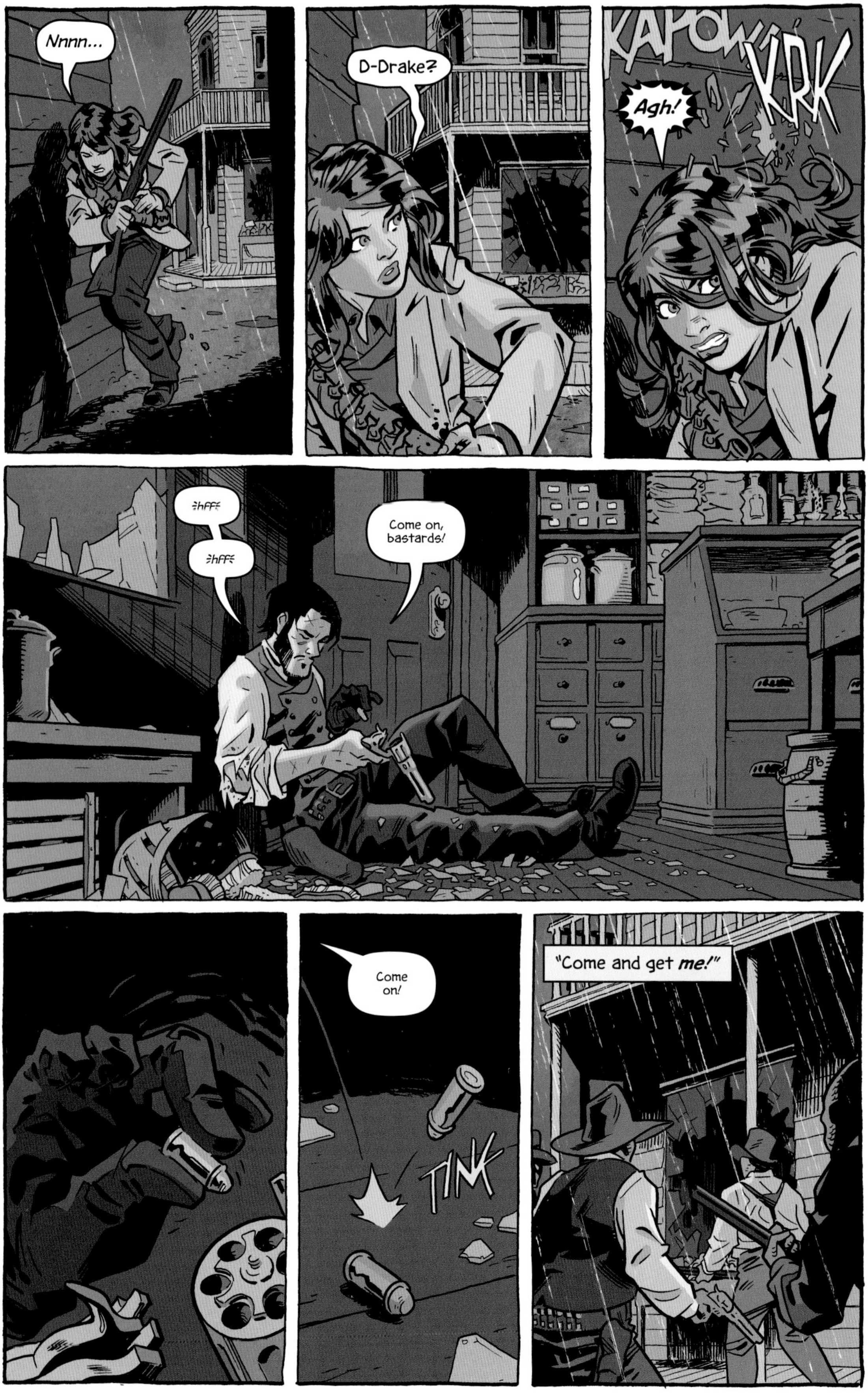
Nnnn...
D-Drake?
KAPOW!
KRK
Agh!
hff
hff
Come on, bastards!
Come on!
TINK
"Come and get me!"

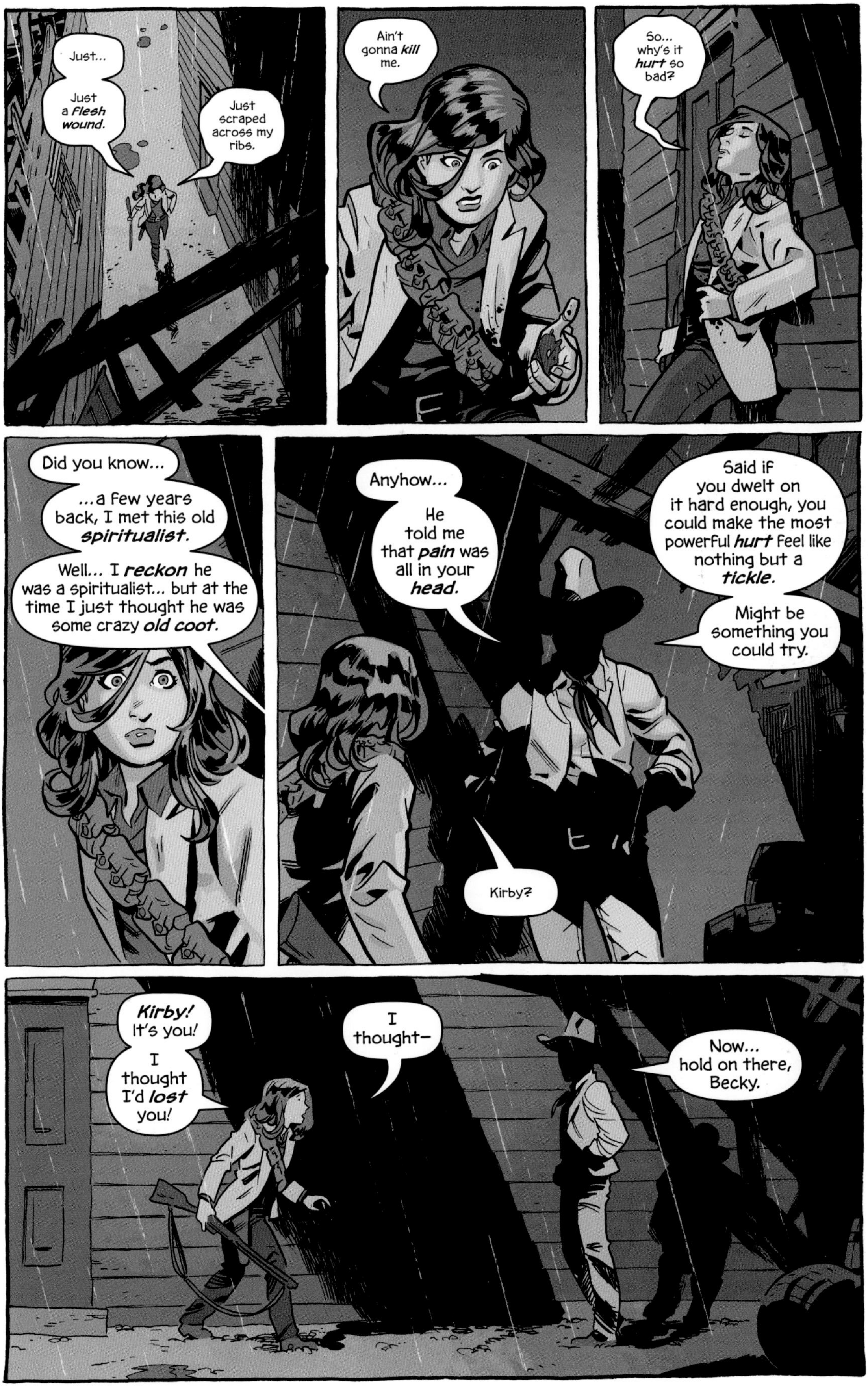
Just...
Just a *flesh wound*.
Just scraped across my ribs.
Ain't gonna *kill* me.
So... why's it *hurt* so bad?
Did you know...
...a few years back, I met this old *spiritualist*.
Well... I *reckon* he was a spiritualist... but at the time I just thought he was some crazy *old coot*.
Anyhow...
He told me that *pain* was all in your *head*.
Said if you dwelt on it hard enough, you could make the most powerful *hurt* feel like nothing but a *tickle*.
Might be something you could try.
Kirby?
Kirby! It's you!
I thought I'd *lost* you!
I thought–
Now... hold on there, Becky.

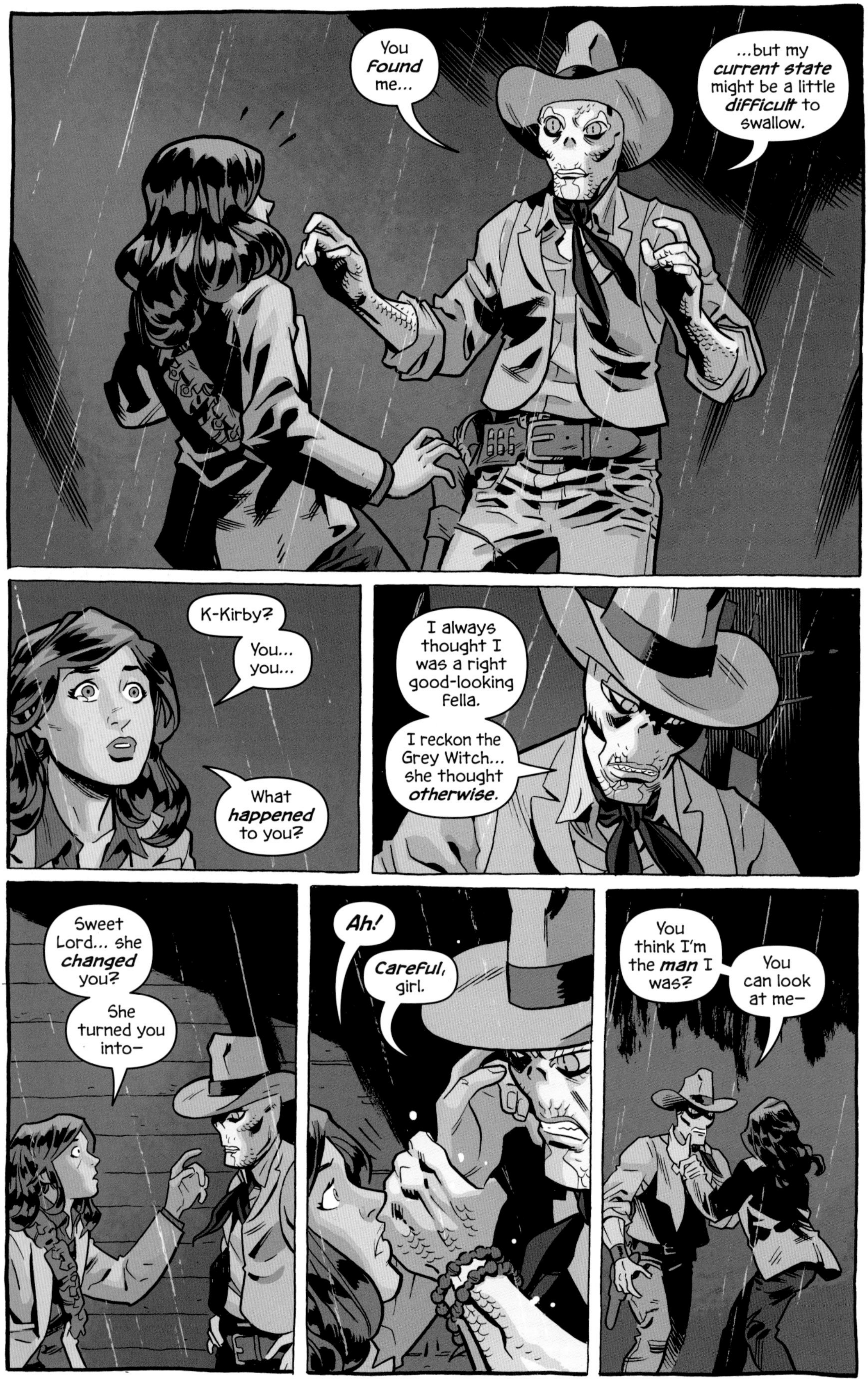
You *found* me...
...but my *current state* might be a little *difficult* to swallow.
K-Kirby?
You... you...
What *happened* to you?
I always thought I was a right good-looking fella.
I reckon the Grey Witch... she thought *otherwise*.
Sweet Lord... she *changed* you?
She turned you into—
Ah!
Careful, girl.
You think I'm the *man* I was?
You can look at me—

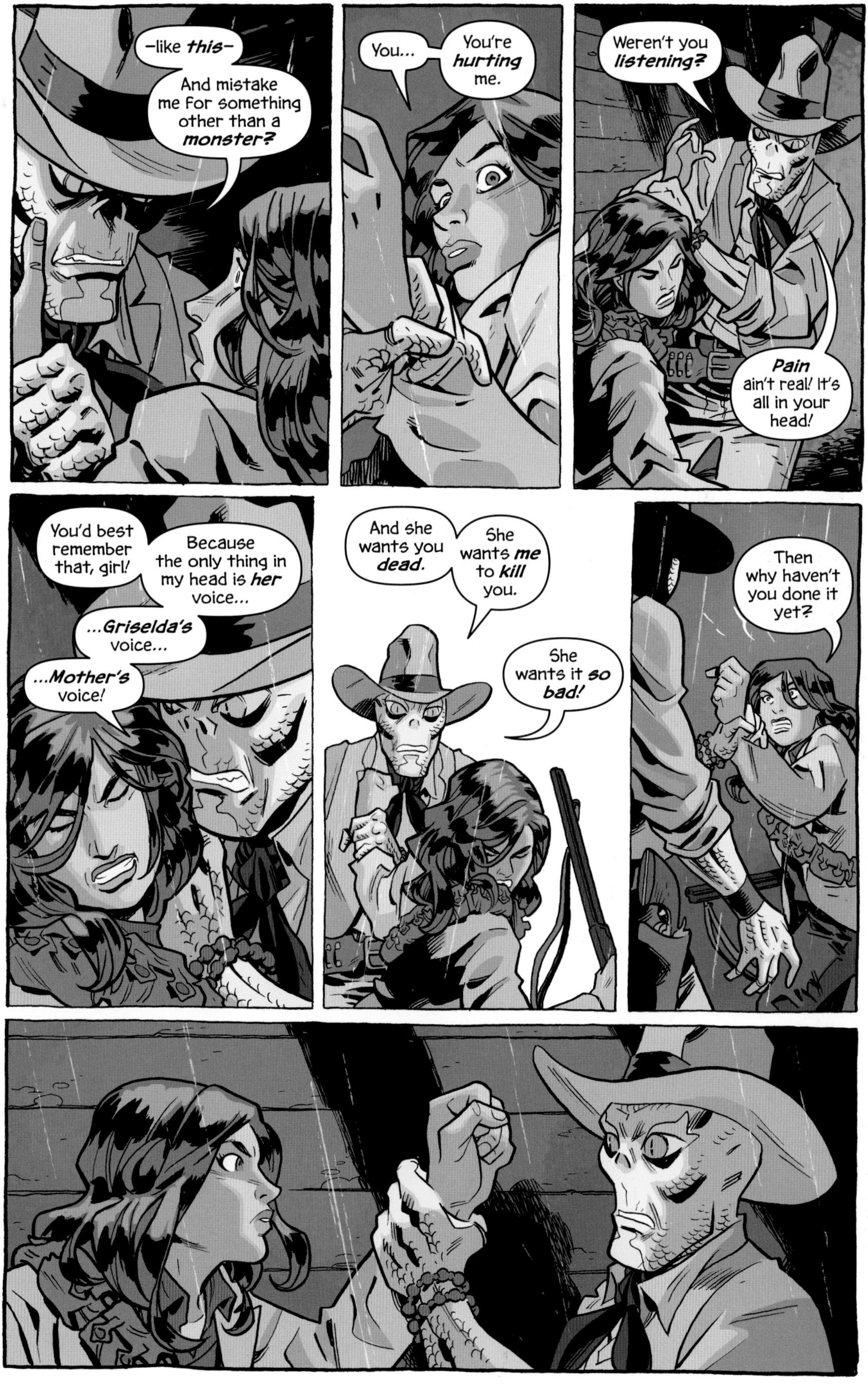

—like *this*—
And mistake me for something other than a *monster?*
You...
You're *hurting* me.
Weren't you *listening?*
Pain ain't real! It's all in your head!
You'd best remember that, girl!
Because the only thing in my head is *her* voice...
...*Griselda's* voice...
...*Mother's* voice!
And she wants you *dead.*
She wants *me* to *kill* you.
She wants it *so bad!*
Then why haven't you done it yet?

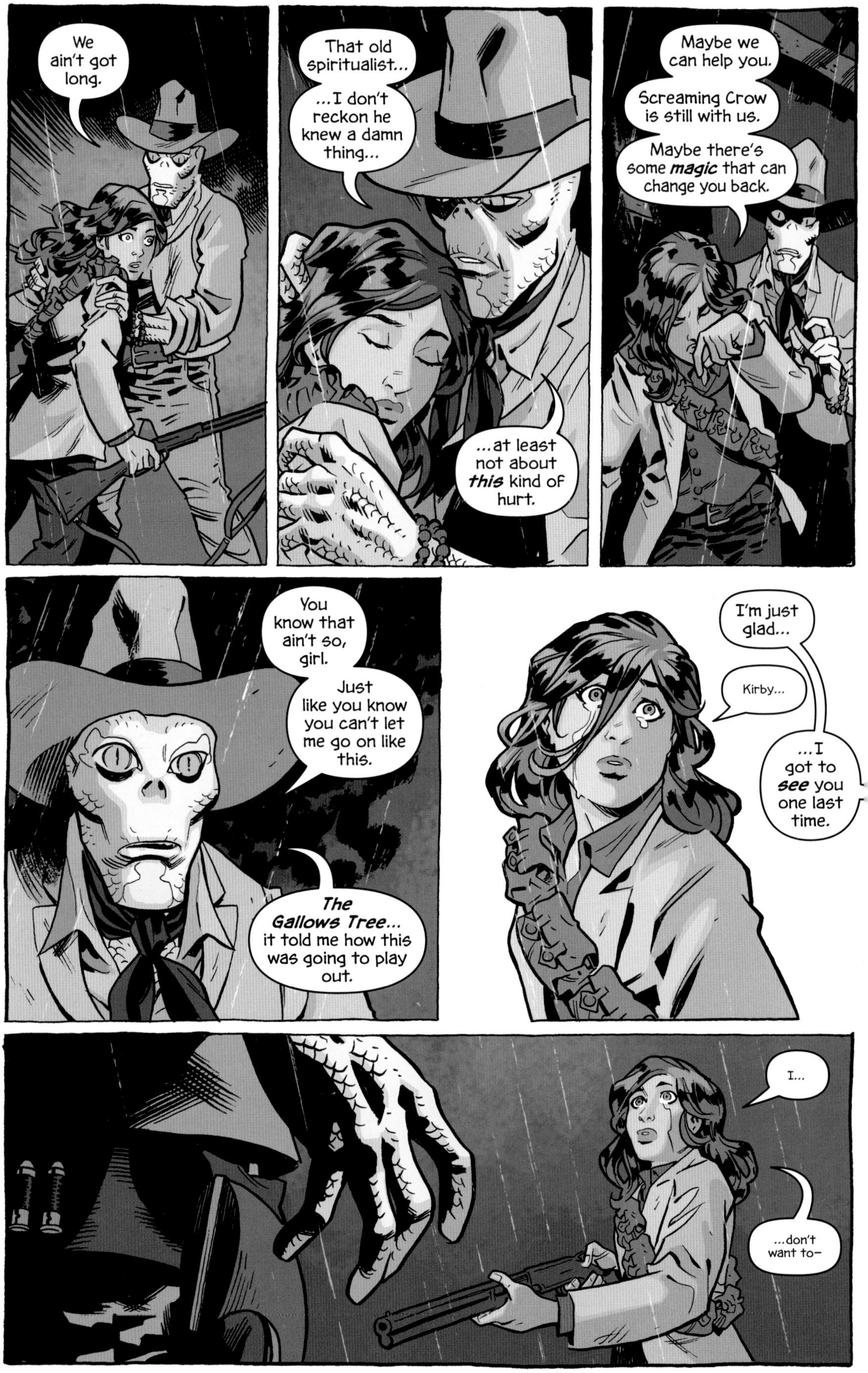
We ain't got long.
That old spiritualist...
...I don't reckon he knew a damn thing...
...at least not about **this** kind of hurt.
Maybe we can help you.
Screaming Crow is still with us.
Maybe there's some **magic** that can change you back.
You know that ain't so, girl.
Just like you know you can't let me go on like this.
The Gallows Tree... it told me how this was going to play out.
Kirby...
I'm just glad...
...I got to **see** you one last time.
I...
...don't want to–

BOOM!

HEAR ME, WAYWARD SPIRIT! HEAR ME, UNBIDDEN THING!

I COMMAND THE ANCIENT POWERS OF THE EARTH AND AIR, WATER AND FLAME!

I ADJURE YOU, WANDERING GHOST!

CLEAR THE WORLD OF THE LIVING! TURN BACK TO WHERE YOU BELONG!

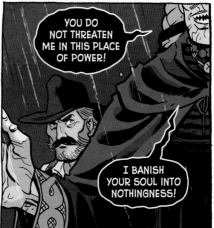

YOU DO NOT THREATEN ME IN THIS PLACE OF POWER!

I BANISH YOUR SOUL INTO NOTHINGNESS!

I REMOVE YOUR POWERS!

I TURN THEM AGAINST YOU!

FLEE THIS PLACE!

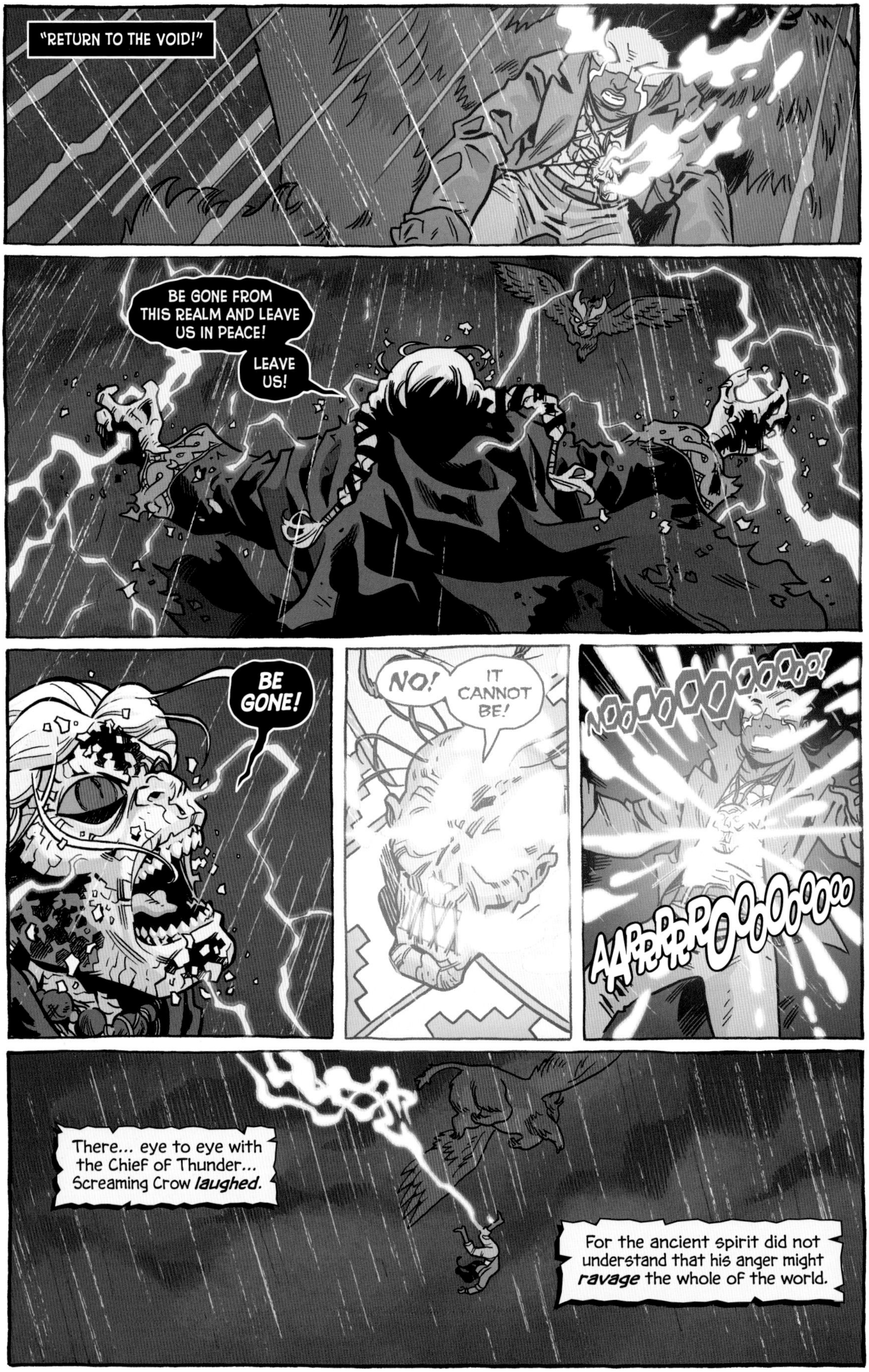
"RETURN TO THE VOID!"
BE GONE FROM THIS REALM AND LEAVE US IN PEACE!
LEAVE US!
BE GONE!
NO!
IT CANNOT BE!
NOOOOOOOOOOOOOO!
AARRRRROOOOOOOO
There... eye to eye with the Chief of Thunder... Screaming Crow *laughed*.
For the ancient spirit did not understand that his anger might *ravage* the whole of the world.

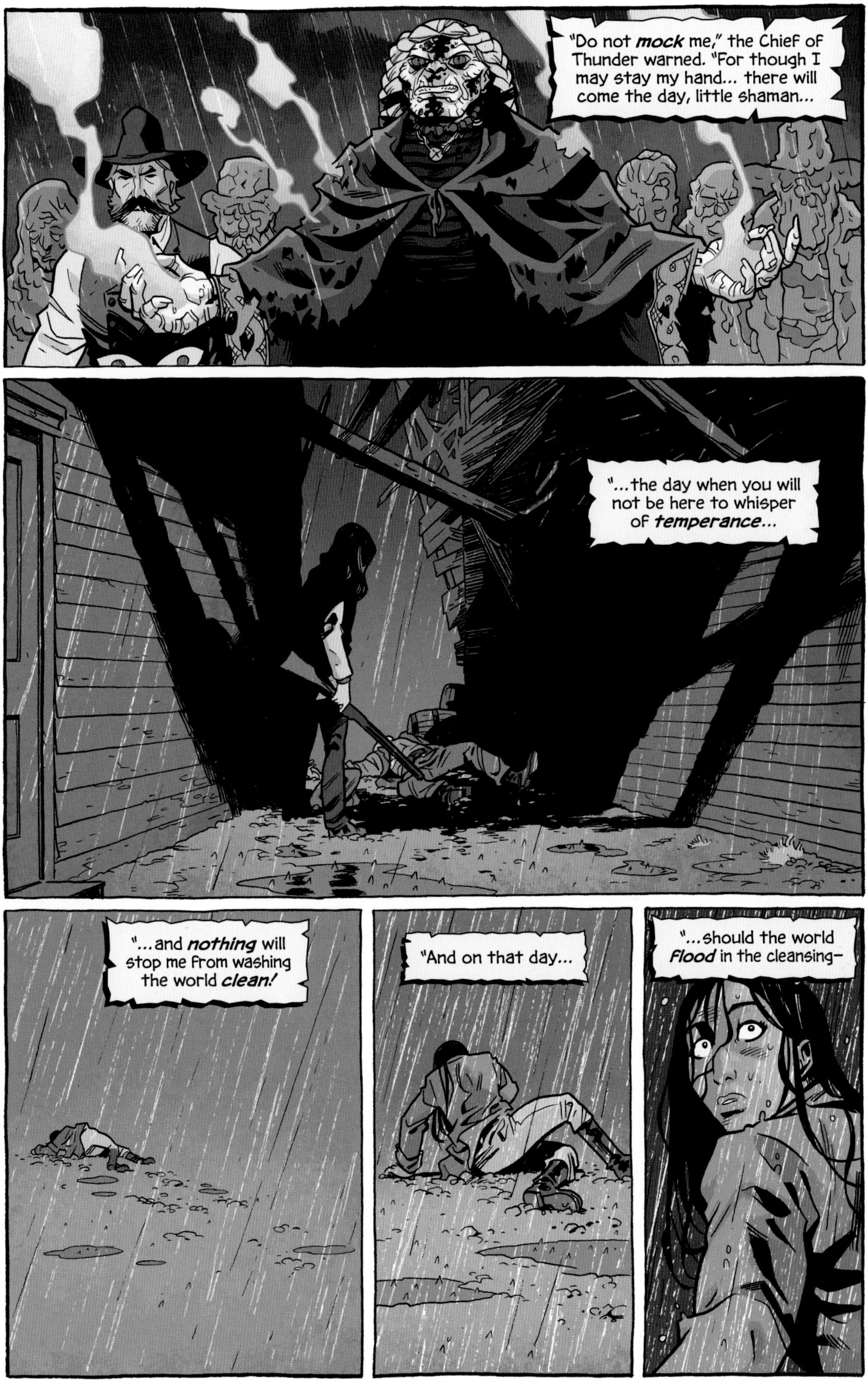
"Do not *mock* me," the Chief of Thunder warned. "For though I may stay my hand... there will come the day, little shaman...
"...the day when you will not be here to whisper of *temperance*...
"...and *nothing* will stop me from washing the world *clean!*
"And on that day...
"...should the world *flood* in the cleansing–

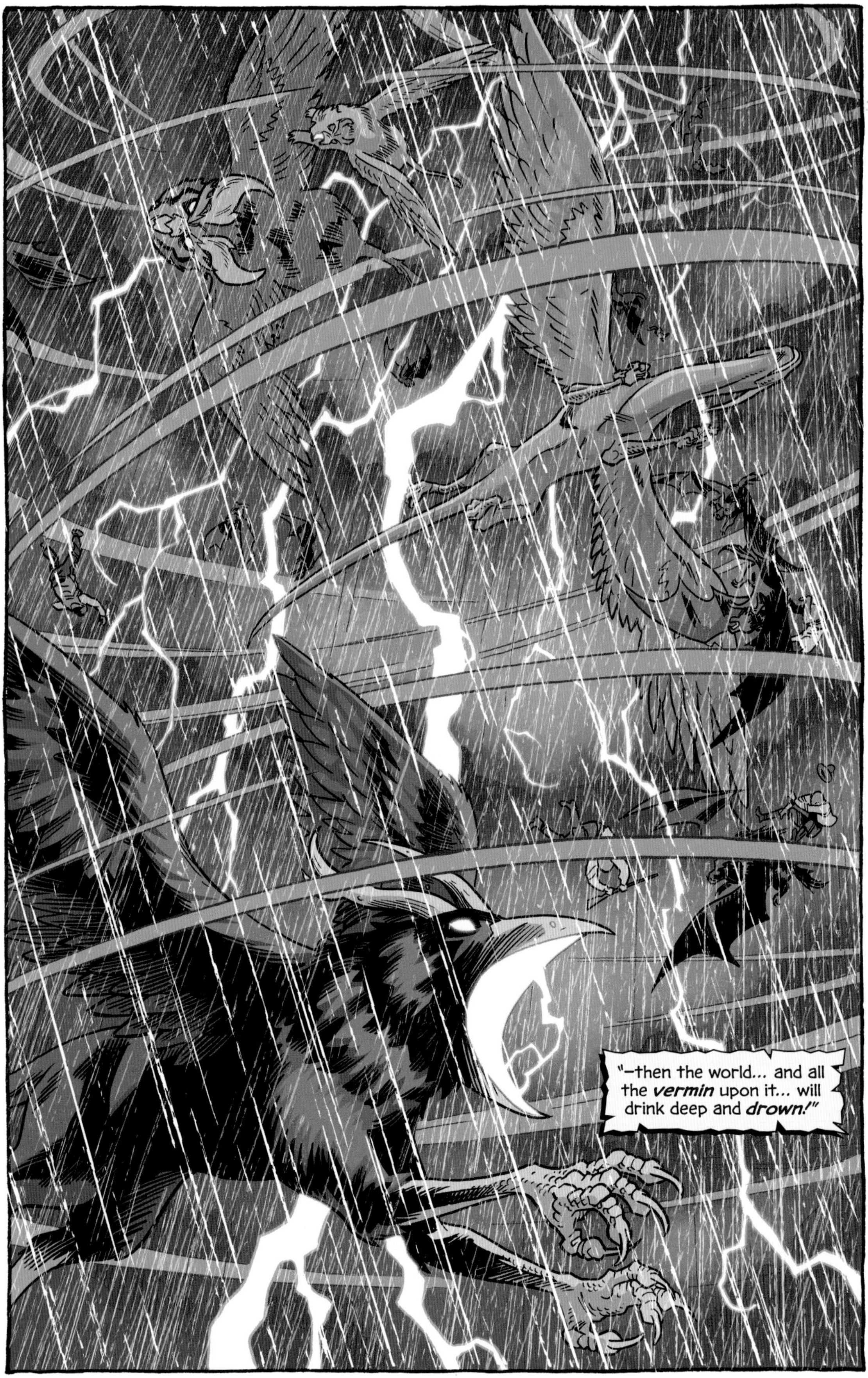
"—then the world... and all the *vermin* upon it... will drink deep and *drown!*"

CHAPTER
FIVE

The *First Gun* strikes with the force of a cannon shell.

The *Second Gun* expels the very flames of Perdition.

The *Third Gun* spreads a flesh-rotting disease.

The *Fourth Gun* calls up the spirits of the men and women it has shot down.

The *Fifth Gun* grants eternal youth and the ability to heal from even a fatal wound.

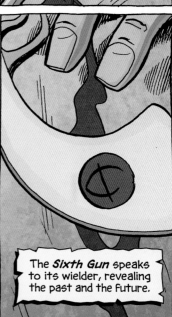

The *Sixth Gun* speaks to its wielder, revealing the past and the future.

Brought together, *the Six* were the keys to *destroying* this world...

...and *rebuilding* the next.

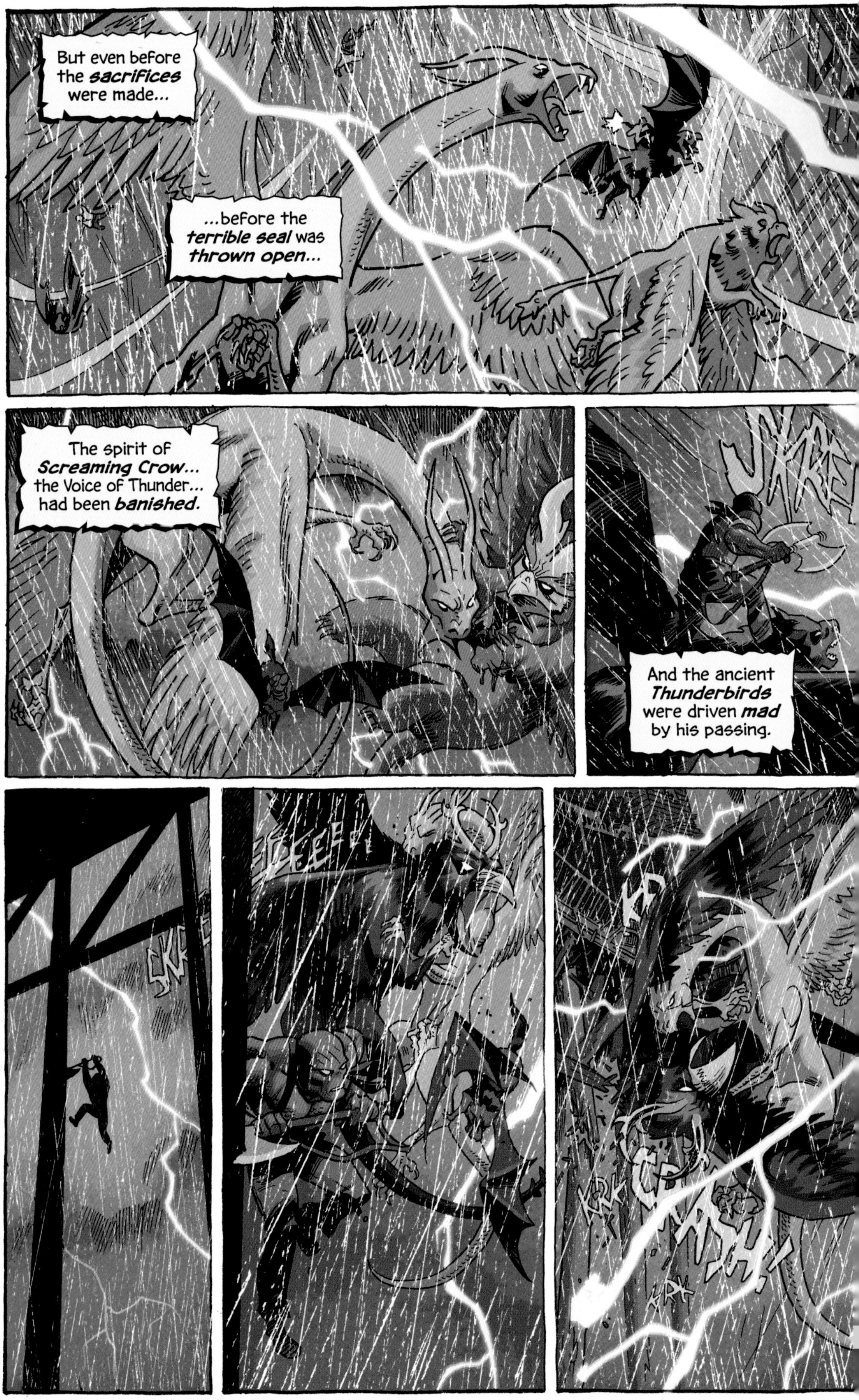
But even before the sacrifices were made...
...before the terrible seal was thrown open...
The spirit of Screaming Crow... the Voice of Thunder... had been banished.
And the ancient Thunderbirds were driven mad by his passing.

...anyone with a pair of eyes could tell this world's time was *done*.

The great creatures shrieked and kicked and lashed out at one another...

SHUNK!

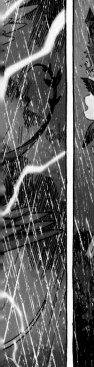

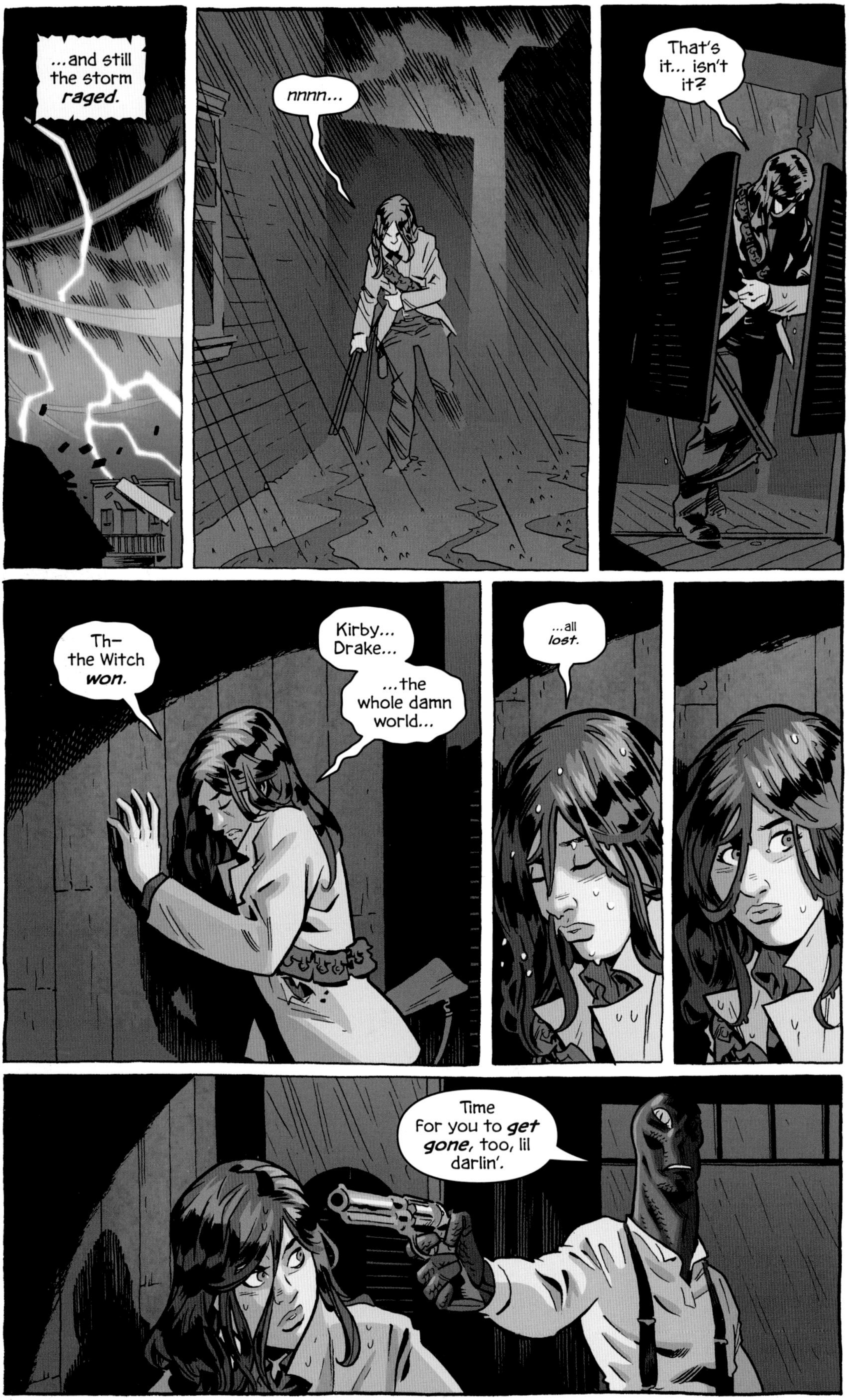
...and still the storm *raged.*
nnnn...
That's it... isn't it?
Th– the Witch *won.*
Kirby... Drake...
...the whole damn world...
...all *lost.*
Time for you to *get gone,* too, lil darlin'.

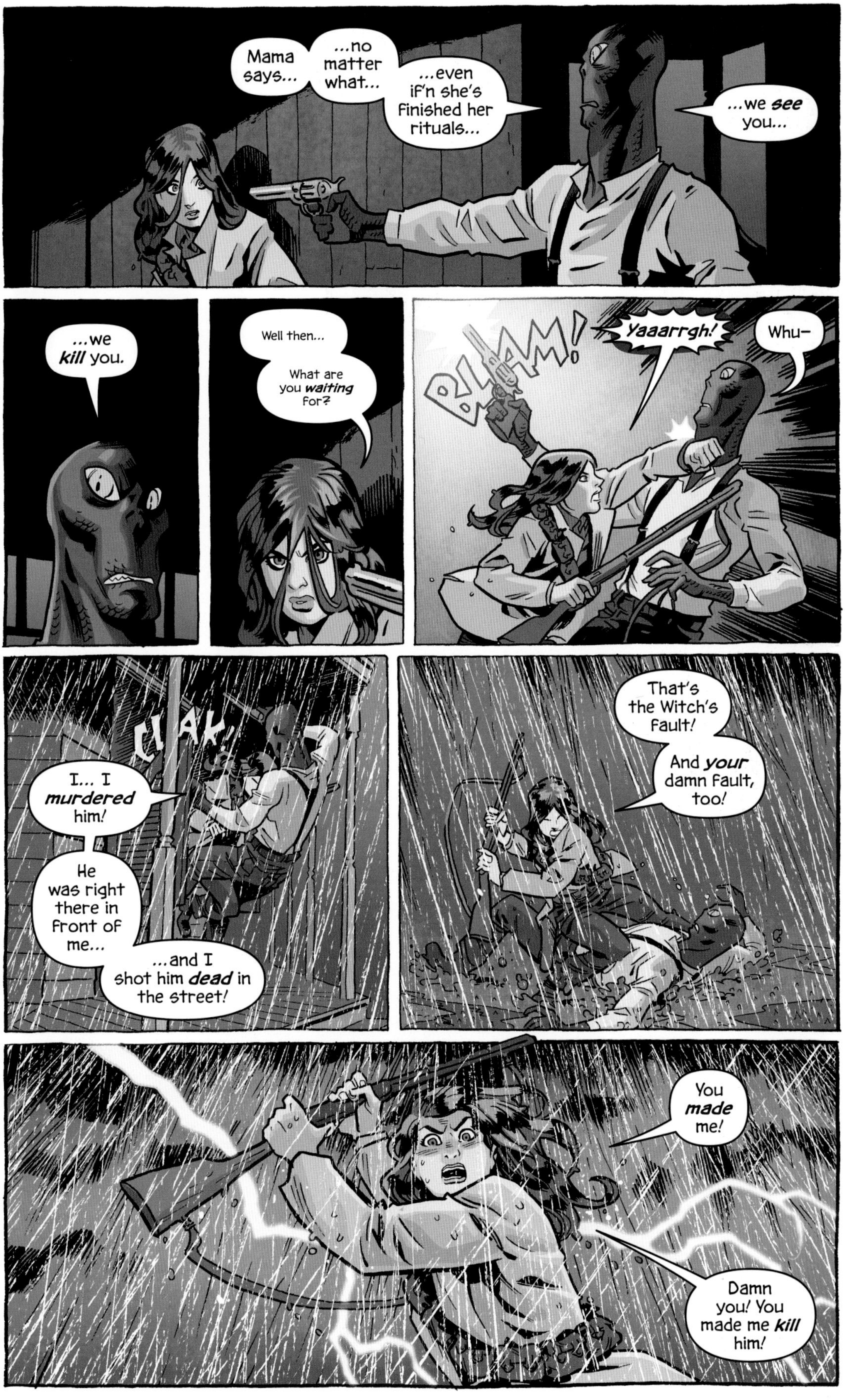
Mama says...
...no matter what...
...even if'n she's finished her rituals...
...we see you...
...we kill you.
Well then...
What are you waiting for?
BLAM!
Yaaarrgh!
Whu-
CLAK!
I... I murdered him!
He was right there in front of me...
...and I shot him dead in the street!
That's the Witch's fault!
And your damn fault, too!
You made me!
Damn you! You made me kill him!

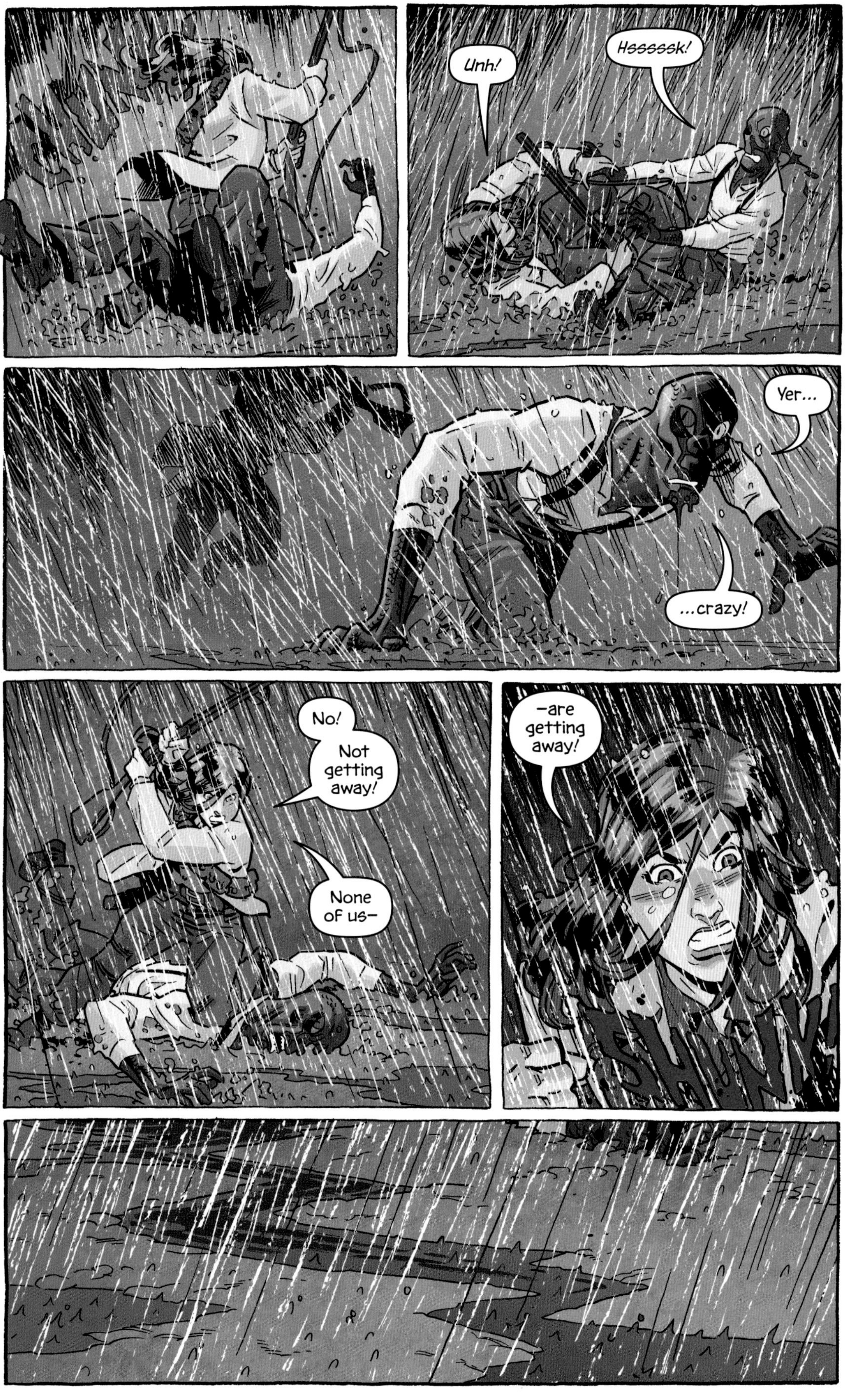
Unh!
Hsssssk!
Yer...
...crazy!
No!
Not getting away!
None of us–
–are getting away!

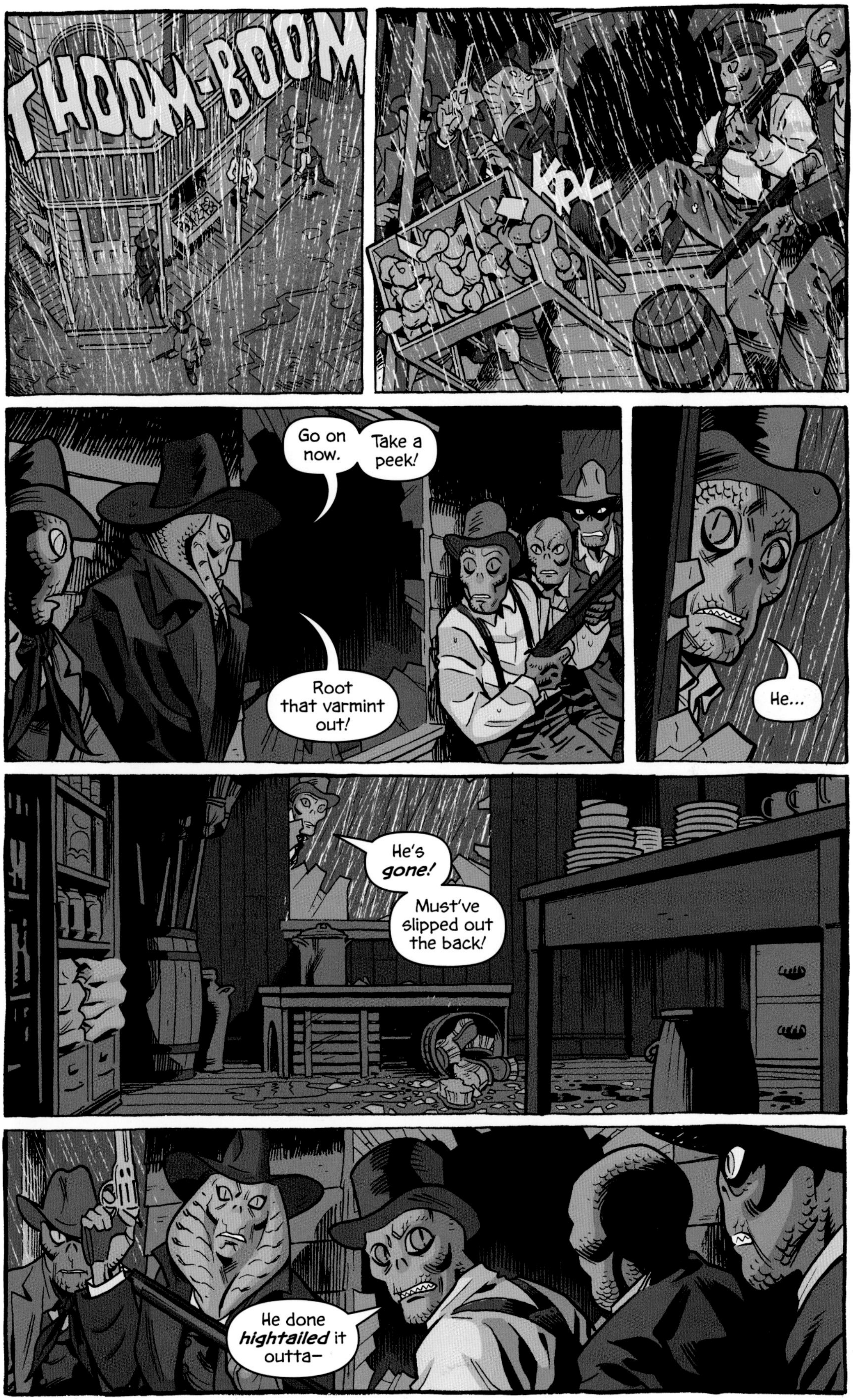
THOOM-BOOM
Go on now.
Take a peek!
Root that varmint out!
He...
He's *gone!*
Must've slipped out the back!
He done *hightailed* it outta—

Tarnation!

Pepper his hide!

Gun him down!

BLAM-KA-BLAM

BLAM-BLAM

POW!

POW!

BLAM!

POW!

KLAM

CLANK

BLAM! LAM

FLUIP

THWF

Hold up!

PFF

THWP

A POW! LAM

KSH!

Hold *up* now, I said!

That ol' boy just got his plow cleaned!

I'd be surprised there's *anything* left of him now.

Why don't you go ahead and have a look-see?

M-me?

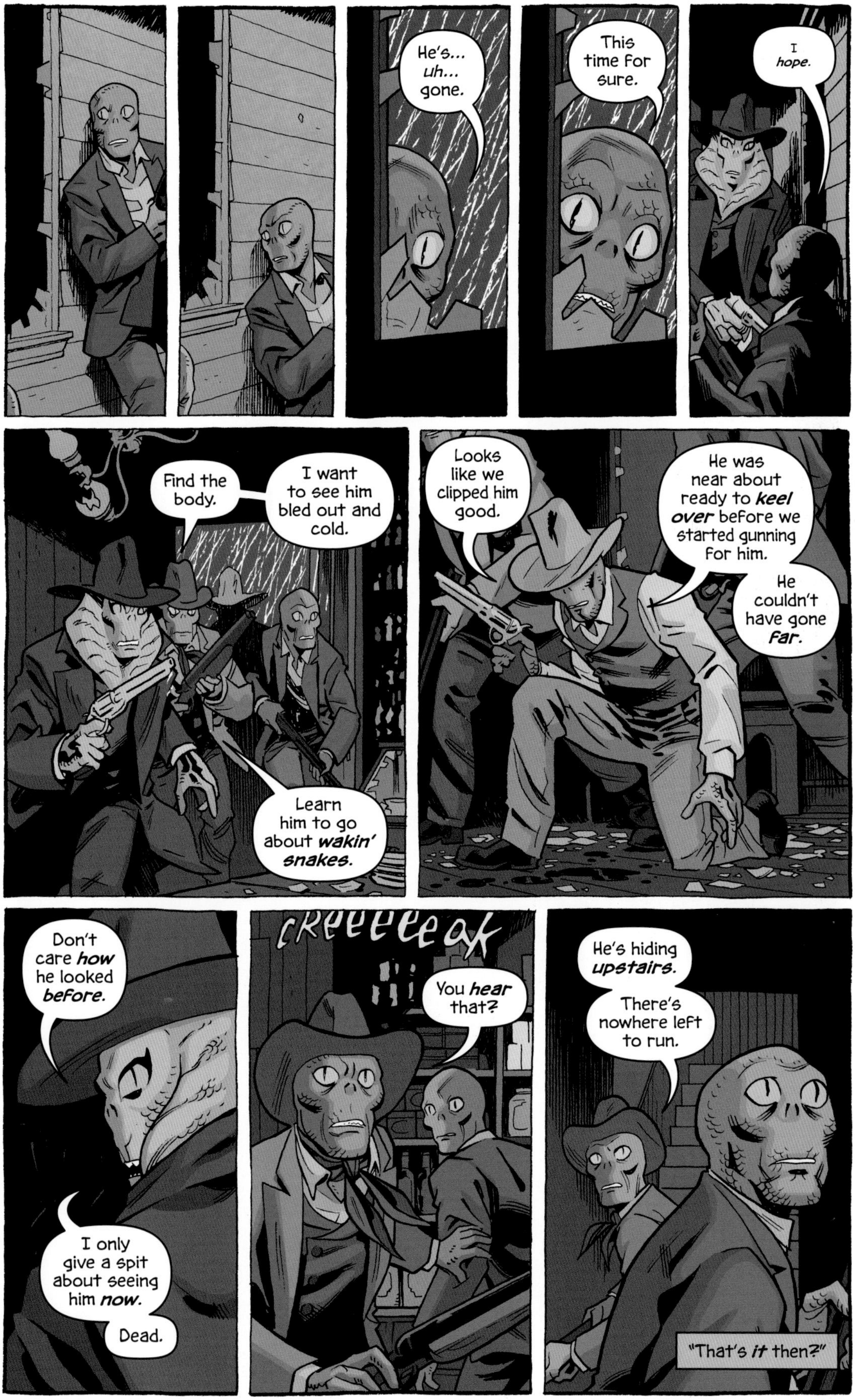
He's... uh... gone.
This time for sure.
I hope.
Find the body.
I want to see him bled out and cold.
Learn him to go about wakin' snakes.
Looks like we clipped him good.
He was near about ready to keel over before we started gunning for him.
He couldn't have gone far.
Don't care how he looked before.
I only give a spit about seeing him now.
Dead.
CREEEEEAK
You hear that?
He's hiding upstairs.
There's nowhere left to run.
"That's it then?"

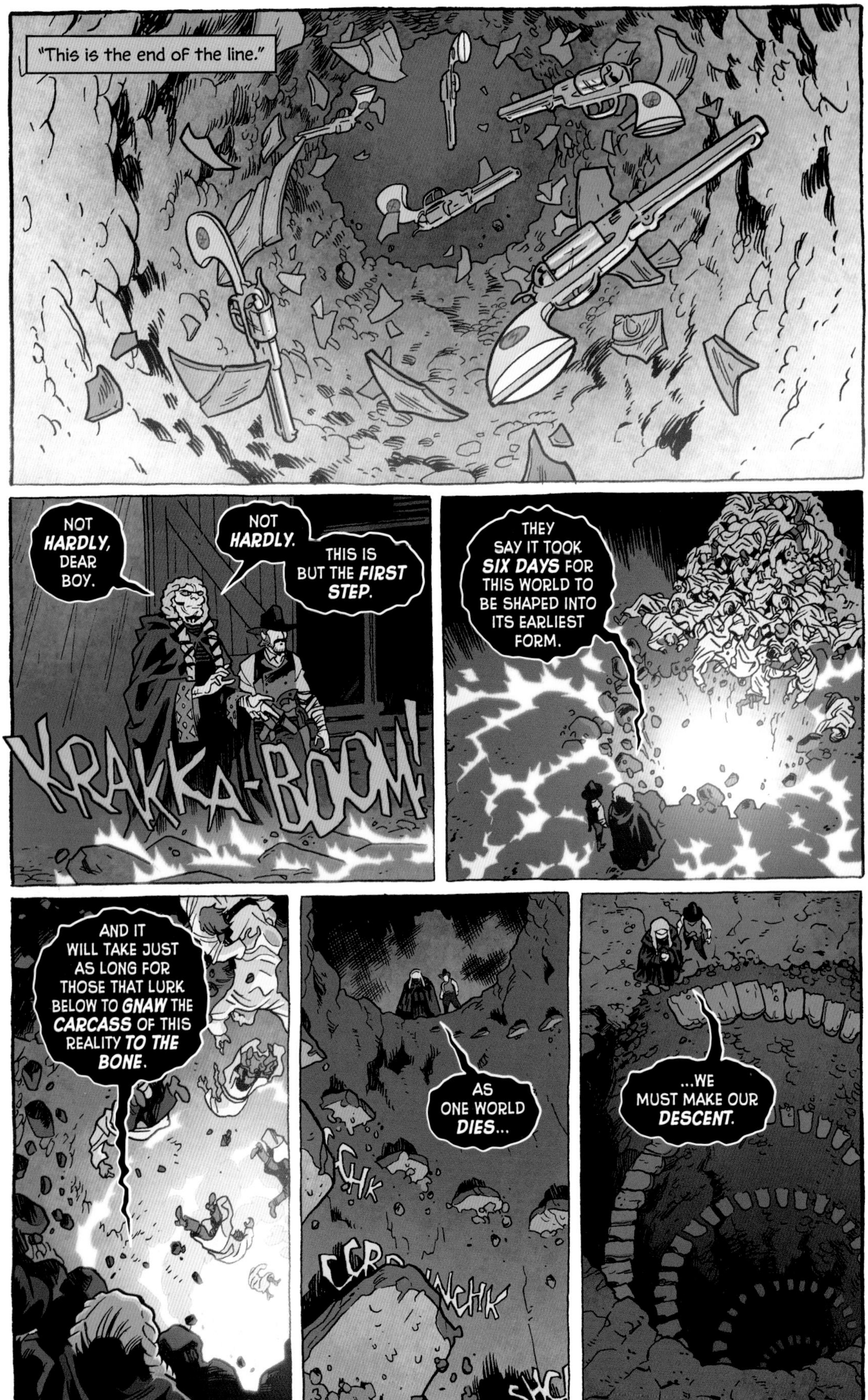
"This is the end of the line."
NOT HARDLY, DEAR BOY.
NOT HARDLY.
THIS IS BUT THE FIRST STEP.
KRAKKA-BOOM!
THEY SAY IT TOOK SIX DAYS FOR THIS WORLD TO BE SHAPED INTO ITS EARLIEST FORM.
AND IT WILL TAKE JUST AS LONG FOR THOSE THAT LURK BELOW TO GNAW THE CARCASS OF THIS REALITY TO THE BONE.
AS ONE WORLD DIES...
CHK
CRUNCHK
...WE MUST MAKE OUR DESCENT.

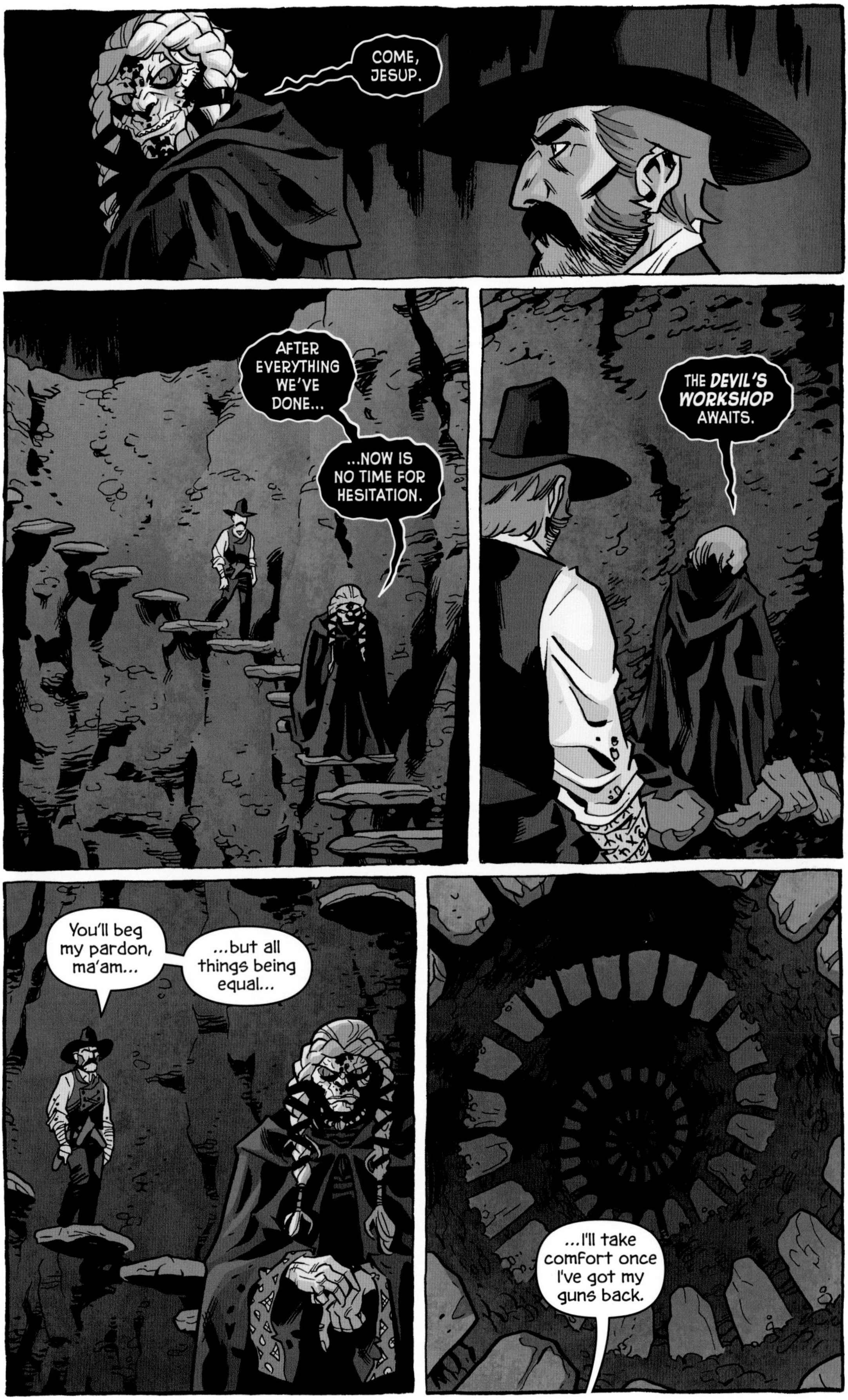
COME, JESUP.
AFTER EVERYTHING WE'VE DONE...
...NOW IS NO TIME FOR HESITATION.
THE DEVIL'S WORKSHOP AWAITS.
You'll beg my pardon, ma'am...
...but all things being equal...
...I'll take comfort once I've got my guns back.

The Thunderbirds could *smell* the *apocalypse* on the winds.

It was a *primordial stink*...

...the reek of times *long forgotten*...

...and it drove them to act as they might in the time before man...

...before they were *tamed*...

...when they were *wild and free*...

KRAK! KRAK! SKREEEEE!

SKK

KRAK!

KRAK-WHOOOOOM!

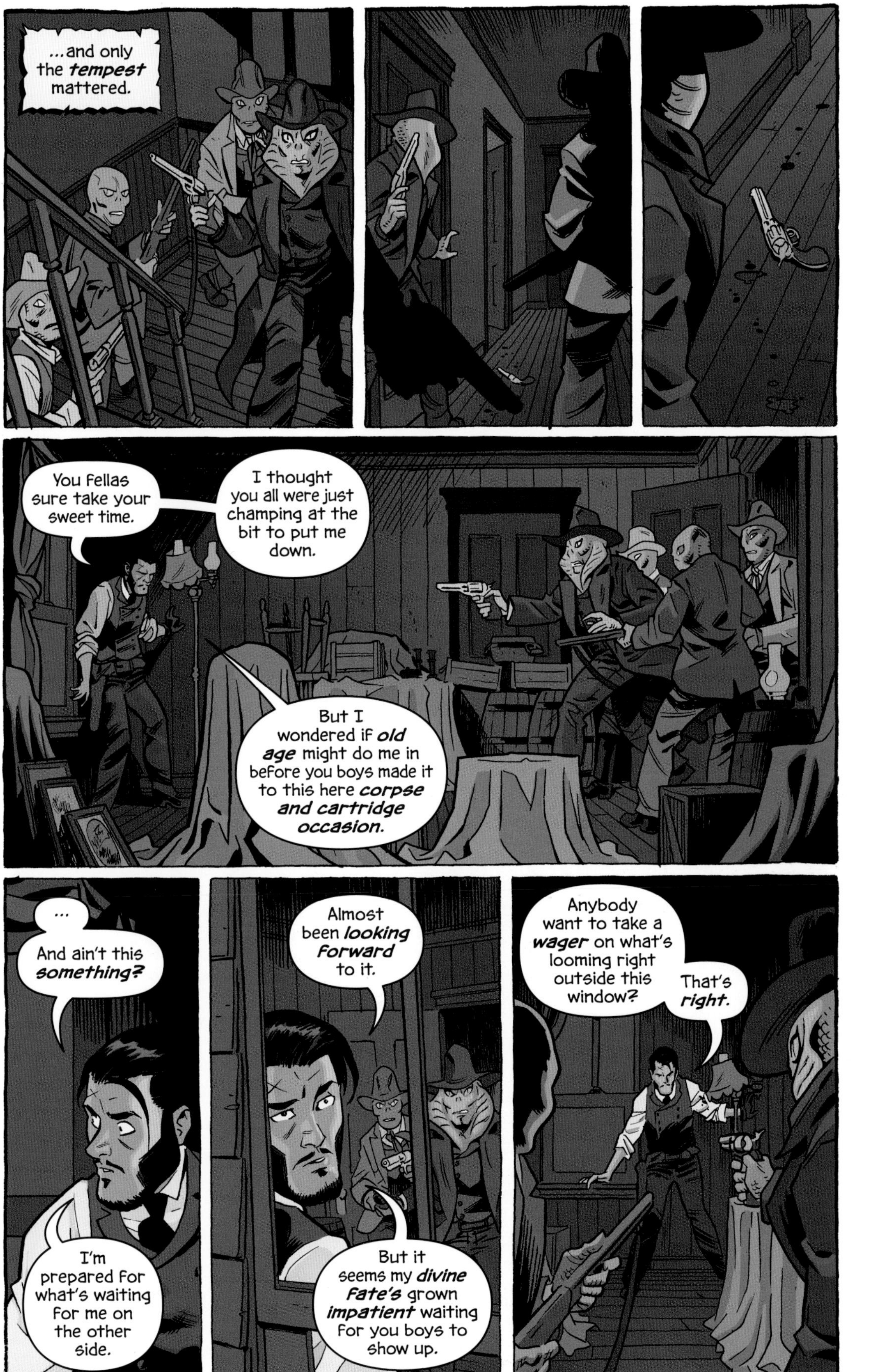
...and only the tempest mattered.
You fellas sure take your sweet time.
I thought you all were just champing at the bit to put me down.
But I wondered if old age might do me in before you boys made it to this here corpse and cartridge occasion.
...
And ain't this something?
I'm prepared for what's waiting for me on the other side.
Almost been looking forward to it.
But it seems my divine fate's grown impatient waiting for you boys to show up.
Anybody want to take a wager on what's looming right outside this window?
That's right.

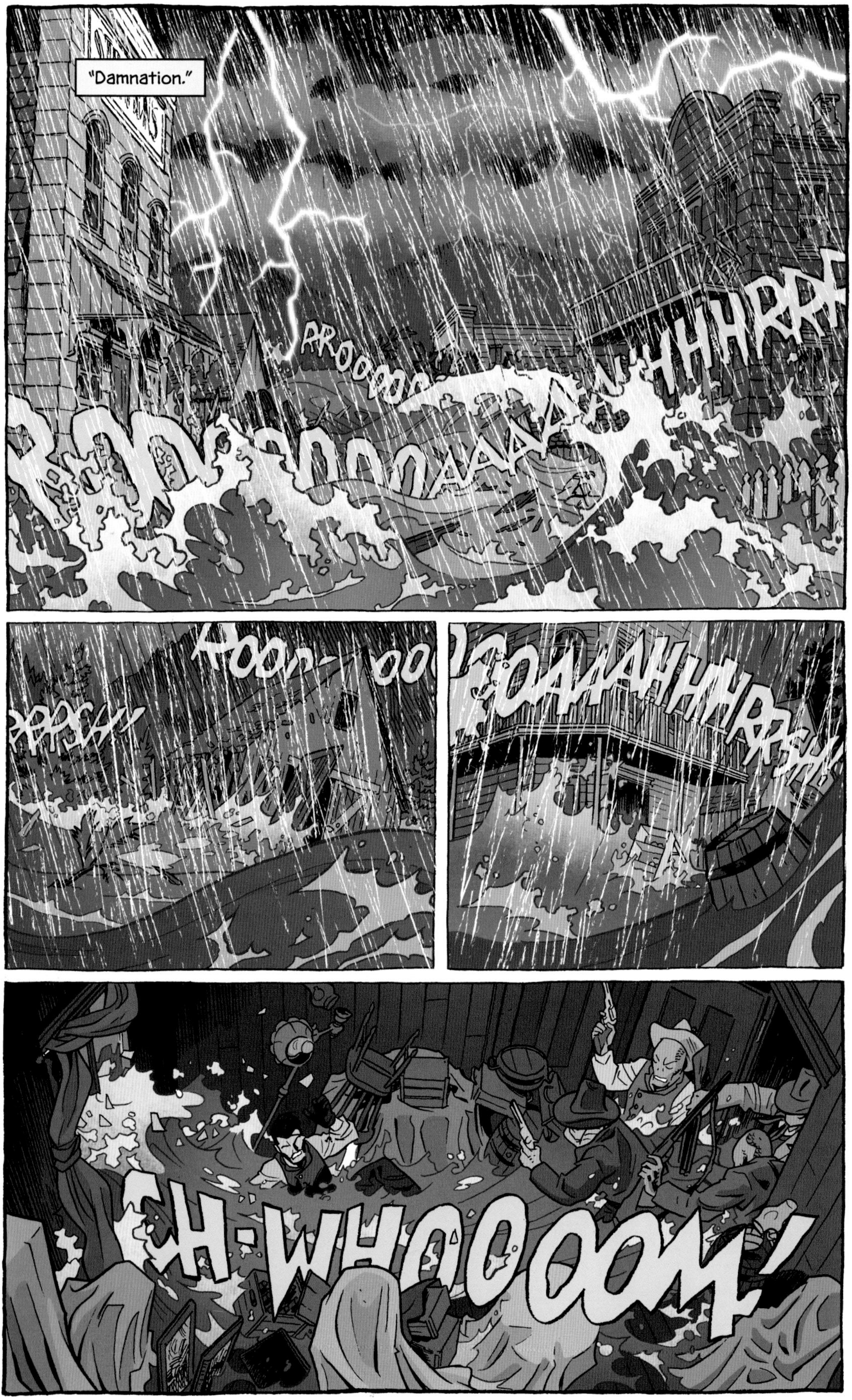
"Damnation."
CH-WHOOOOOM!

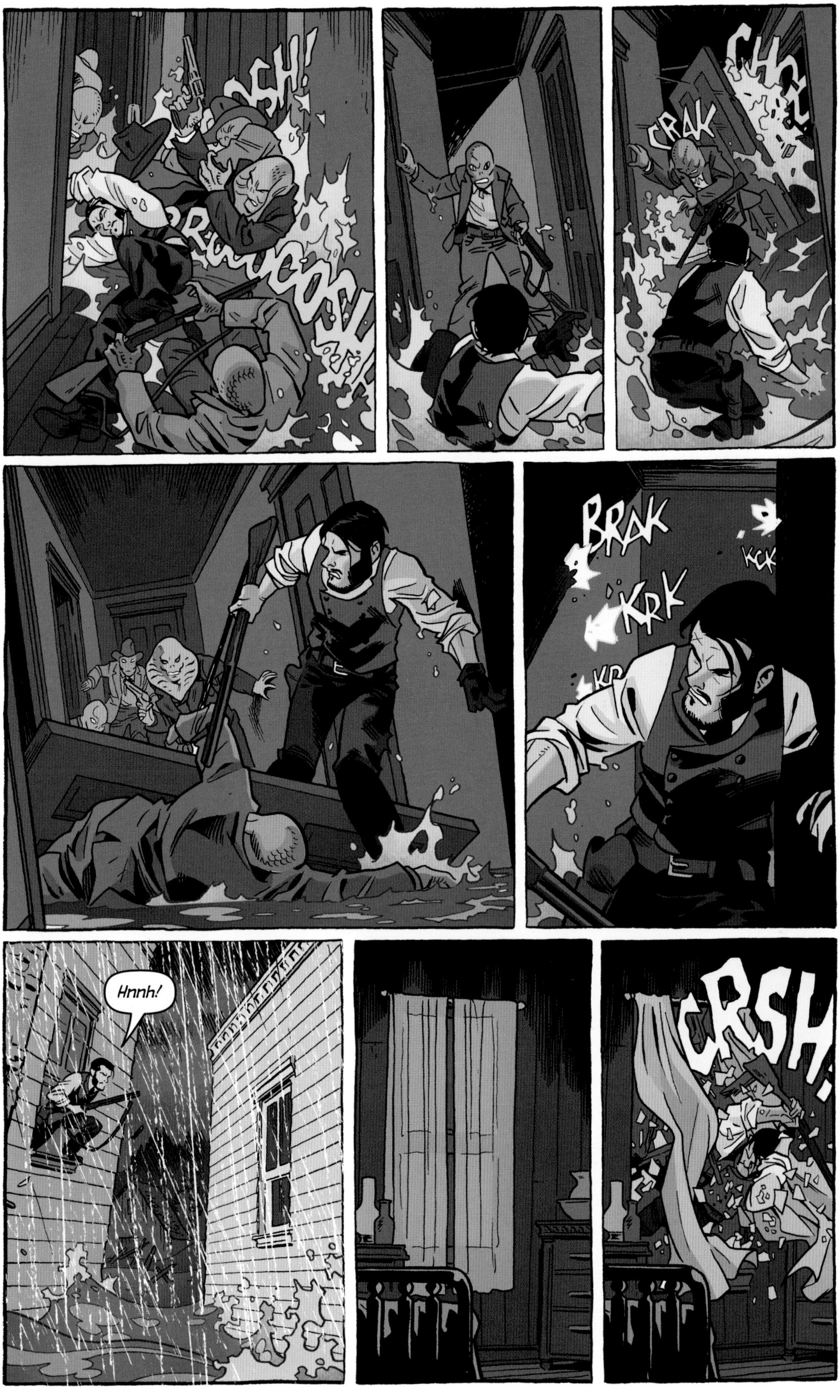
CRAK
BRAK
KCK
KRK
KR
Hnnh!
CRSH!

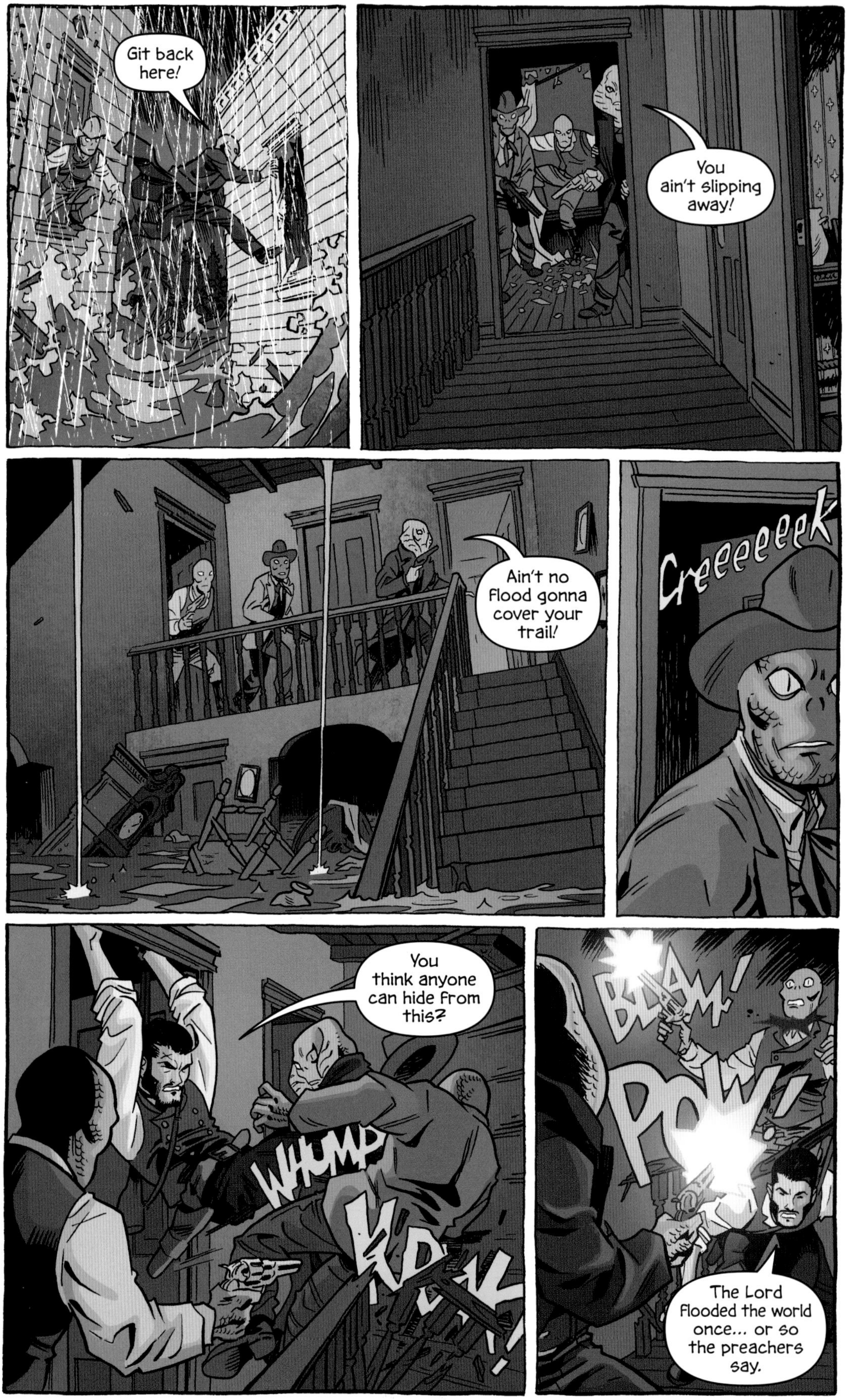
Git back here!
You ain't slipping away!
Ain't no flood gonna cover your trail!
Creeeeeek
You think anyone can hide from this?
WHUMP
BLAM!
POW!
The Lord flooded the world once... or so the preachers say.

Cleaned out all the wicked men.

SHOOM

But this...

...this time...

KRROOM

KAK

KRSH

...the high water's come for the angels and the devils both!

BLAM

KRK

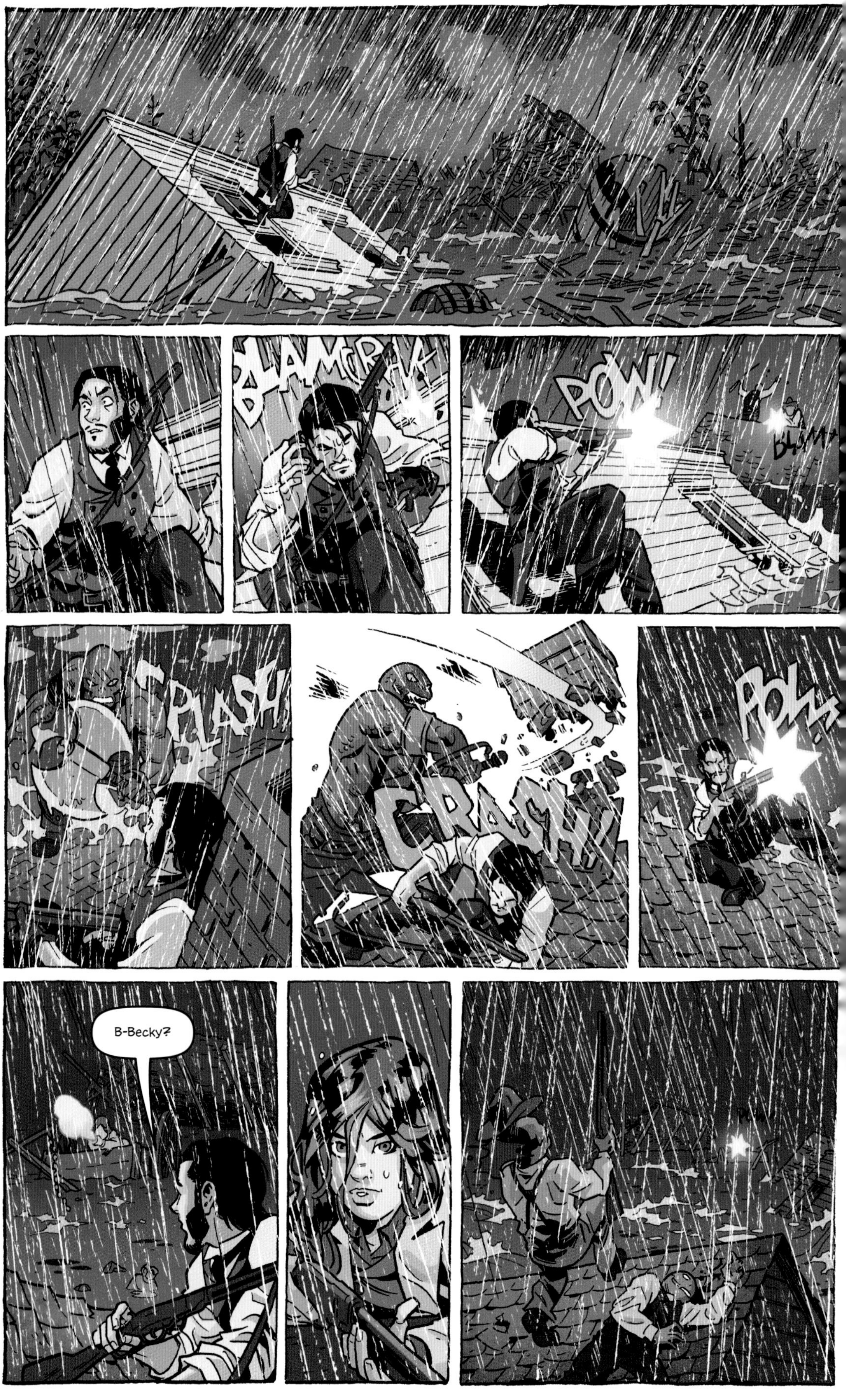
BLAMCRAK
POW!
SPLASH
CRASH!
POW
B-Becky?

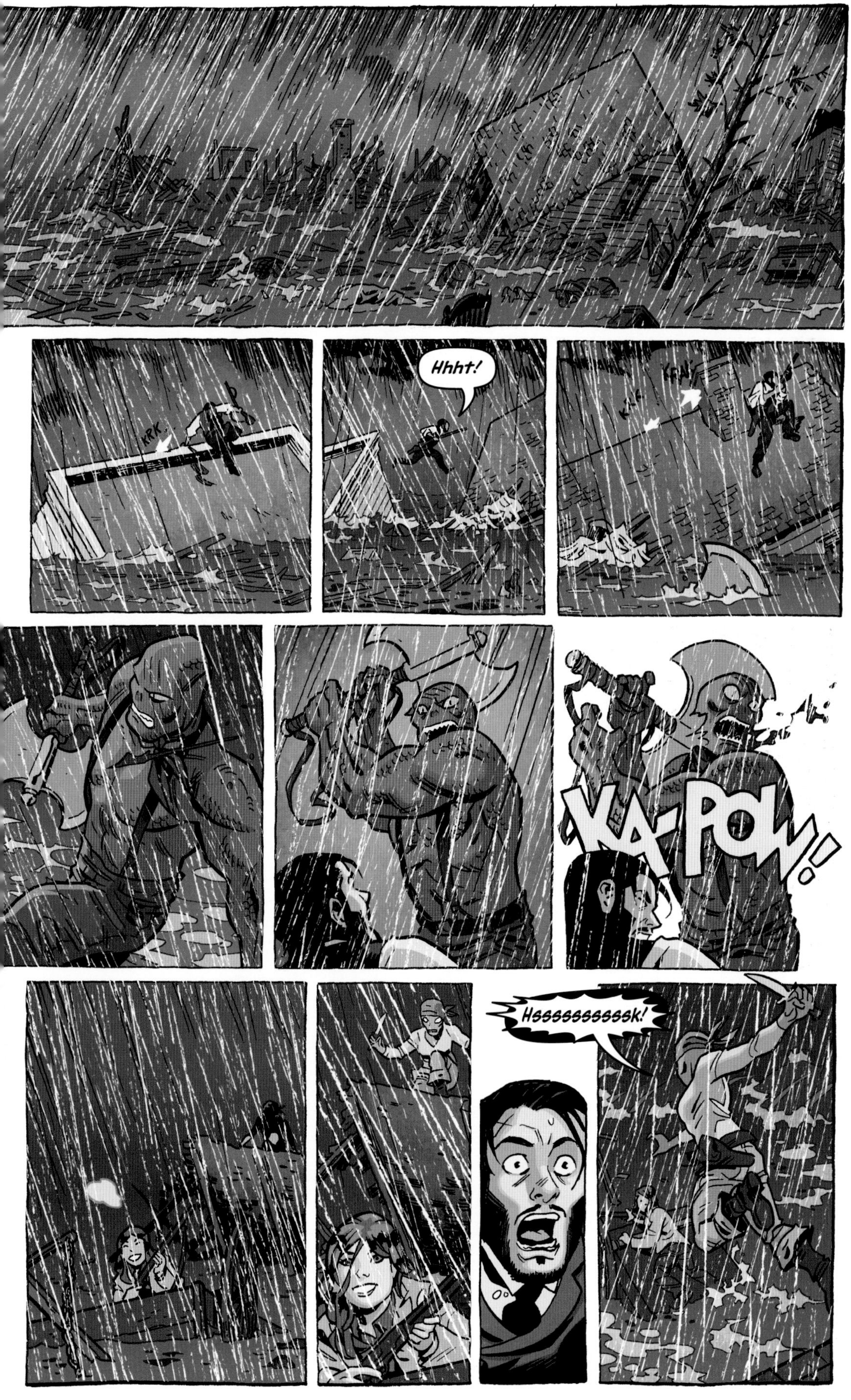
KRK
Hhht!
KA-POW!
Hsssssssssssk!

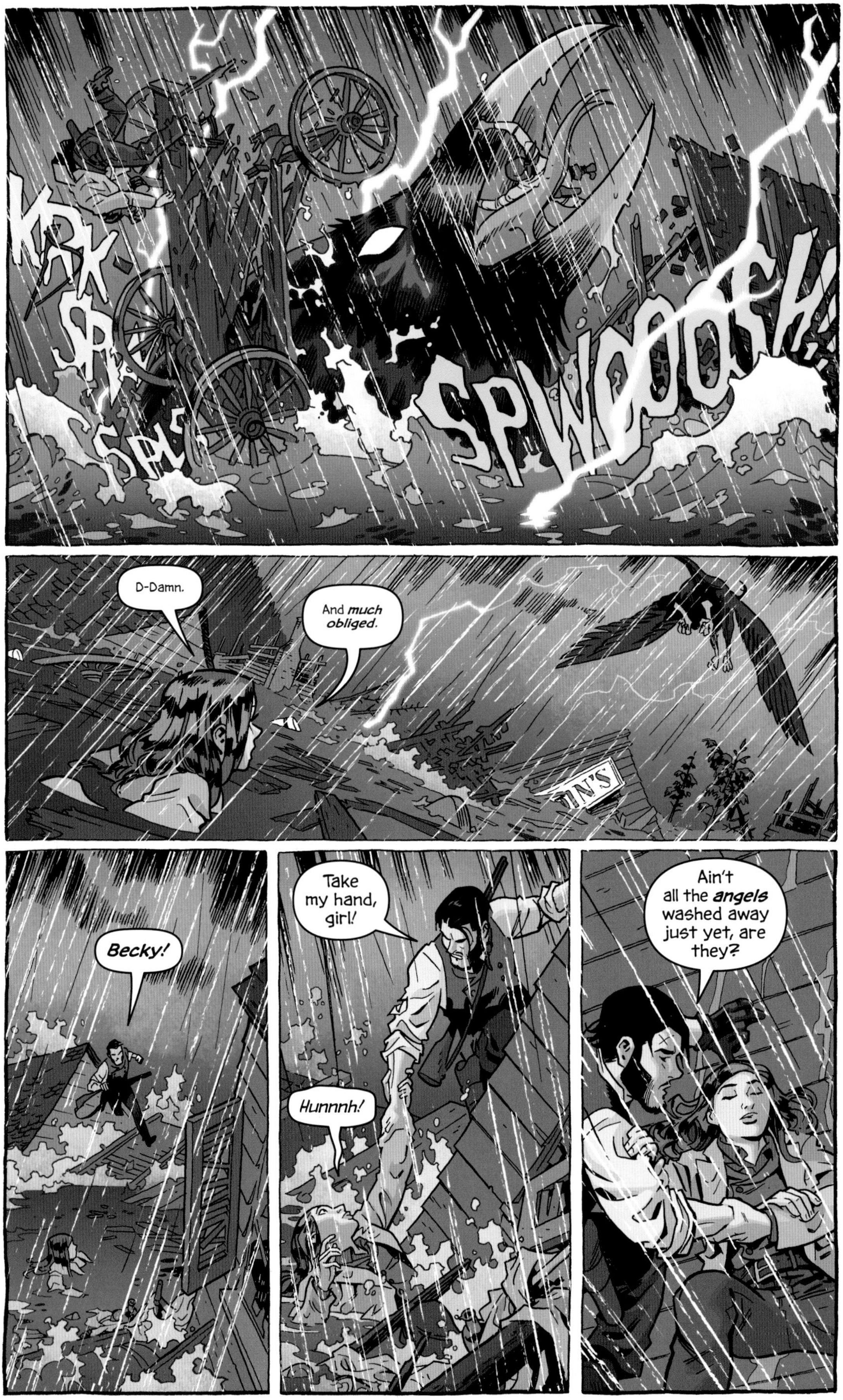
SPWOOOSH!!
D-Damn.
And *much* obliged.
Becky!
Take my hand, girl!
Hunnnh!
Ain't all the *angels* washed away just yet, are they?

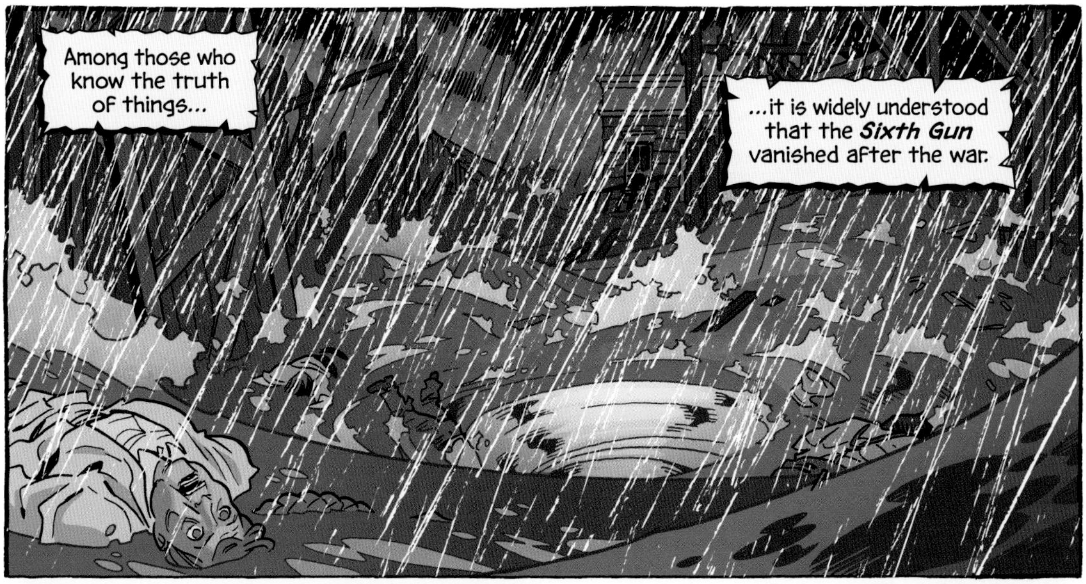

Among those who know the truth of things...
...it is widely understood that the *Sixth Gun* vanished after the war.

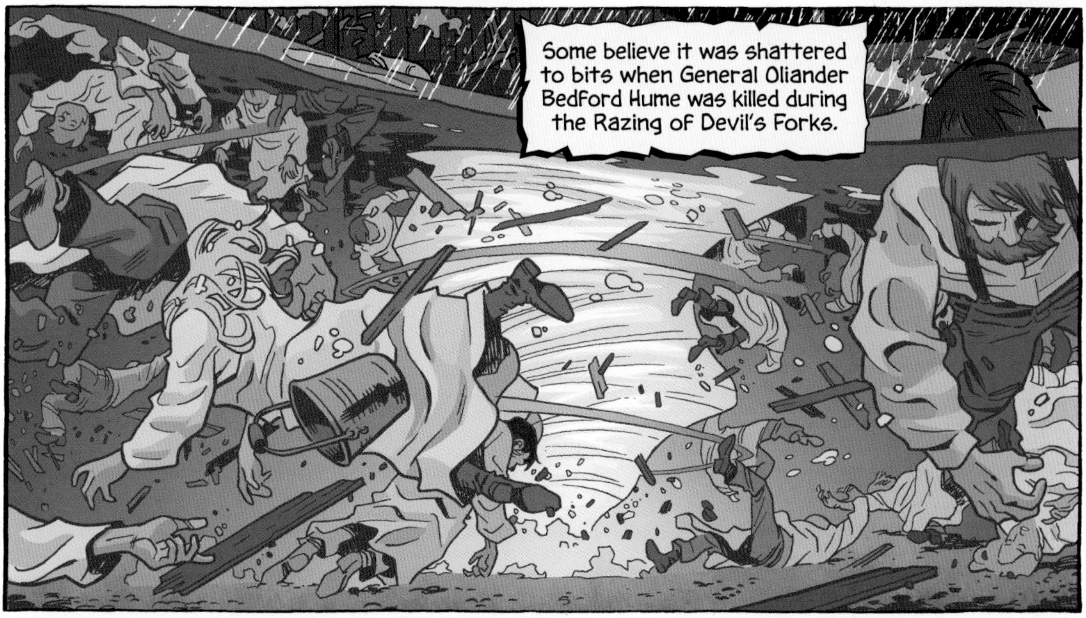

Some believe it was shattered to bits when General Oliander Bedford Hume was killed during the Razing of Devil's Forks.

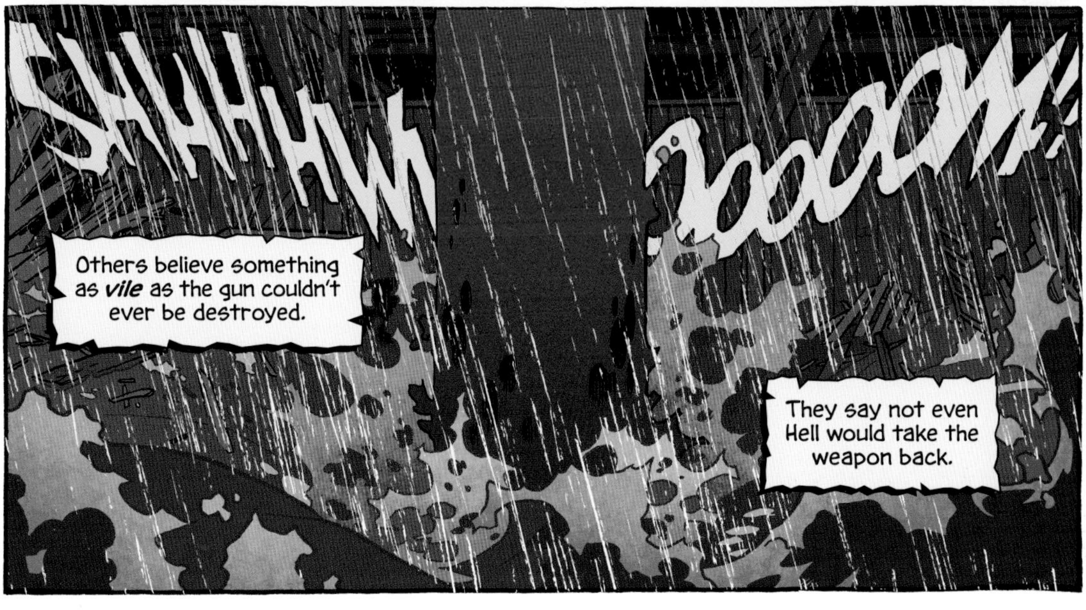

SHHHWWOOOOM!
Others believe something as *vile* as the gun couldn't ever be destroyed.
They say not even Hell would take the weapon back.

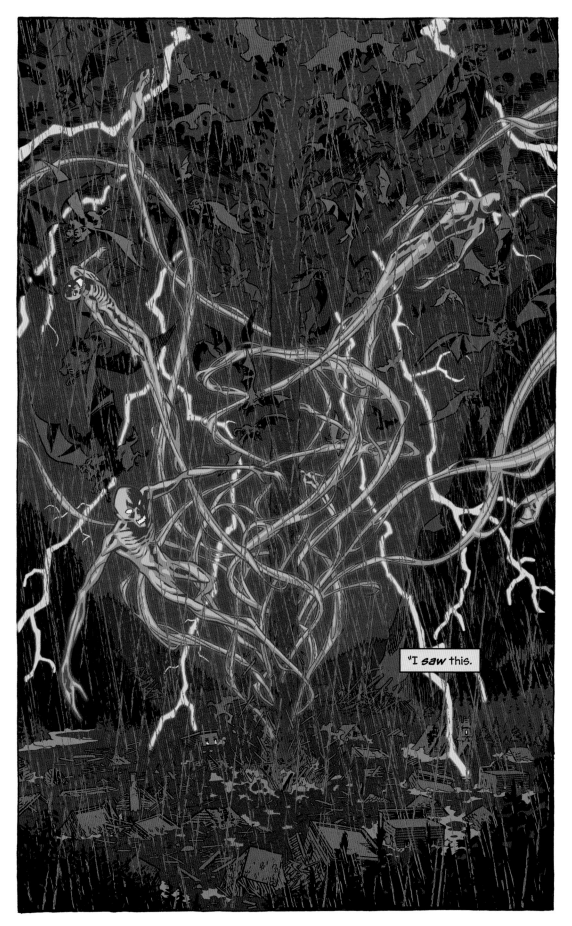

"I *saw* this.

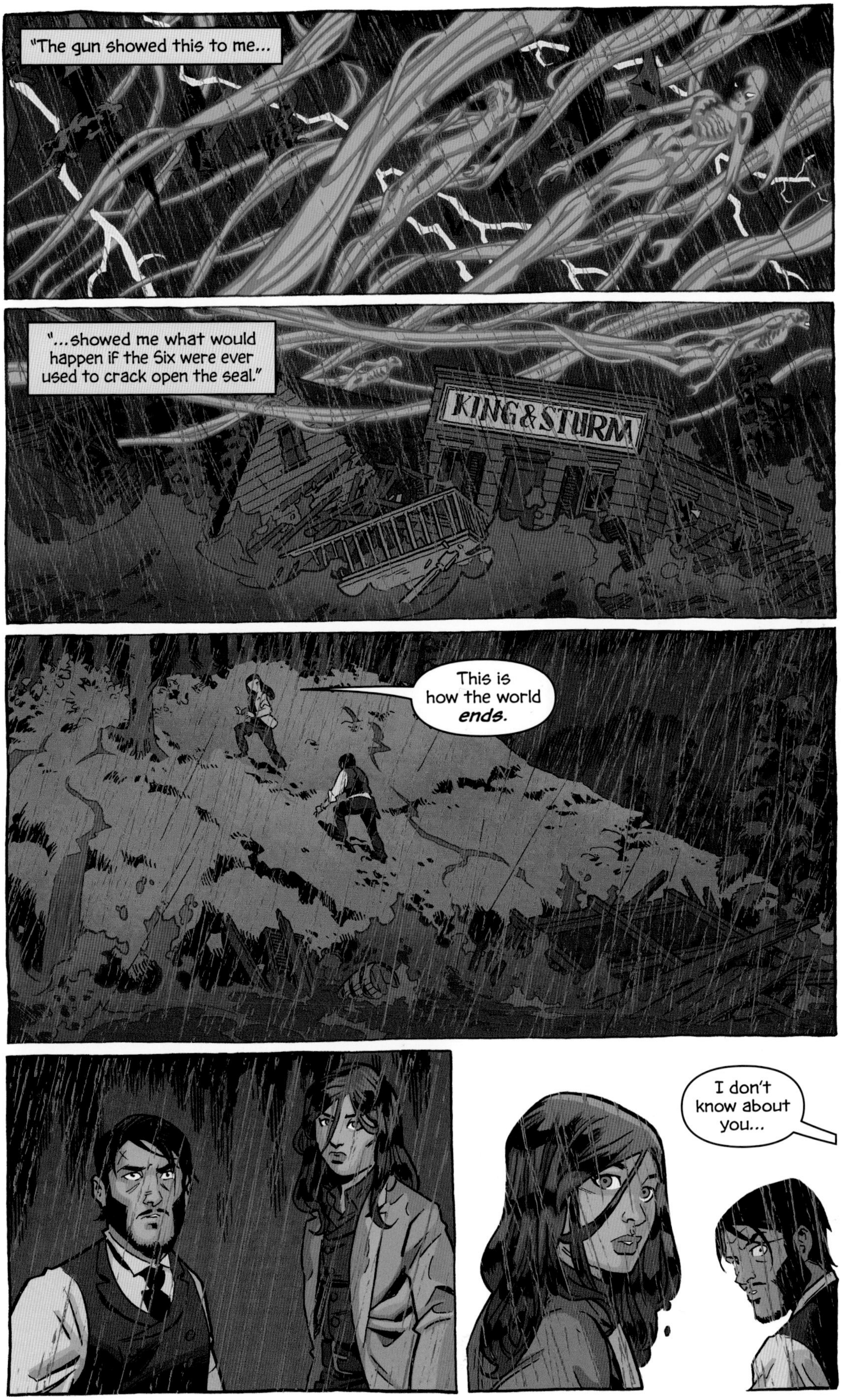
"The gun showed this to me...
"...showed me what would happen if the Six were ever used to crack open the seal."
KING & STURM
This is how the world *ends.*
I don't know about you...

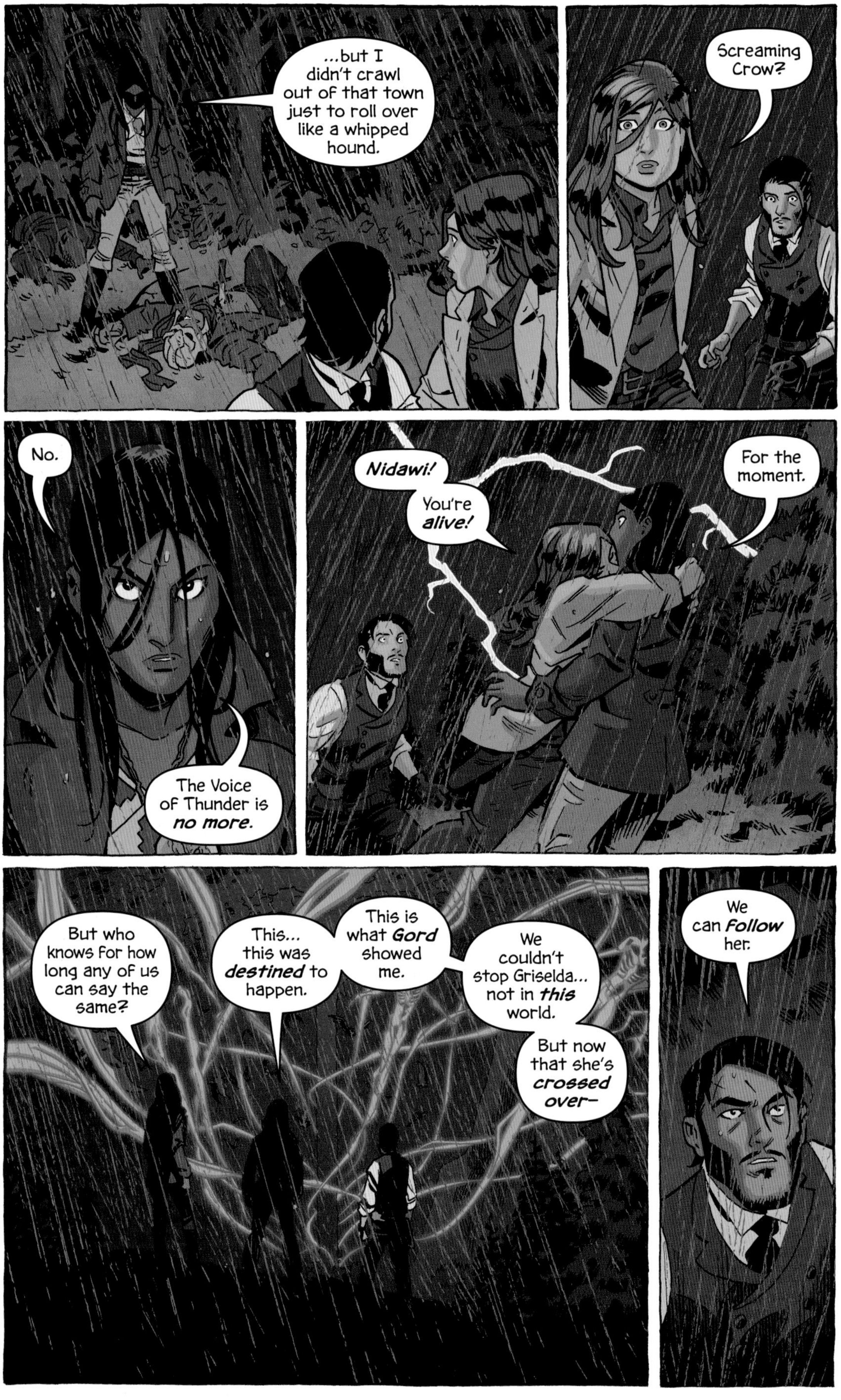
...but I didn't crawl out of that town just to roll over like a whipped hound.
Screaming Crow?
No.
The Voice of Thunder is *no more.*
Nidawi!
You're *alive!*
For the moment.
But who knows for how long any of us can say the same?
This... this was *destined* to happen.
This is what *Gord* showed me.
We couldn't stop Griselda... not in *this* world.
But now that she's *crossed over*—
We can *follow* her.

CHAPTER SIX

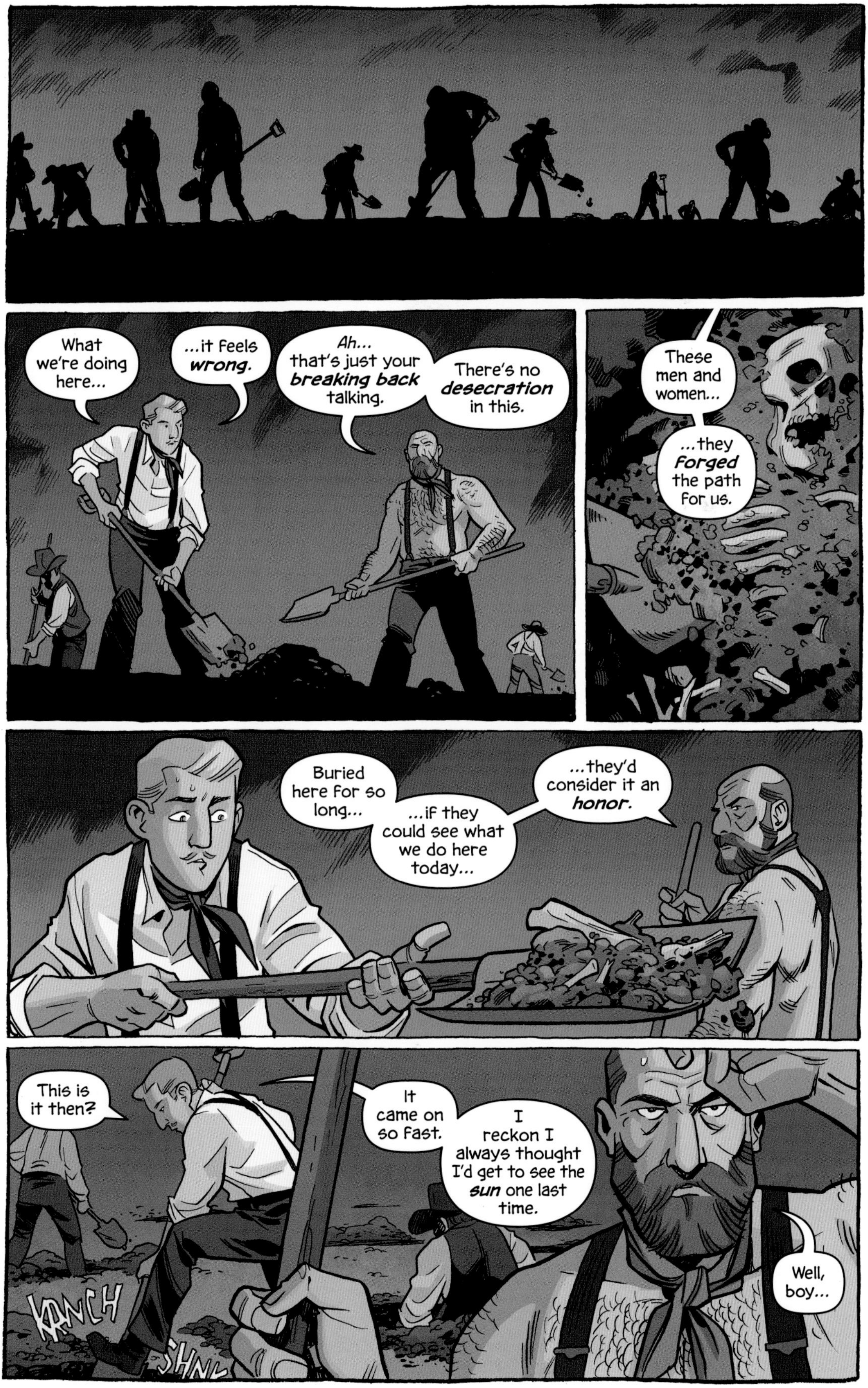

What we're doing here...
...it feels wrong.
Ah... that's just your breaking back talking.
There's no desecration in this.
These men and women...
...they forged the path for us.
Buried here for so long...
...if they could see what we do here today...
...they'd consider it an honor.
This is it then?
It came on so fast.
I reckon I always thought I'd get to see the sun one last time.
Well, boy...
KRNCH
SHNK

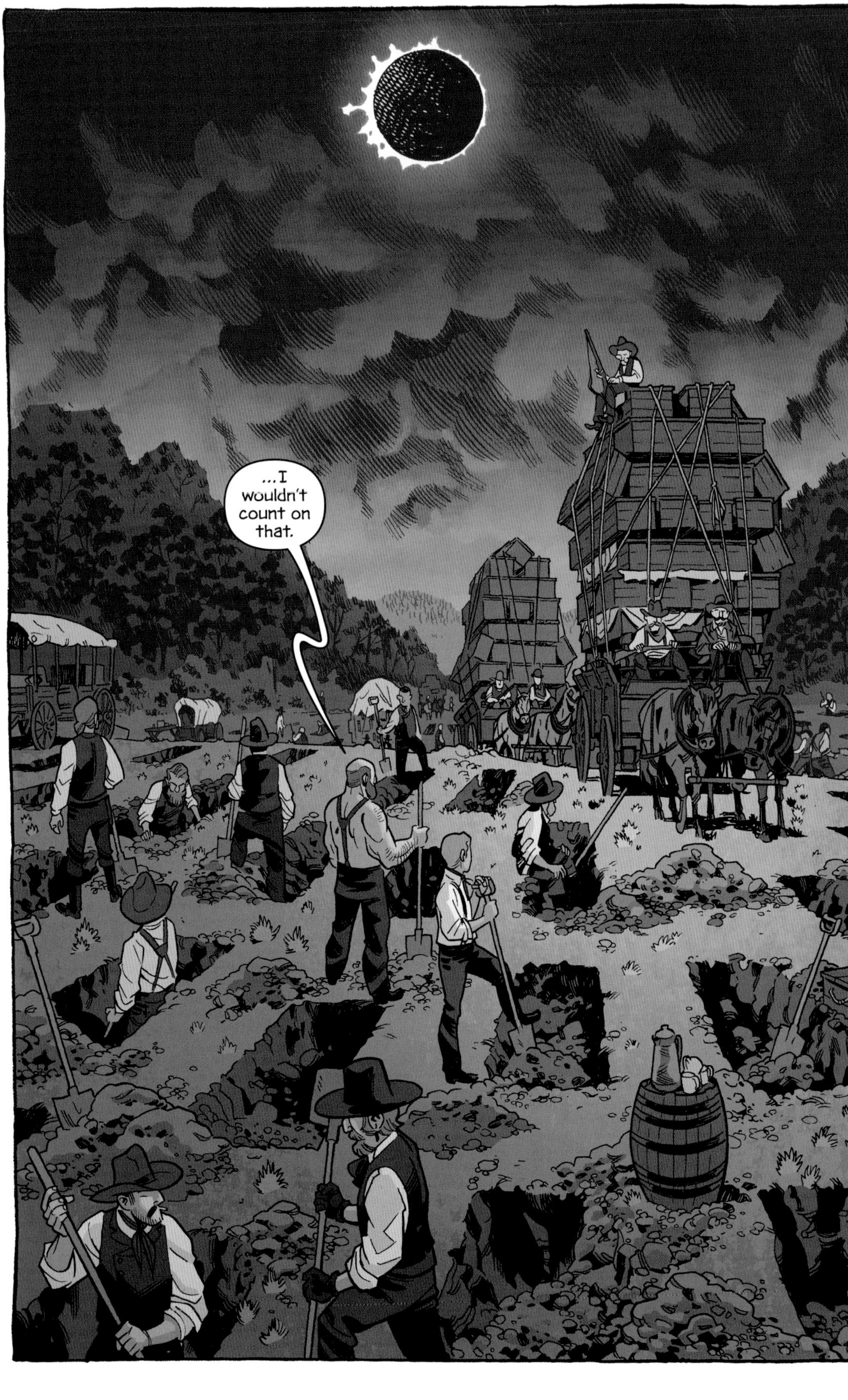
...I wouldn't count on that.

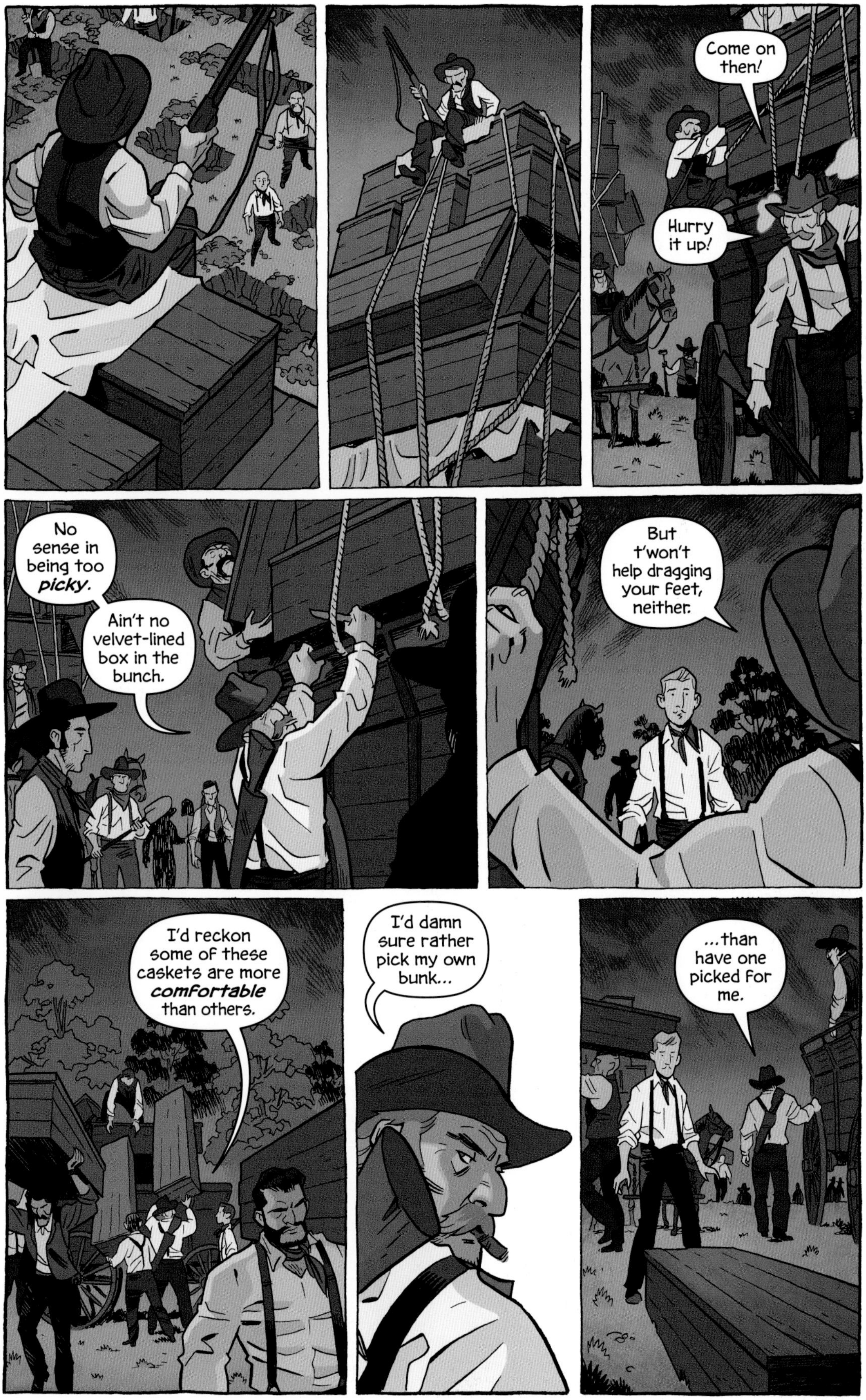

Come on then!
Hurry it up!
No sense in being too **picky**.
Ain't no velvet-lined box in the bunch.
But t'won't help dragging your feet, neither.
I'd reckon some of these caskets are more **comfortable** than others.
I'd damn sure rather pick my own bunk...
...than have one picked for me.

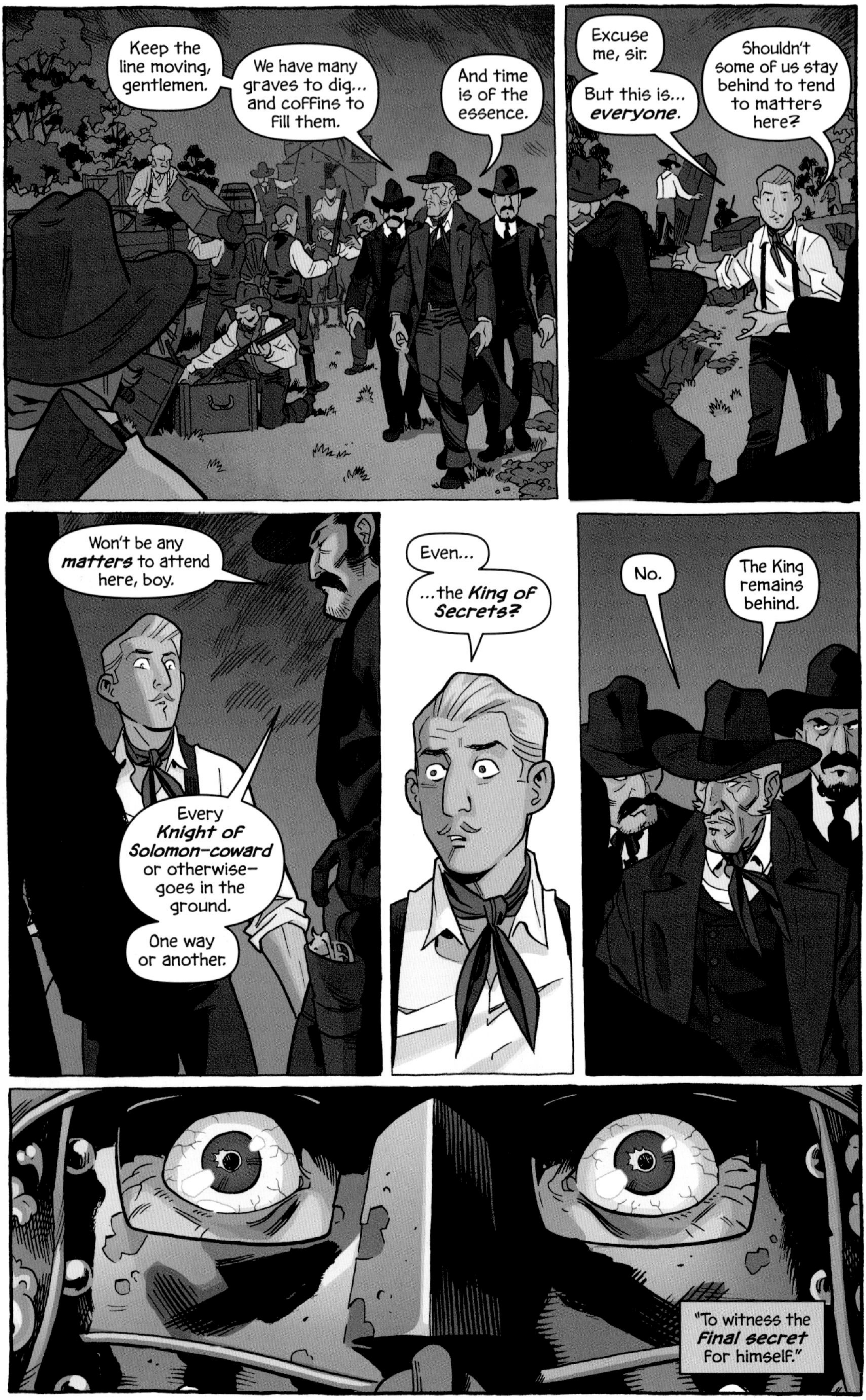
Keep the line moving, gentlemen.
We have many graves to dig... and coffins to fill them.
And time is of the essence.
Excuse me, sir.
But this is... *everyone.*
Shouldn't some of us stay behind to tend to matters here?
Won't be any *matters* to attend here, boy.
Every *Knight of Solomon*—coward or otherwise—goes in the ground.
One way or another.
Even...
...the *King of Secrets?*
No.
The King remains behind.
"To witness the *Final secret* for himself."

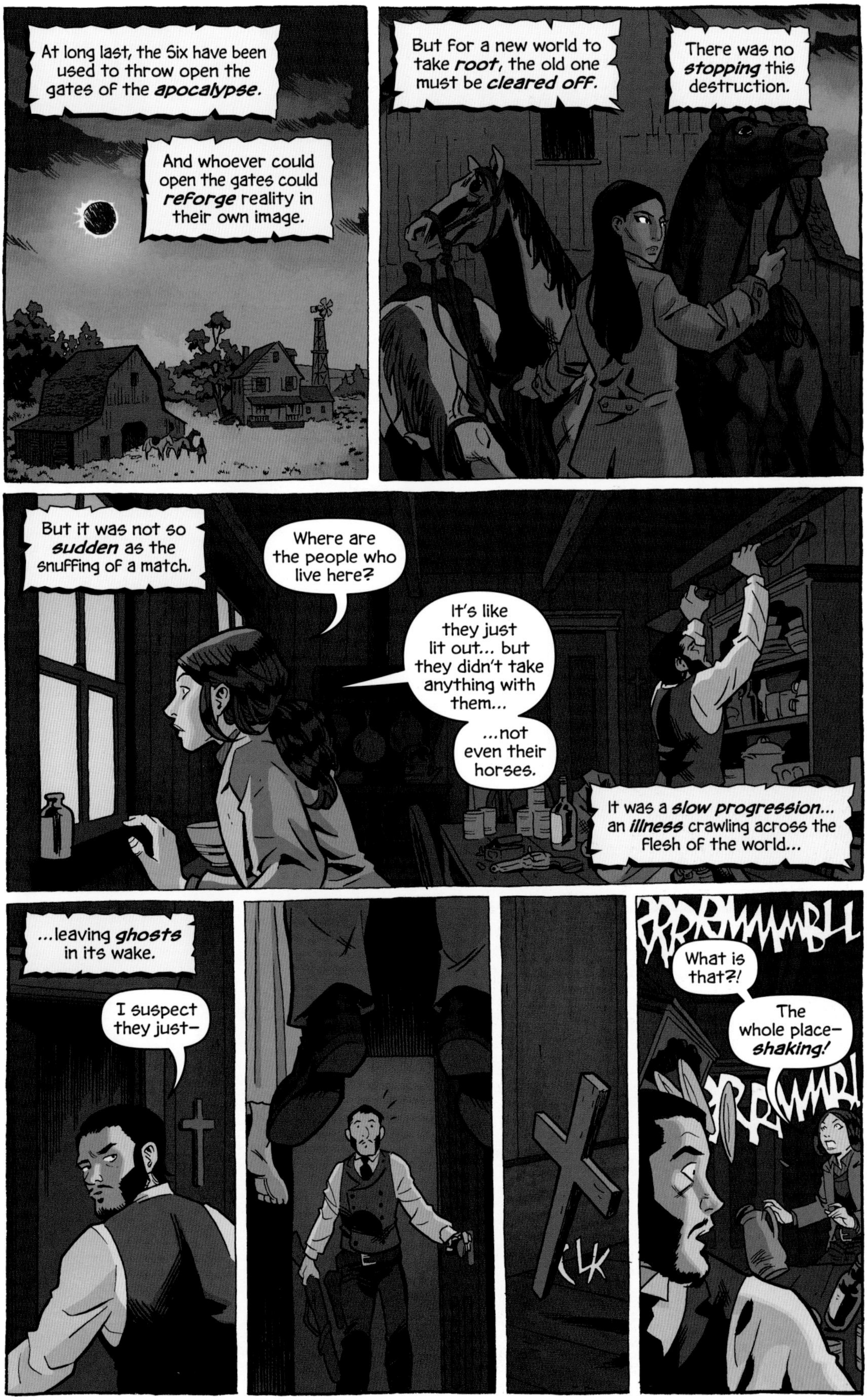
At long last, the Six have been used to throw open the gates of the apocalypse.
And whoever could open the gates could reforge reality in their own image.
But for a new world to take root, the old one must be cleared off.
There was no stopping this destruction.
But it was not so sudden as the snuffing of a match.
Where are the people who live here?
It's like they just lit out... but they didn't take anything with them...
...not even their horses.
It was a slow progression... an illness crawling across the flesh of the world...
...leaving ghosts in its wake.
I suspect they just—
CLK
RRRMMMMBLL
What is that?!
The whole place— shaking!
RRRMMBL

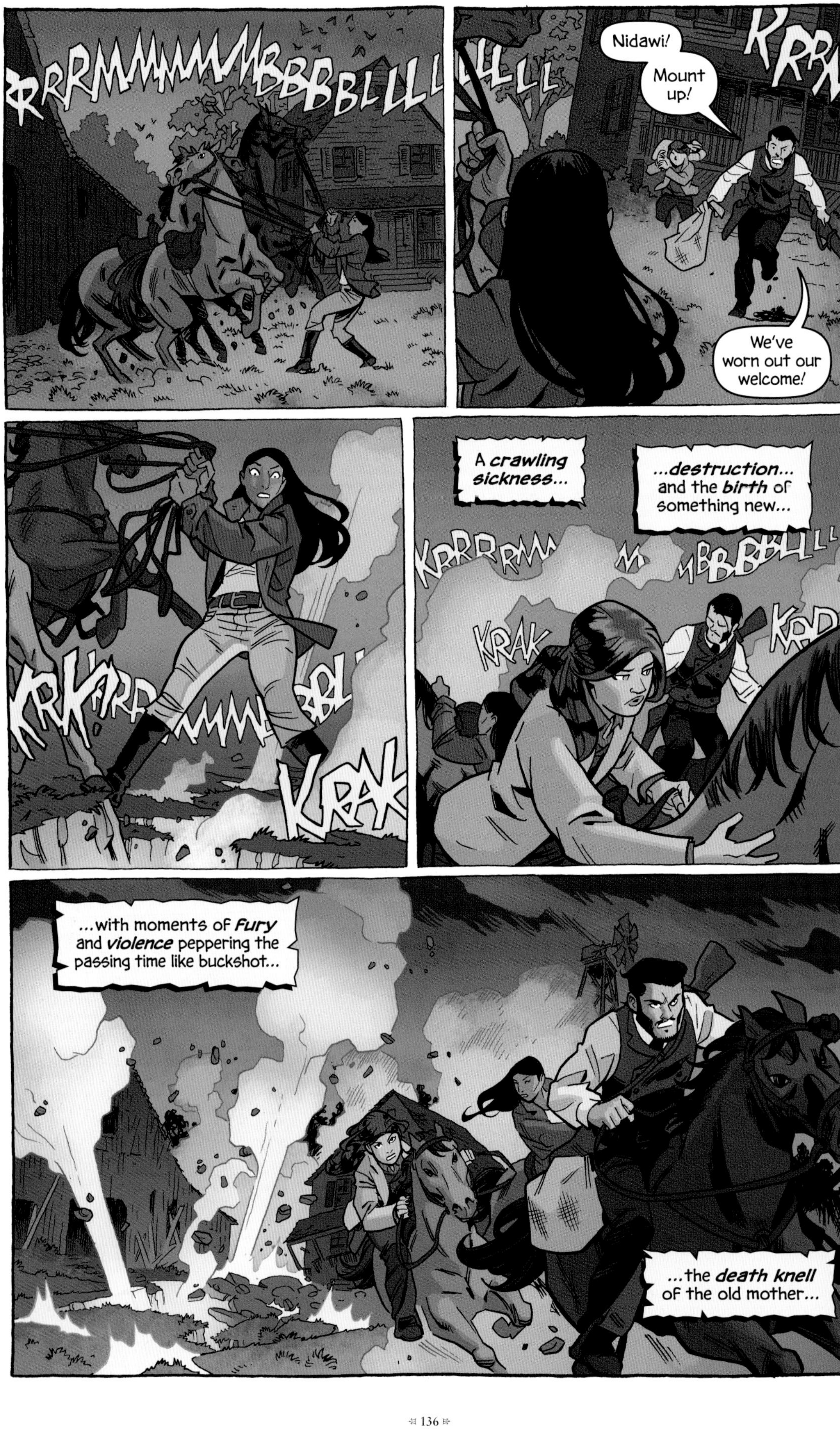
RRRMMMMMMBBBBLLLLLLLLL
Nidawi!
Mount up!
KRRN
We've worn out our welcome!
KRKARRMMMMBBBL
KRAK
A crawling sickness...
...destruction... and the birth of something new...
KRRRRMMMMBBBBLLLL
KRAK
KRAK
...with moments of fury and violence peppering the passing time like buckshot...
...the death knell of the old mother...

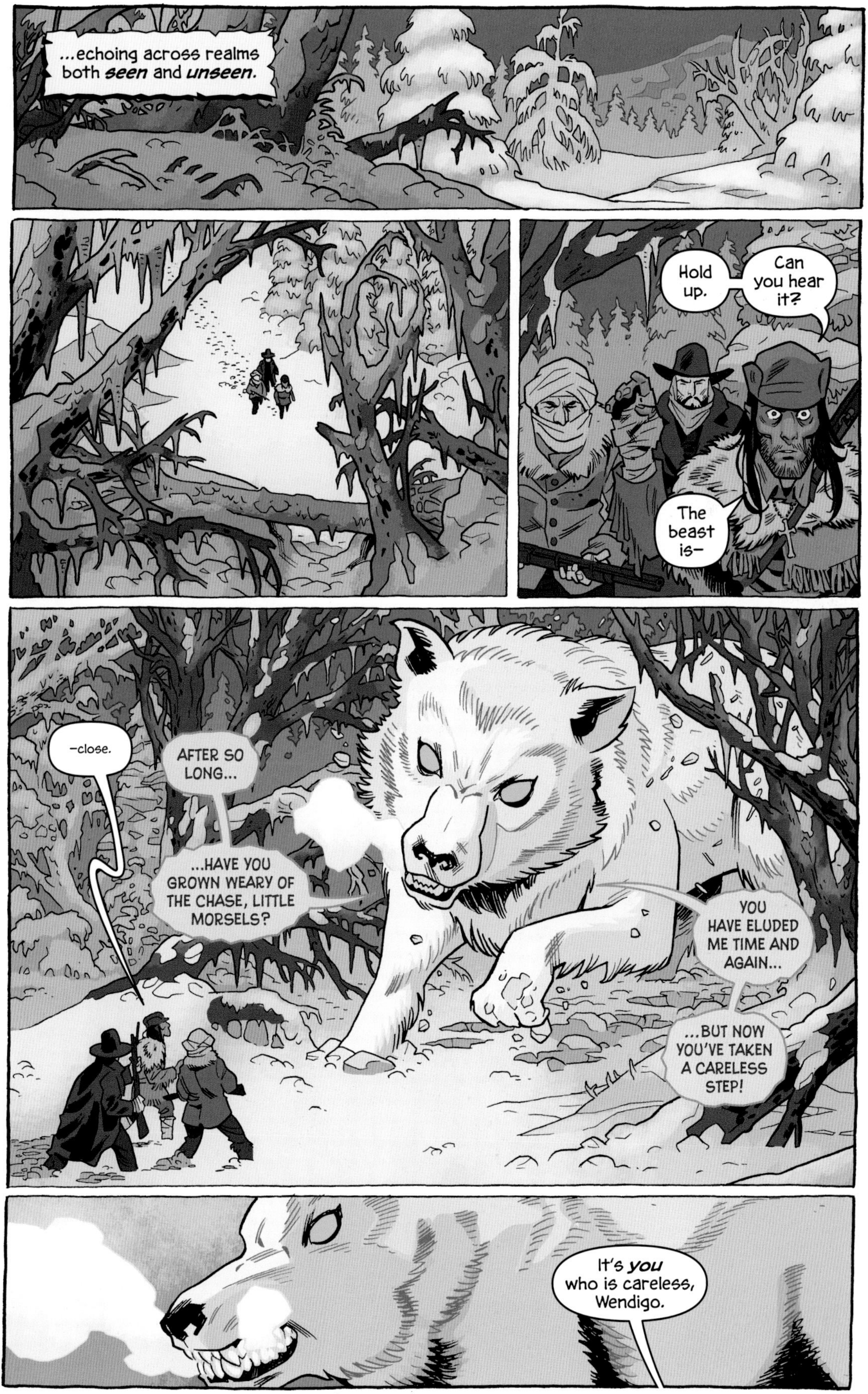
...echoing across realms both *seen* and *unseen*.
Hold up.
Can you hear it?
The beast is–
–close.
AFTER SO LONG...
...HAVE YOU GROWN WEARY OF THE CHASE, LITTLE MORSELS?
YOU HAVE ELUDED ME TIME AND AGAIN...
...BUT NOW YOU'VE TAKEN A CARELESS STEP!
It's *you* who is careless, Wendigo.

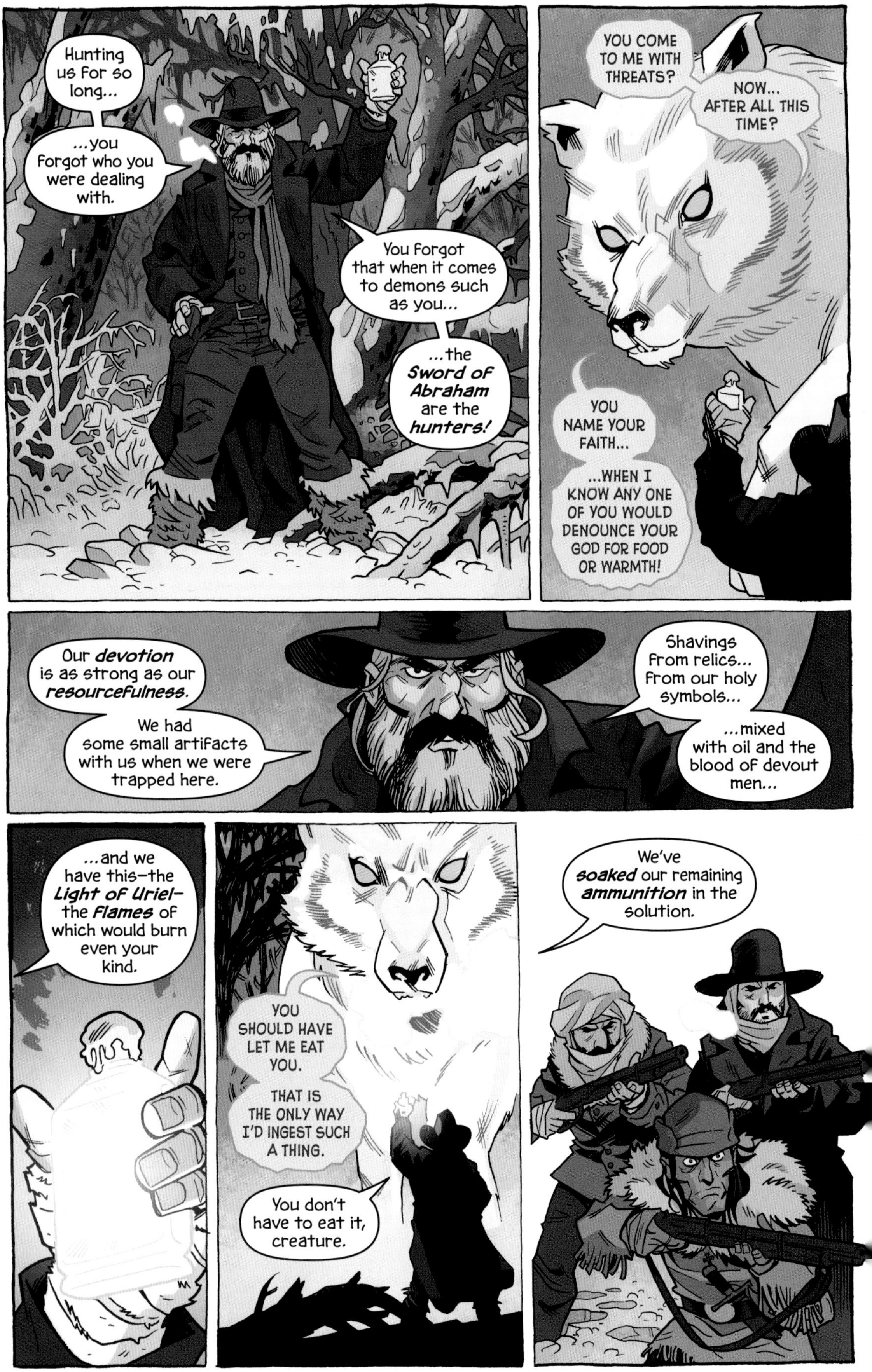
Hunting us for so long...
...you forgot who you were dealing with.
You forgot that when it comes to demons such as you...
...the *Sword of Abraham* are the *hunters!*
YOU COME TO ME WITH THREATS?
NOW... AFTER ALL THIS TIME?
YOU NAME YOUR FAITH...
...WHEN I KNOW ANY ONE OF YOU WOULD DENOUNCE YOUR GOD FOR FOOD OR WARMTH!
Our *devotion* is as strong as our *resourcefulness*.
We had some small artifacts with us when we were trapped here.
Shavings from relics... from our holy symbols...
...mixed with oil and the blood of devout men...
...and we have this—the *Light of Uriel*—the *Flames* of which would burn even your kind.
YOU SHOULD HAVE LET ME EAT YOU.
THAT IS THE ONLY WAY I'D INGEST SUCH A THING.
You don't have to eat it, creature.
We've *soaked* our remaining *ammunition* in the solution.

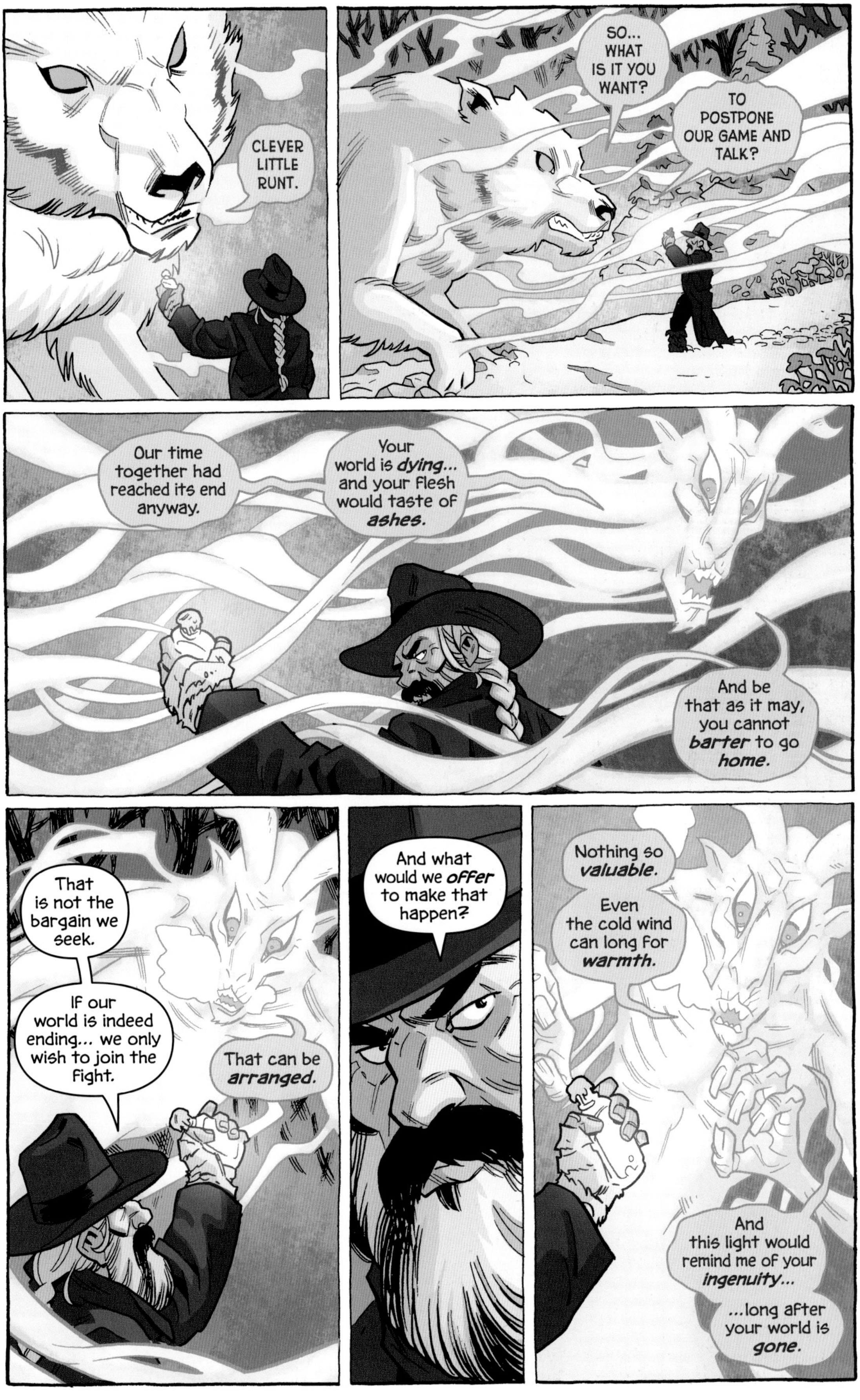
CLEVER LITTLE RUNT.
SO... WHAT IS IT YOU WANT?
TO POSTPONE OUR GAME AND TALK?
Our time together had reached its end anyway.
Your world is *dying*... and your flesh would taste of ***ashes.***
And be that as it may, you cannot ***barter*** to go ***home.***
That is not the bargain we seek.
If our world is indeed ending... we only wish to join the fight.
That can be ***arranged.***
And what would we ***offer*** to make that happen?
Nothing so ***valuable.***
Even the cold wind can long for ***warmth.***
And this light would remind me of your ***ingenuity...***
...long after your world is ***gone.***

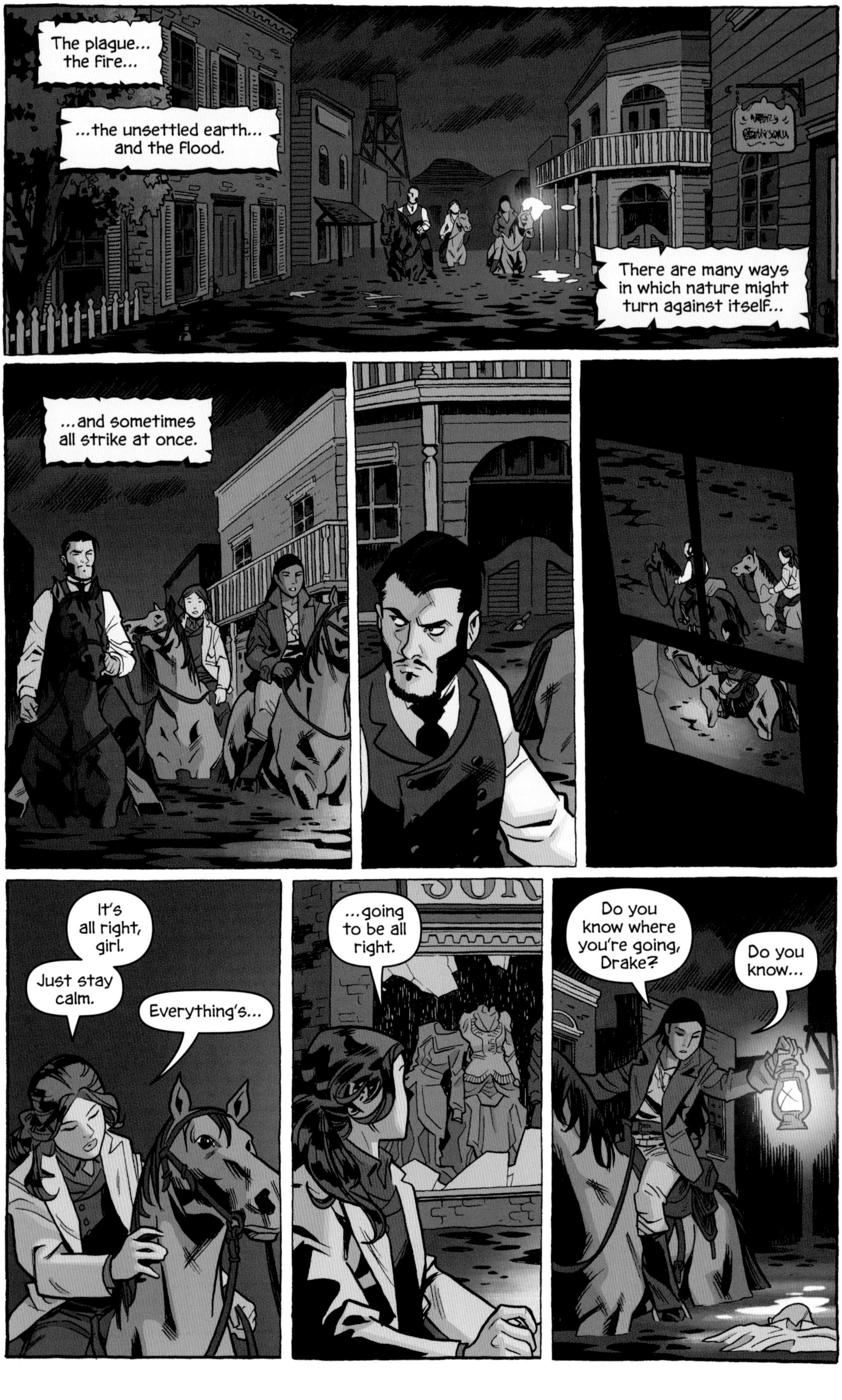

The plague... the fire...
...the unsettled earth... and the flood.
There are many ways in which nature might turn against itself...
...and sometimes all strike at once.
It's all right, girl.
Just stay calm.
Everything's...
...going to be all right.
Do you know where you're going, Drake?
Do you know...

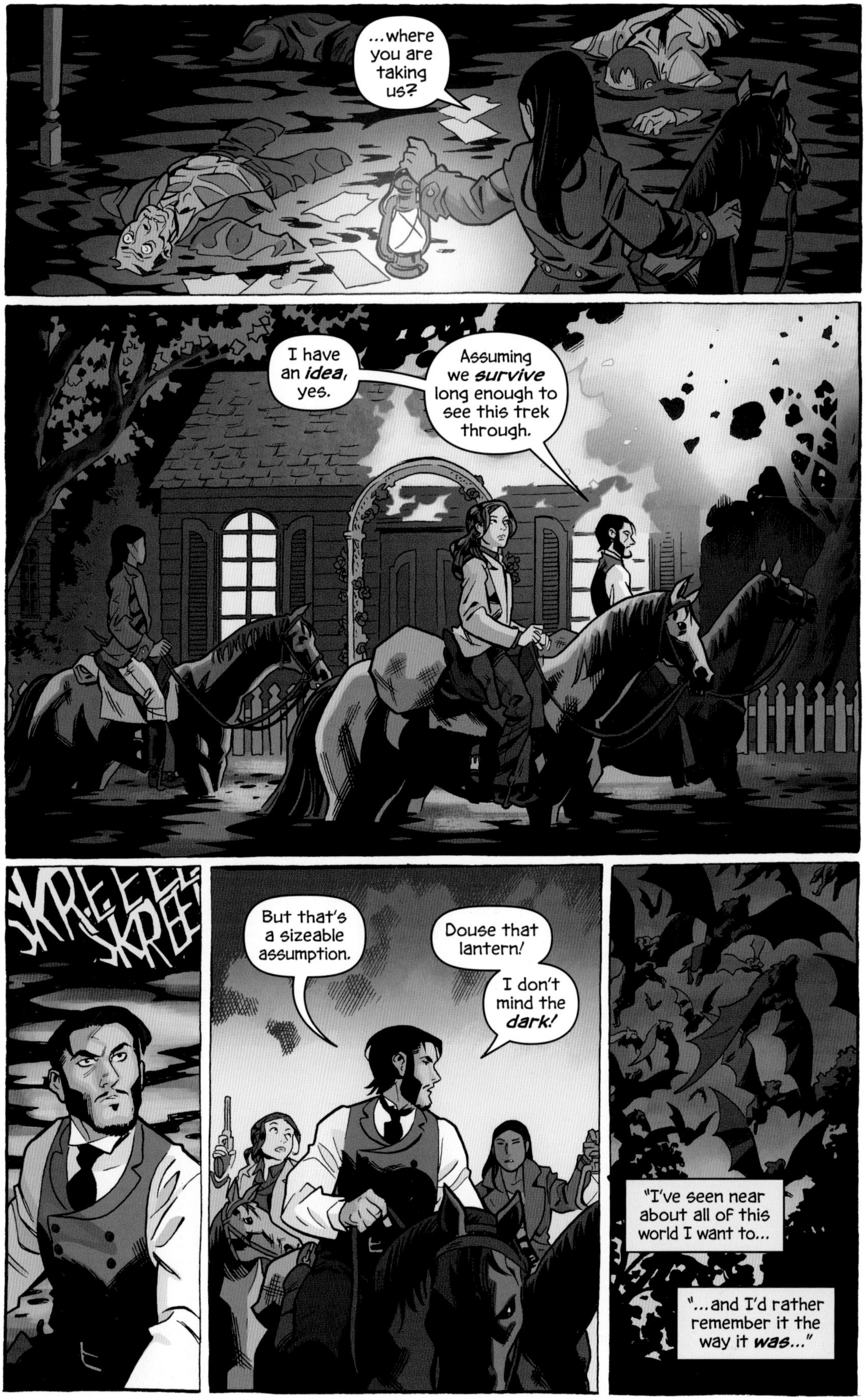
...where you are taking us?
I have an *idea*, yes.
Assuming we *survive* long enough to see this trek through.
SKREEE SKREEE
But that's a sizeable assumption.
Douse that lantern!
I don't mind the *dark!*
"I've seen near about all of this world I want to...
"...and I'd rather remember it the way it *was*..."

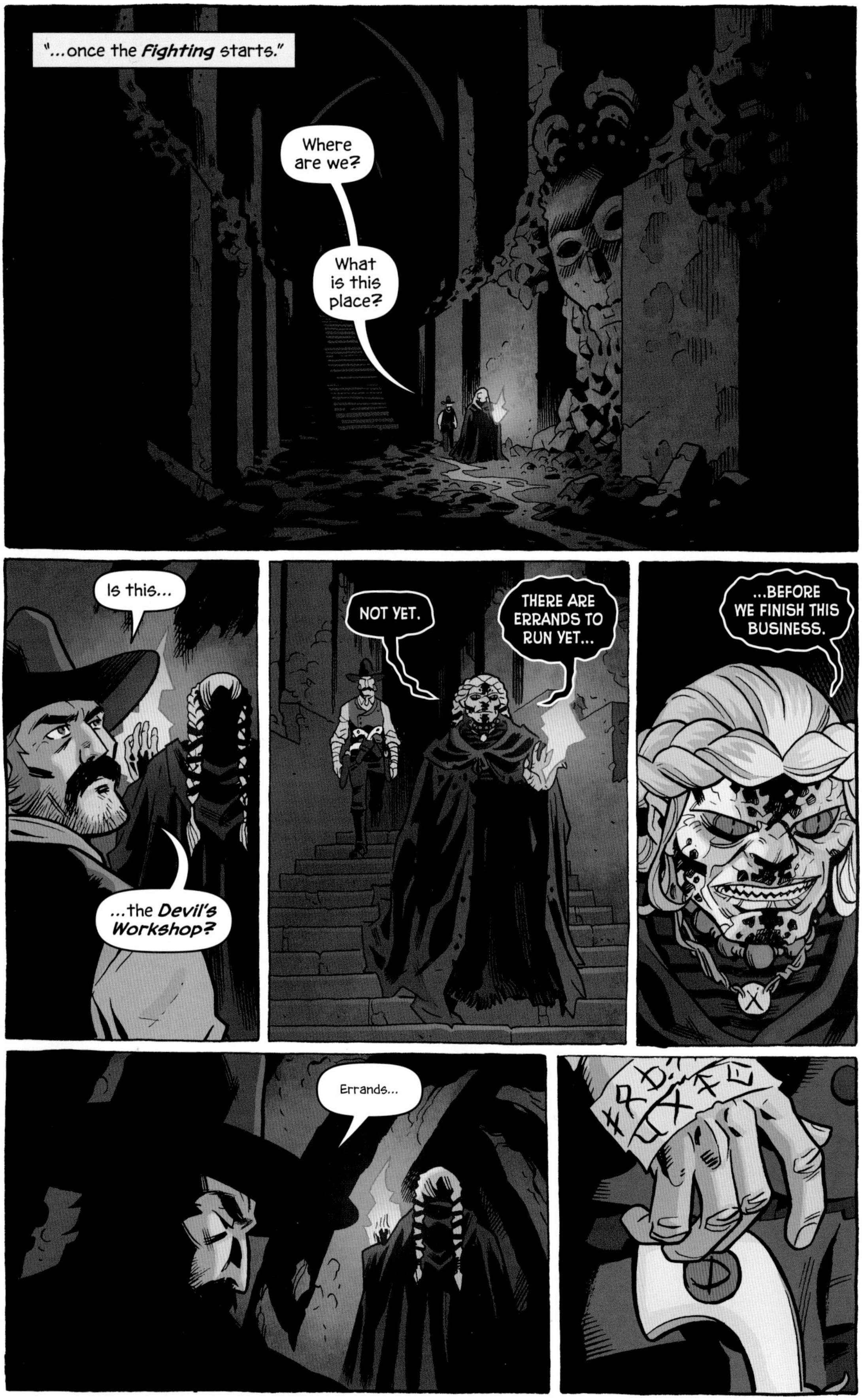
"...once the *Fighting* starts."
Where are we?
What is this place?
Is this...
...the *Devil's Workshop?*
NOT YET.
THERE ARE ERRANDS TO RUN YET...
...BEFORE WE FINISH THIS BUSINESS.
Errands...

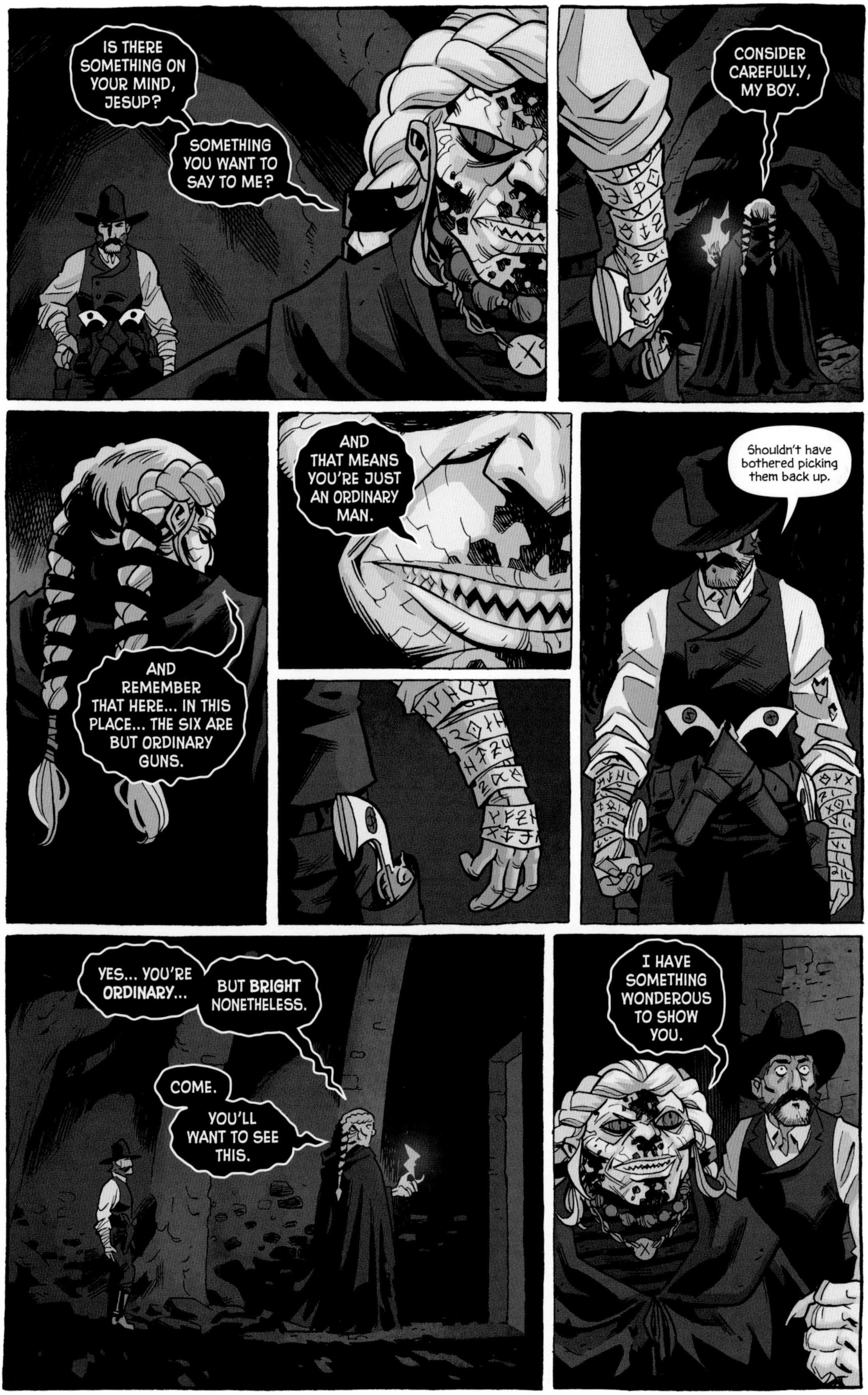

IS THERE SOMETHING ON YOUR MIND, JESUP?
SOMETHING YOU WANT TO SAY TO ME?
CONSIDER CAREFULLY, MY BOY.
AND REMEMBER THAT HERE... IN THIS PLACE... THE SIX ARE BUT ORDINARY GUNS.
AND THAT MEANS YOU'RE JUST AN ORDINARY MAN.
Shouldn't have bothered picking them back up.
YES... YOU'RE ORDINARY...
BUT BRIGHT NONETHELESS.
COME.
YOU'LL WANT TO SEE THIS.
I HAVE SOMETHING WONDEROUS TO SHOW YOU.

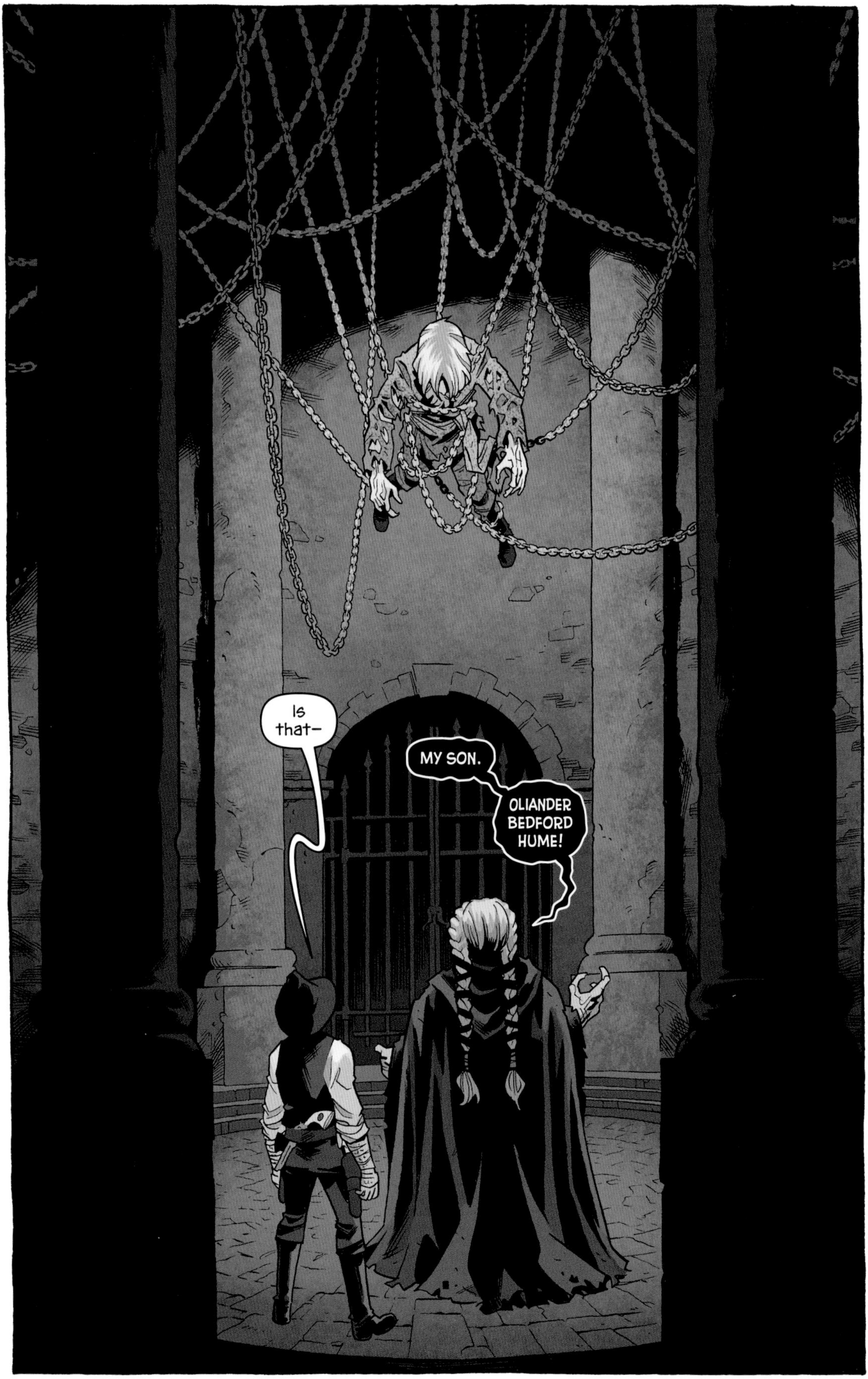
Is that–
MY SON.
OLIANDER BEDFORD HUME!

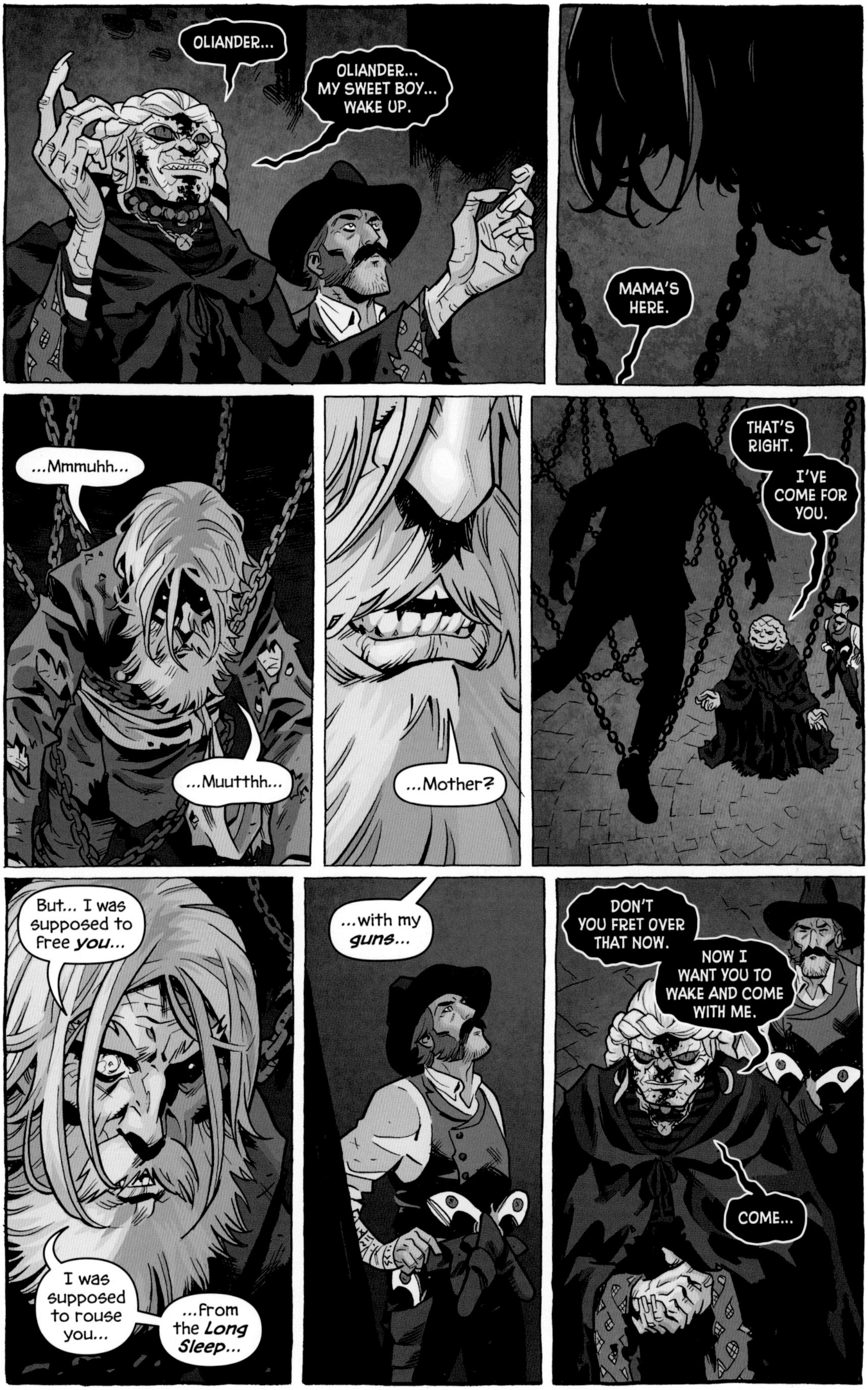
OLIANDER...
OLIANDER... MY SWEET BOY... WAKE UP.
MAMA'S HERE.
...Mmmuhh...
...Muutthh...
...Mother?
THAT'S RIGHT.
I'VE COME FOR YOU.
But... I was supposed to free *you*...
I was supposed to rouse you...
...from the *Long Sleep*...
...with my *guns*...
DON'T YOU FRET OVER THAT NOW.
NOW I WANT YOU TO WAKE AND COME WITH ME.
COME...

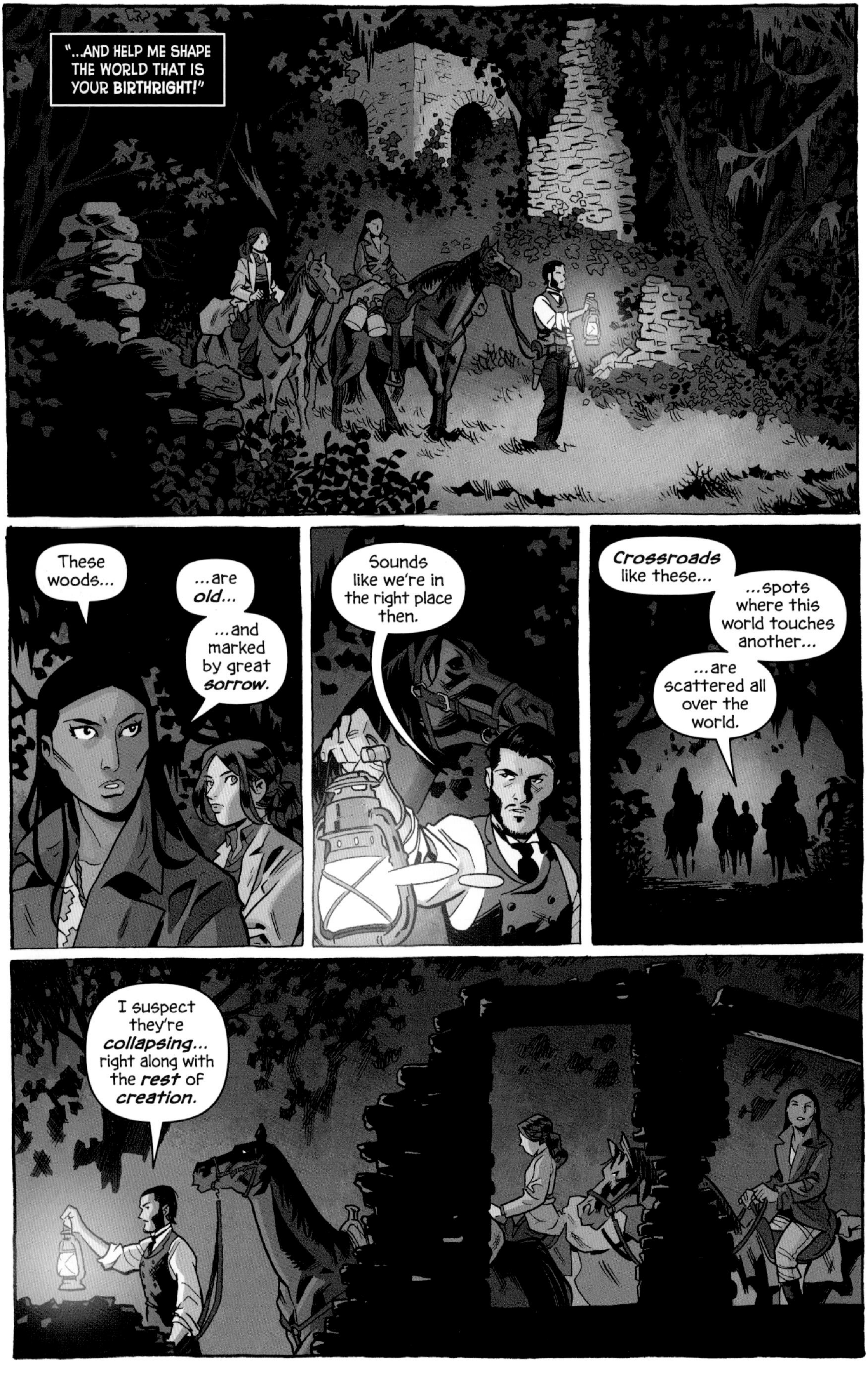
"...AND HELP ME SHAPE THE WORLD THAT IS YOUR BIRTHRIGHT!"
These woods...
...are old...
...and marked by great sorrow.
Sounds like we're in the right place then.
Crossroads like these...
...spots where this world touches another...
...are scattered all over the world.
I suspect they're collapsing... right along with the rest of creation.

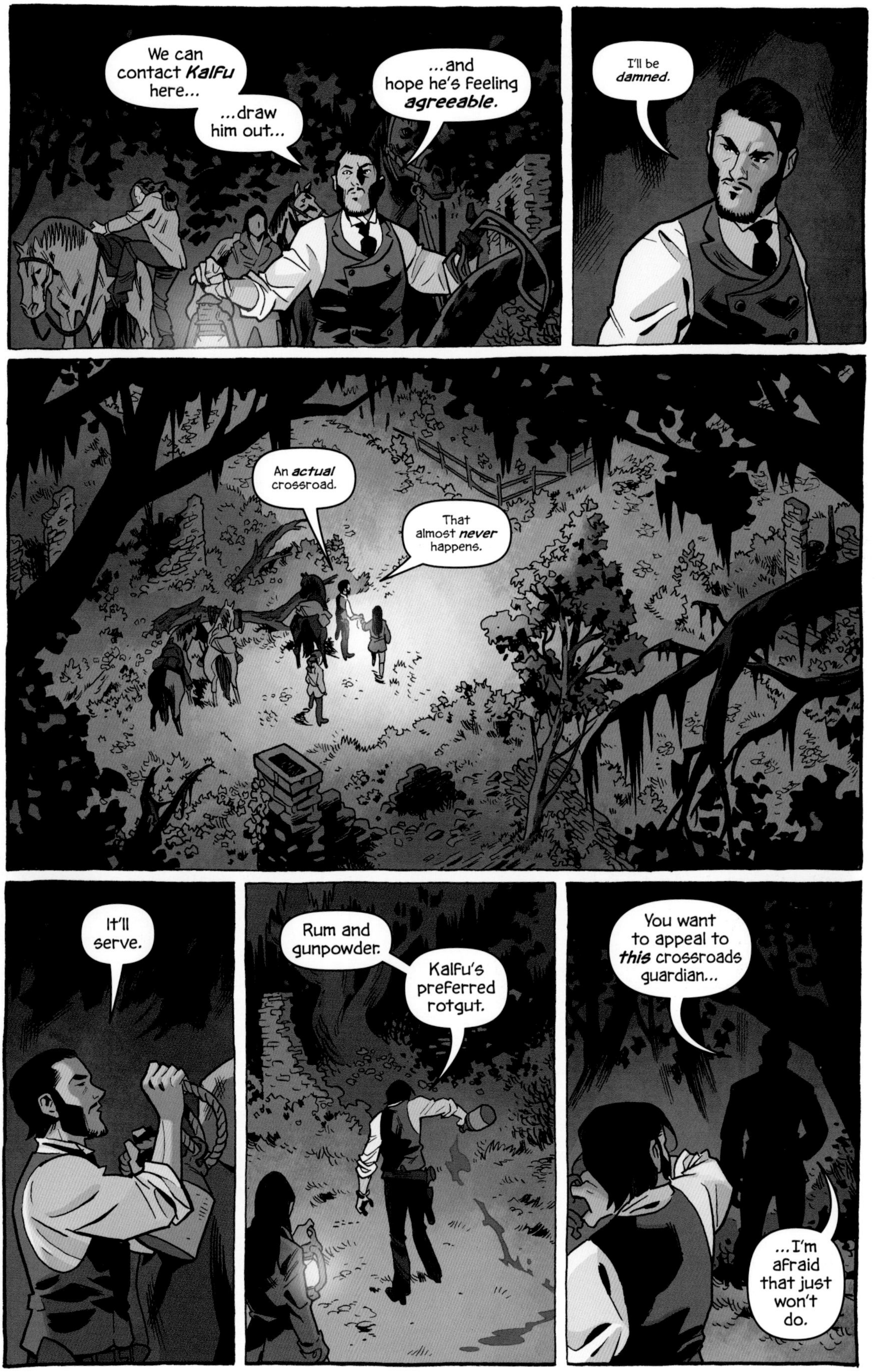

We can contact *Kalfu* here...
...draw him out...
...and hope he's feeling *agreeable.*
I'll be *damned*.
An *actual* crossroad.
That almost *never* happens.
It'll serve.
Rum and gunpowder.
Kalfu's preferred rotgut.
You want to appeal to *this* crossroads guardian...
...I'm afraid that just won't do.

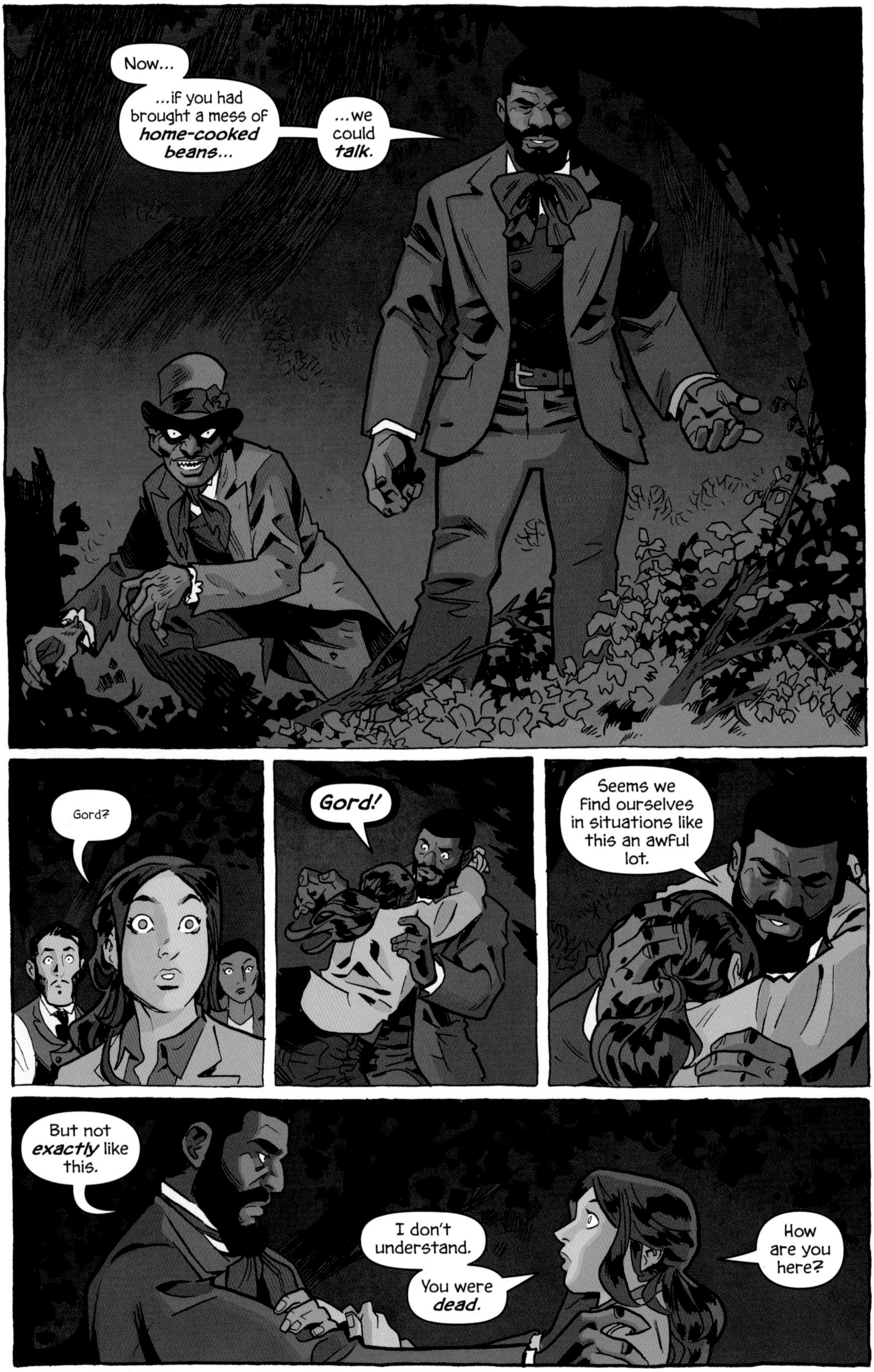
Now...
...if you had brought a mess of *home-cooked beans...*
...we could *talk.*
Gord?
Gord!
Seems we find ourselves in situations like this an awful lot.
But not *exactly* like this.
I don't understand.
You were *dead.*
How are you here?

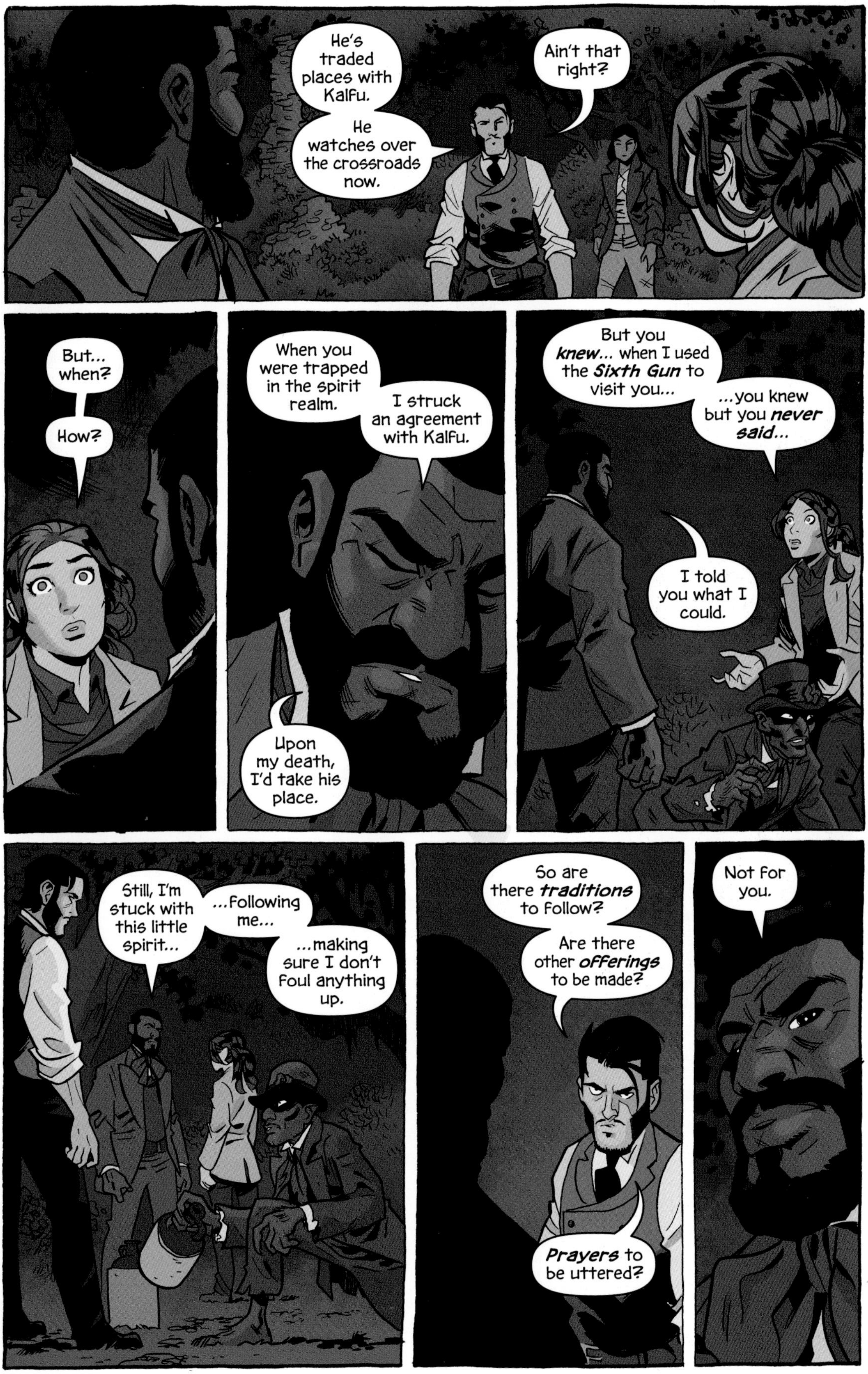
He's traded places with Kalfu.
He watches over the crossroads now.
Ain't that right?
But... when?
How?
When you were trapped in the spirit realm.
I struck an agreement with Kalfu.
Upon my death, I'd take his place.
But you *knew*... when I used the *Sixth Gun* to visit you...
...you knew but you *never said*...
I told you what I could.
Still, I'm stuck with this little spirit...
...following me...
...making sure I don't foul anything up.
So are there *traditions* to follow?
Are there other *offerings* to be made?
Prayers to be uttered?
Not for you.

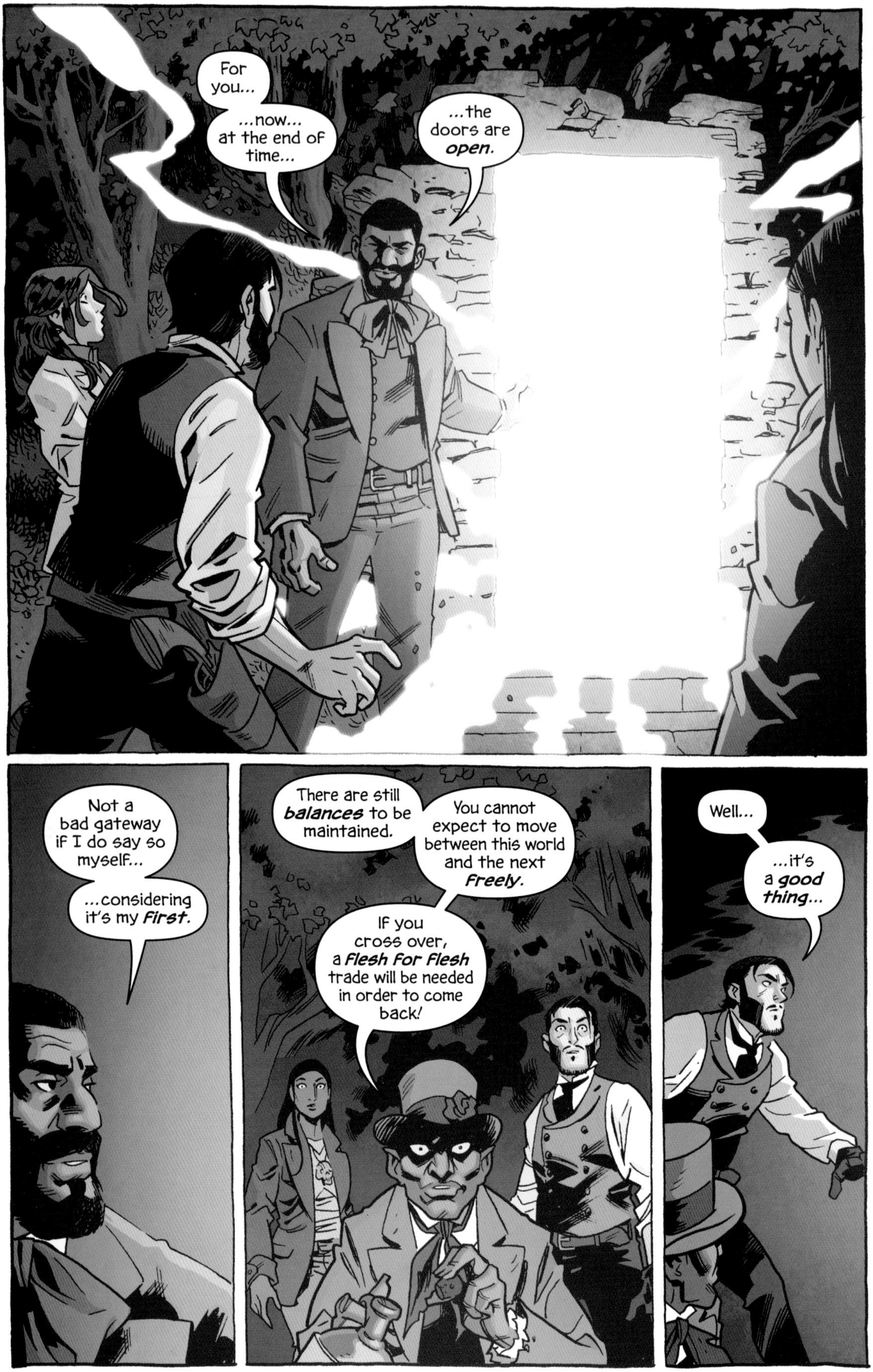
For you...
...now... at the end of time...
...the doors are *open*.
Not a bad gateway if I do say so myself...
...considering it's my *first*.
There are still *balances* to be maintained.
You cannot expect to move between this world and the next *freely*.
If you cross over, a *flesh for flesh* trade will be needed in order to come back!
Well...
...it's a *good thing*...

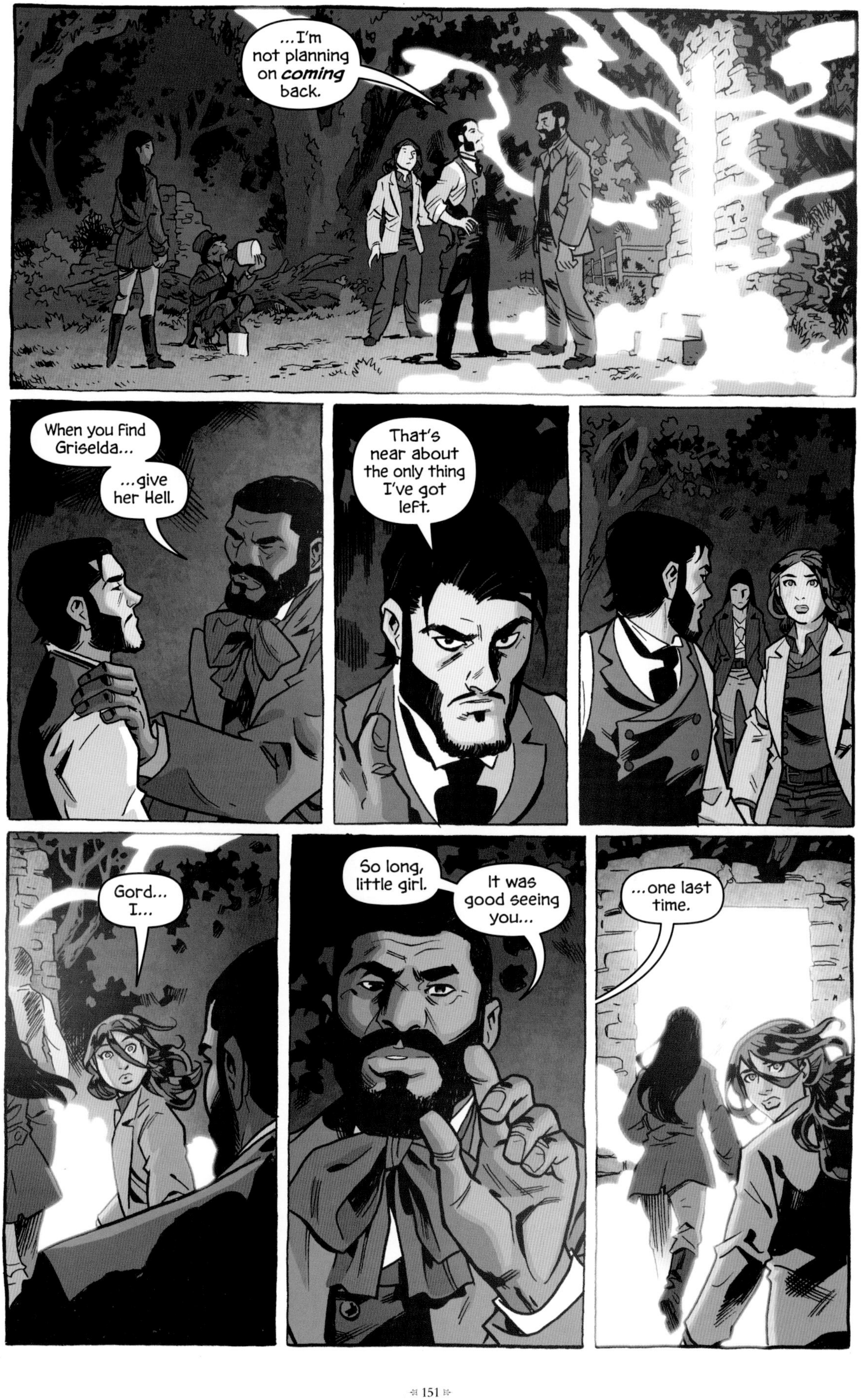
...I'm not planning on *coming* back.
When you find Griselda...
...give her Hell.
That's near about the only thing I've got left.
Gord... I...
So long, little girl.
It was good seeing you...
...one last time.

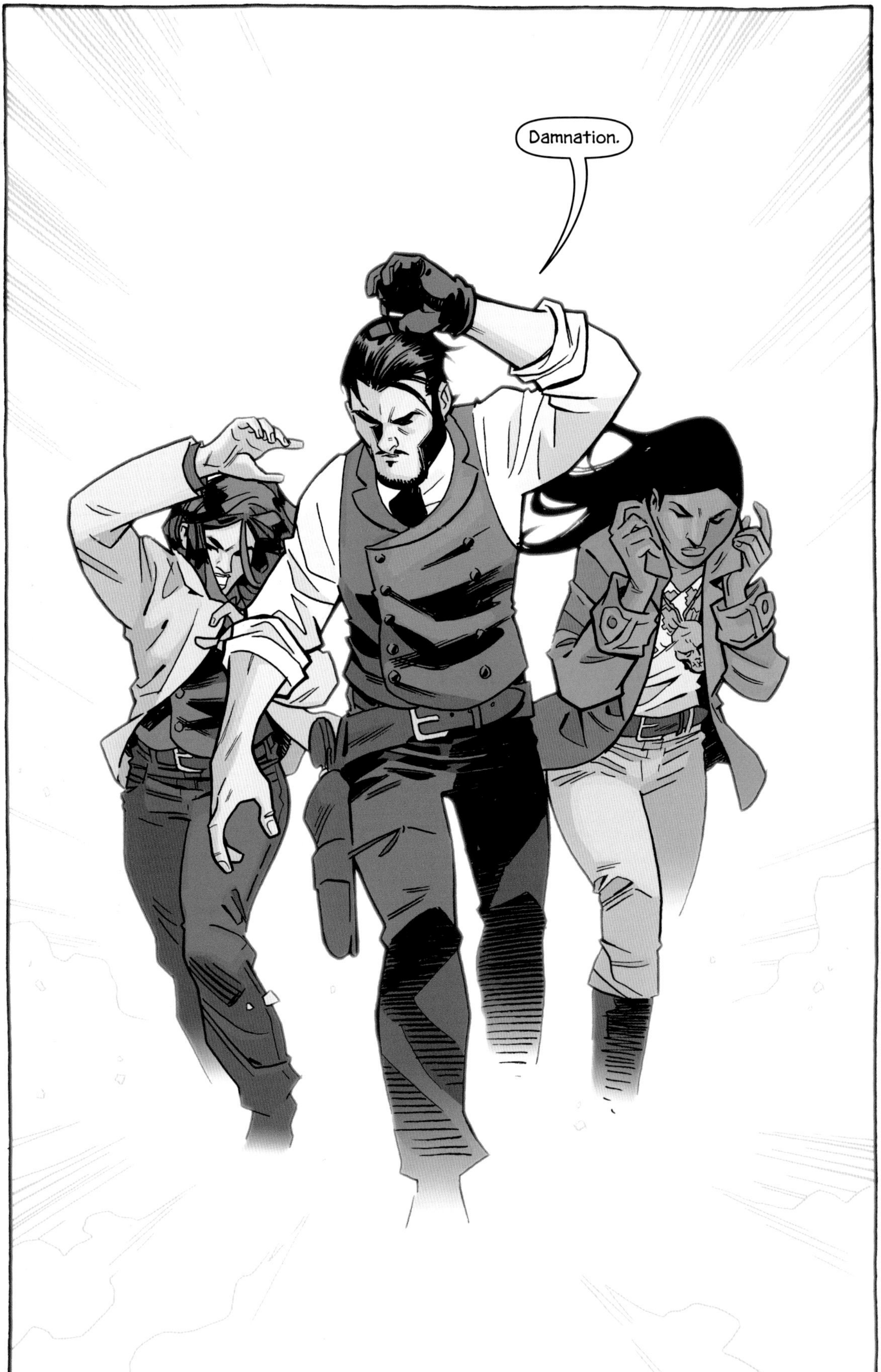
Damnation.

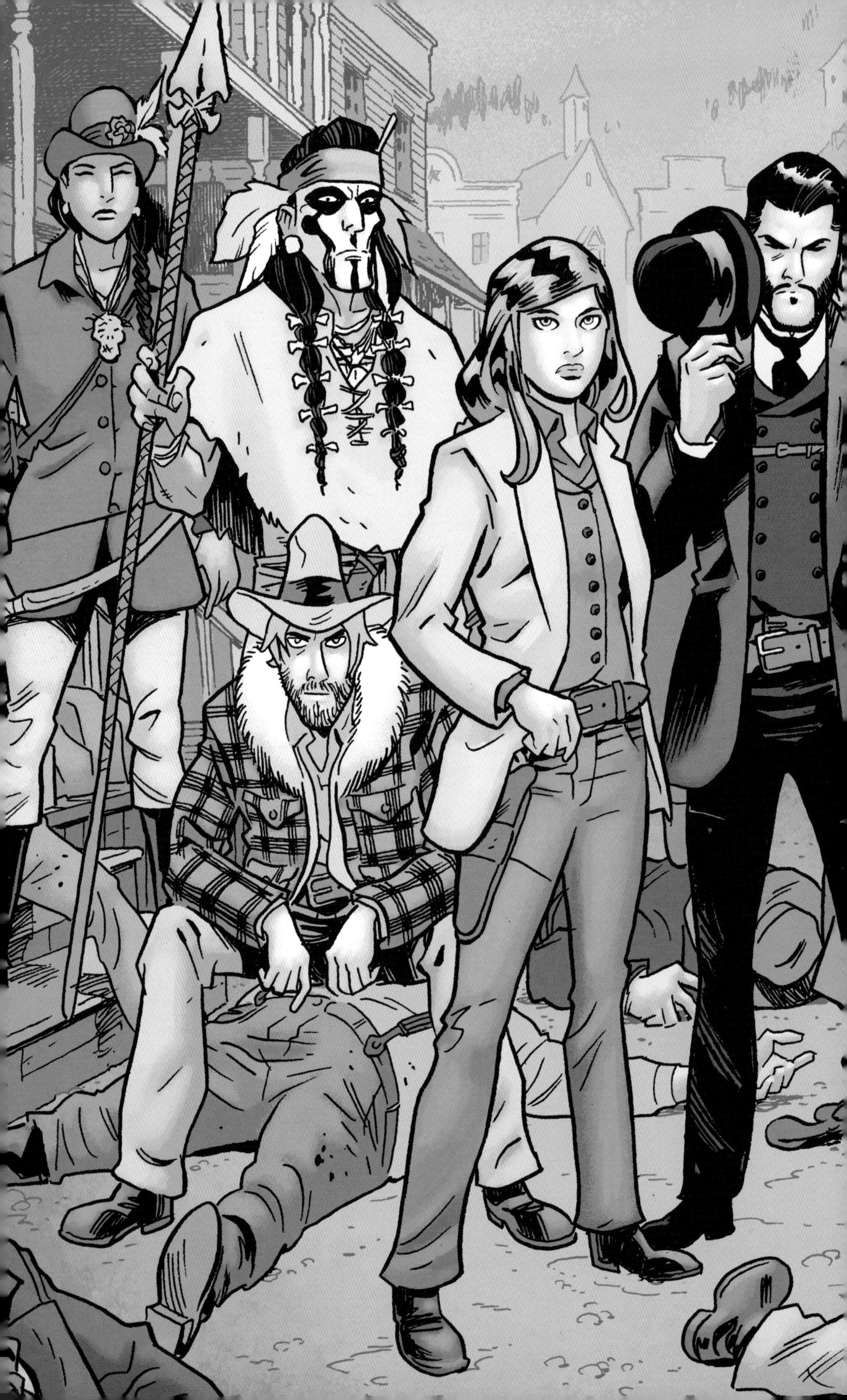

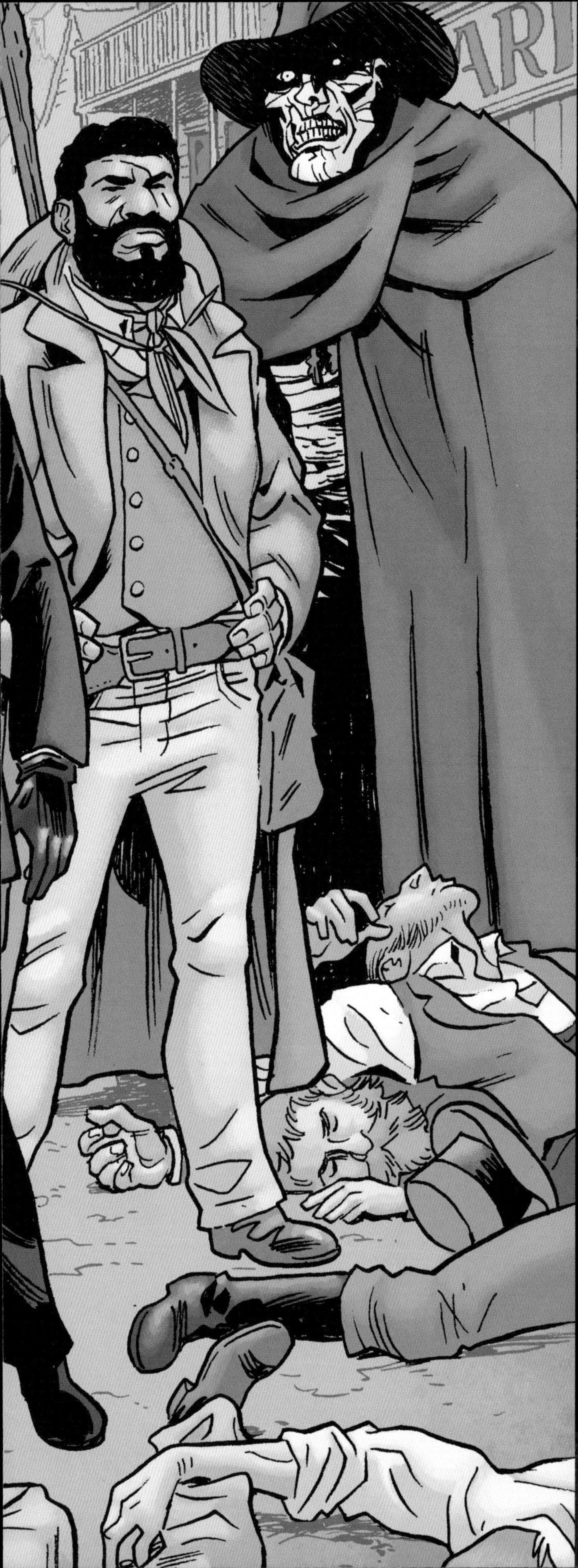

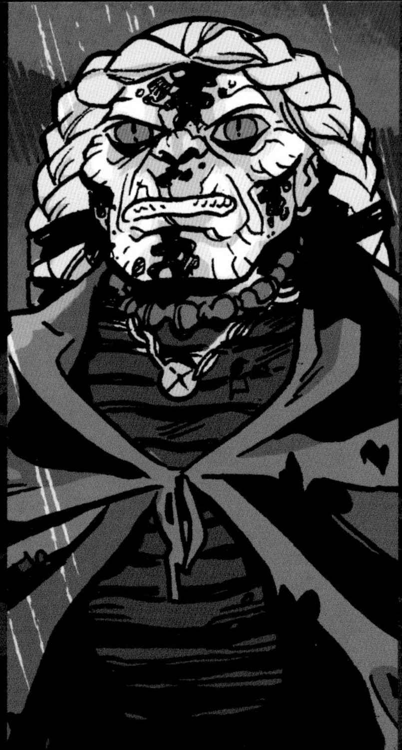

THE ADVENTURE CONCLUDES!

The forces of darkness have thrown open the gates of Hell, and our world is no more. Now, the Grey Witch makes ready to cast herself as the god of her own nightmare realm. With nothing left to lose, Drake Sinclair and Becky Montcrief pursue Griselda into the spirit realm. There, they are reunited with old friends and tormented by enemies thought long dead.

The final battle for the fate of all Creation begins now.

Cullen Bunn is the writer of comic books such *The Damned*, *The Sixth Gun*, *Helheim*, *The Tooth* and *Terrible Lizard* for Oni Press. He has also written titles including *Wolverine*, *Fearless Defenders*, *Venom*, *Deadpool Killustrated*, and *Magneto* for Marvel Comics.

In addition, he is the author of the middle reader horror novel, *Crooked Hills*, and the collection of short fiction, *Creeping Stones and Other Stories*.

His prose work has appeared in numerous magazines and anthologies. Somewhere along the way, he founded Undaunted Press and edited the critically acclaimed horror zine *Whispers From the Shattered Forum*.

Cullen claims to have worked as an Alien Autopsy Specialist, Rodeo Clown, Pro Wrestling Manager, and Sasquatch Wrangler. He has fought for his life against mountain lions and performed on stage as the World's Youngest Hypnotist. Buy him a drink sometime, and he'll tell you all about it.

cullenbunn.com / @cullenbunn.

Author portrait illustrations by Jason Latour, jasonlatour.com

Brian Hurtt got his start in comics pencilling the second arc of Greg Rucka's *Queen & Country*. This was followed by art duties on several projects including *Queen & Country: Declassified*, *Three Strikes*, and Steve Gerber's critically acclaimed series *Hard Time*.

In 2006, Brian teamed with Cullen Bunn to create the Prohibition-era monster-noir sensation *The Damned*. The two found that their unique tastes and storytelling sensibilities were well-suited to one another and were eager to continue that relationship.

The Sixth Gun is their sophomore endeavor together and the next in what looks to be many years of creative collaboration.

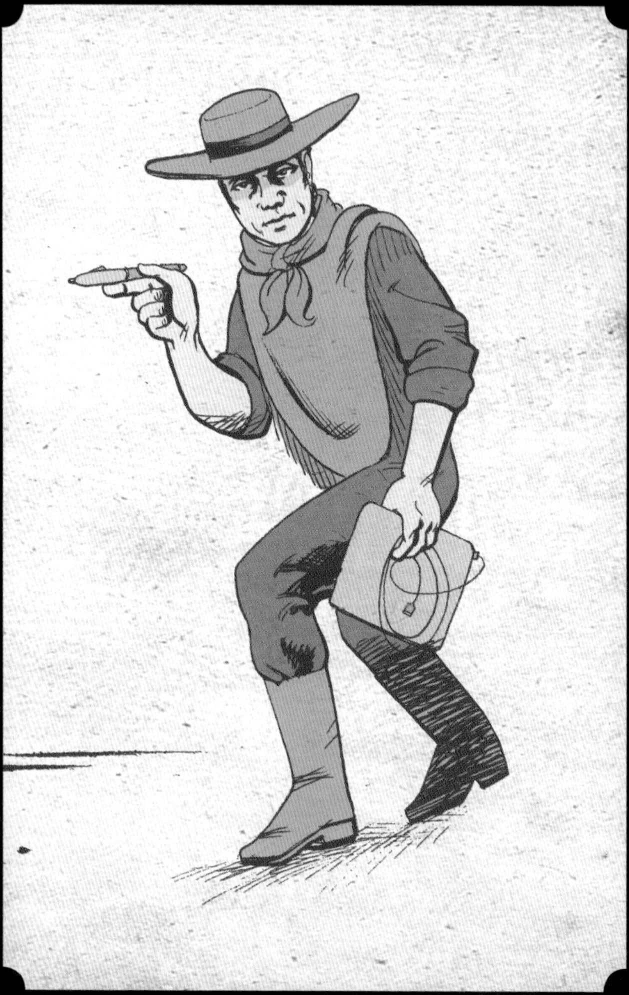

Illustration by Bill Crabtree.

Bill Crabtree's career as a colorist began in 2003 with the launch of Image Comic's *Invincible* and *Firebreather*. He was nominated for a Harvey Award for his work on *Invincible*, and he went on to color the first 50 issues of what would become a flagship Image Comics title. He continues to color *Firebreather*, which was recently made into a feature film on Cartoon Network, *Godland*, and *Jack Staff*.

Perhaps the highlight of his comics career, his role as colorist on *The Sixth Gun* began with issue 6, and has since been described as "like Christmas morning, but with guns."

@crabtree_bill

THE DAMNED
VOLUME ONE
"THREE DAYS DEAD"

HELHEIM
CULLEN BUNN • JOËLLE JONES • NICK FILARDI
BOOK 1: THE WITCH WAR

CULLEN BUNN DREW MOSS RYAN HILL
TERRIBLE LIZARD

ONI PRESS
the Tooth
A New Beginning! The Tooth Unleashed!

MIKE NORTON'S
THE CURSE

THE SECRET HISTORY OF
COOPER
BY BRIAN CHURILLA

PETROGRAD
PHILIP GELATT • TYLER CROOK

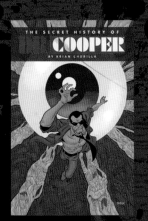

Also Available From Oni Press...

CIUDAD
By Ande Parks, Joe and Anthony Russo, Fernando León González
168 pages • Hardcover
Black and White
ISBN 978-1-62010-146-9

GHOST PROJEKT
By Joe Harris & Steve Rolston
152 pages • Hardcover
Color
ISBN 978-1-934964-42-2

GUERILLAS: VOLUME 1
By Brahm Revel
168 pages • 6"x9" Trade Paperback
Black and White
ISBN 978-1-934964-43-9

PRINCESS UGG: VOLUME 1
By Ted Naifeh and Warren Wucinich
120 pages • Trade Paperback
Color
ISBN 978-1-62010-178-0

QUEEN & COUNTRY DEFINITIVE EDITION: VOLUME 1
By Greg Rucka with Steve Rolston, Brian Hurtt, and Leandro Fernandez
376 pages • 6"x9" • Trade Paperback
Black and White
ISBN 978-1-932664-87-4

STUMPTOWN: VOLUME 1
By Greg Rucka & Matthew Southworth
160 pages • Hardcover
Color
ISBN 978-1-934964-37-8

WASTELAND, VOLUME 1: CITIES IN DUST
By Antony Johnston & Christopher Mitten
160 pages • Trade Paperback
Black and White
ISBN 978-1-932664-59-1

ONE SOUL
By Ray Fawkes
176 pages • Hardcover
Black and White
ISBN 978-1-934964-66-8

CIUDAD

GHOST PЯOJEKT
VOLUME ONE

GUERILLAS
INTRODUCTION BY JACKSON PUBLICK (CREATOR OF THE VENTURE BROS.)
VOLUME 1
BRAHM REVEL

PRINCESS UGG

GREG RUCKA
QUEEN & COUNTRY
DEFINITIVE EDITION
VOLUME 01

"STUMPTOWN IS, FOR MY MONEY, THE PERFECT RUCKA BOOK."
STUMPTOWN
GREG RUCKA • MATTHEW SOUTHWORTH

WASTELAND
ANTONY JOHNSTON
CHRISTOPHER MITTEN
BOOK 01
CITIES IN DUST

Ray Fawkes
ONE SOUL

ONI PRESS

For more information on these and other fine Oni Press comic books and graphic novels visit www.onipress.com. To find a comic shop specialty store in your area visit www.comicshops.us.

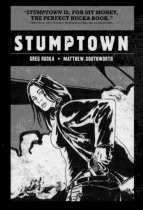